# LaTeX quick reference

# LaTeX quick reference

Herbert Voss

UIT
CAMBRIDGE, ENGLAND

Published by
UIT Cambridge Ltd.
PO Box 145
Cambridge
CB4 1GQ
England

Tel: +44 1223 302 041
Web: www.uit.co.uk

ISBN 978-1-906860-21-9

10 9 8 7 6 5 4 3 2 1

# Contents

# Preface

Far more people use LaTeX nowadays, in part thanks to the development of TeX Live and MiKTeX, which provide automatic package management, long-desired by many users. The "real" TeX or LaTeX user, on the other hand, still deals with `.dtx` formats, texhash for the file tree, or updmap for the directory of fonts. It remains to be seen which user group gains the deeper understanding. Since this TeX renaissance, many more publications have been produced about using the program, with the number available more than doubling in recent years. However, there are still holes in the coverage, especially when it comes to practical things, which can often be the cause of users failing or matters where even the skilled user doesn't want to search through a thick standard volume to find the answer. This has prompted UIT to commission English translations of my series of German workbooks published by DANTE e.V. that aim to provide an entirely practical reference for the user, addressing topics of and around TeX, LaTeX, pdfTeX or related systems like ConTeXt, $\Omega$ or later LuaTeX and $\varepsilon_{\chi}$TeX.

This book was the initial publication in the DANTE series, but it is meant as a reference for LaTeX, not as an introduction. An immediate question that sprang up when writing this book was what is LaTeX and what is not – the border with TeX is fluid and packages can be based on LaTeX, TeX or both. We decided to cover here the environments and commands defined in the `latex.ltx` base file (CTAN: macros/latex/base/) that are of practical relevance to the user. This book therefore does not provide comprehensive coverage of all the commands that can be found there; for anyone looking for more in-depth explanations, there is the standard volume for LaTeX, the Companion [16].

The focus of this book is to summarize all interesting environments and commands in tables that you can then use to check easily how many parameters a command takes and/or in which form they should be used. Optional parameters always have a *[grey]* background.

The first part of this compilation describes the programs and their optional parameters, which are often not known. The next part gives a summary of all document classes on the current TeX Live; some of these will also be unknown – it isn't easy to keep an overview on CTAN. A similar summary is presented for the style files of bibliographies. The given fonts are a summary of the commonly used and freely available fonts. Then we reach the main part of the book, which is the summary of environments and commands that are available for LATEX. The chapter on commonly-used packages presents an arbitrary but important selection. Please note that if class-specific values for lengths and counters are used, they refer to the document class being used there; if you use other classes instead, the results could be different.

All examples in this book are on CTAN – CTAN: `info/examples/LaTeX-Reference/`. Each one consists of a complete set of LATEX files that should work with every TEX distribution.

Thanks must go to Ralf Heckmann, Lutz Ihlenburg, Markus Kohm, Lars Madsen (for `memoir`), Günter Milde, Rolf Niepraschk, Dominik Waßenhoven (for `biblatex`), Uwe Ziegenhagen, Volker RW Schaa and expecially to Lars Kotthoff, who did the translation and Christine Jagger for her excellent job of proofreading.

Berlin, November 2011                                        Herbert Voß

# The programs

The first part of this reference guide to LaTeX describes the relationship between the various programs, and lists their optional parameters. The main program nowadays is pdftex, which can run in different modes, just like luatex and xetex.

The flow from creating the source code to the final PostScript or PDF document is shown in Figure 1.1 on the following page. The programs and options described in the following sections are usually the TeX Live versions and can't be carried over to MiKTeX (http://docs.miktex.org/manual).

```
tex      ⇒ tex, "the program ..."
etex     ⇒ pdftex in dvi (device independent) mode
latex    ⇒ pdftex with latex format in dvi mode
pdftex   ⇒ pdftex in pdf mode
pdflatex ⇒ pdftex with latex format in pdf mode
xetex    ⇒ xetex in dvi or pdf mode
xelatex  ⇒ xetex with latex format in dvi or pdf mode
luatex   ⇒ luatex in dvi or pdf mode
lualatex ⇒ luatex with latex format in dvi or pdf mode
```

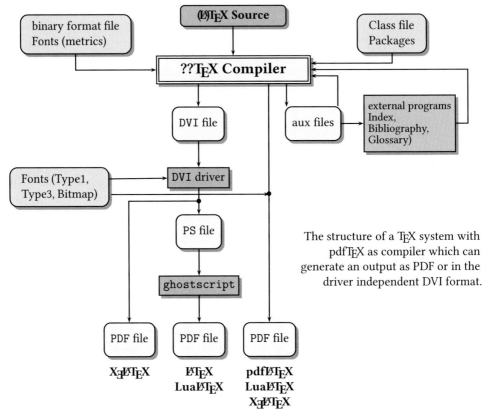

Figure 1.1: "From spring to spout…"

## 1.1 TₑX and ᴌᴬTₑX

tex is the main program, though it has been superseded by etex (extended TₑX) and pdftex.

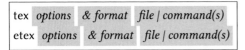

| tex | options | & format | file | command(s) |
| etex | options | & format | file | command(s) |

The options listed below are also valid for ᴌᴬTₑX, which is just a special TₑX format. You can output the list of possible options to the console, for example through tex –help. Most affect the kernel of TₑX and are therefore applicable to ᴌᴬTₑX and pdfTₑX as well.

**-enc** Activates the encTeX extensions (http://www.olsak.net/); only makes sense in conjunction with the ini option.

**-file-line-error** Prints error messages in the form file:line:error, as is common for compilers.

**-no-file-line-error** Prints error messages unformatted.

**-file-line-error-style** Obsolete name of the file-line-error option.

**-fmt** *format* Takes format as the name of the format to load instead of the one specified in the program line or on the first line of the document through `%& format`.

**-halt-on-error** Exit with the corresponding error code if an error occurs during compilation.

**-help** Outputs a short help and terminates the program.

**-ini** Starts in INI mode, which is required for a format dump. You can use INI mode for a compilation pass if you aren't loading a format and are specifying catcodes manually.

**-interaction** *mode* Starts `interaction` mode, which can be specified as `batchmode`, `nonstopmode`, `scrollmode` or `errorstopmode`. The meaning of these options is the same as for the TEX commands of the same name.

**-ipc** Sends DVI output to a defined socket as well as to the default output file. The availability of this option depends on the TEX installation.

**-ipc-start** The same as `ipc`, except that it additionally starts the server on the other end. Again the availability depends on the TEX installation.

**-jobname** *name* Lets you specify a different name than the default `\jobname`.

**-kpathsea-debug** *bitmask* Sets the debugging flags for the search path to the specified bitmask. More information can be found in the kpathsea manual.

**-mktex** *fmt* Activates mktexfmt; allowed values for `fmt` are `tex` or `tfm`.

**-mltex** Activates the MLTEX extensions (only possible in conjunction with the option `ini`).

**-no-mktex** *fmt* Deactivates mktexfmt; allowed values for `fmt` are `tex` or `tfm`.

**-output-comment** *string* Replaces the default output of the date in the DVI file by *string*.

**-output-directory** *directory* Uses *directory* instead of the current directory. Input files are first looked for in *directory*, then in the normal search path.

**-parse-first-line** Starts the first line of a document with `%&`, then evaluates it.

**-no-parse-first-line** If the first line starts with a comment character %, it is not evaluated.

**-progname** *name* Uses *name* instead of the actual program name, including TEX format and search path.

**-recorder** Activates the file recorder and saves all information in file operations in a file with extension `.fls`.

**-shell-escape** Activates the `\write18` command, which allows TEX to start external programs. This option is disabled by default for security reasons.

**-no-shell-escape** Deactivates the `\write18` command if it was activated in the `texmf.cnf` configuration file.

**-src-specials** Adds "source specials" to the DVI file.

**-src-specials** *where* Adds "source specials" to the DVI file at position *where*. One or more of the following values, separated by comma, may be specified: `cr`, `display`, `hbox`, `math`, `par`, `parent` or `vbox`.

**-translate-file** *tcxname* Uses the transformation table *tcxname* for mapping the input characters and remapping the output characters.

**-default-translate-file** *tcxname* As above, but can be overwritten by a first `%&` line.

**-version** Outputs the version number and terminates TEX.

If you specify `\& format` explicitly, then TEX uses the specified precompiled format, which must have the extension `.fmt`. It is more sensible, however, to use the `-fmt format` option.

You can choose anything for the file name of the source document as long as it doesn't correspond to a TEX file that already exists in the search path of TEX. It can be specified with or without the `.tex` extension. Internally, this name is saved as `\jobname` and can be used within the document.

```
voss@shania:~> tex
This is TeX, Version 3.1415926 (TeX Live 2010)
**
```

This mode is nowadays only used to test short command sequences and to output command definitions.

```
voss@shania:~> tex
This is TeX, Version 3.1415926 (TeX Live 2010)
**\show\bigskip
> \bigskip=macro:
->\vskip \bigskipamount .
<*> \show\bigskip
```

\end or \bye terminate the interactive mode and create the default output file texput.dvi.

TeX refers to the environment variables listed below and evaluates them accordingly. Where default values are not given, they are either empty or too large. You can use kpsewhich (cf. Section 1.8.1 on page 11) to show the values of any of these variables, as in the following example:

```
voss@shania:~> kpsewhich -var-value TEXMFHOME
/home/voss/texmf
voss@shania:~> kpsewhich -var-value TEXMFLOCAL
/usr/local/texlive/2010/../texmf-local
```

**TEXINPUTS** This determines the search path for \input and \openin files. These should start with ./ by default so that user files are found before system files. An empty path is replaced by the specification in the texmf.cnf configuration file.

**TEXMFOUTPUT** Usually, TeX writes all output files to the current directory. If one of these files can't be opened for writing, the directory defined by the TEXMFOUTPUT is used instead. This environment variable does not usually have a default value.

**TEXFORMATS** Search path for the format files.

**TEXPOOL** Search path for the TeX internal strings.

**TEXEDIT** Command that is executed when TeX changes to the editor; vi by default.

**TFMFONTS** Search path for the font metrics with the extension .tfm.

**TEXMF** Main search path for the TeX installation with the default value given on page 12.

**TEXMFLOCAL** Search path for the local TeX directories; default value /usr/local/texlive/<year>/../texmf-local for TeX Live.

latex is not a stand-alone program, but a special format. In recent distributions it is read and interpreted not by tex but by pdftex to create DVI output automatically. LaTeX can only process external PostScript or EPS files, so all graphics files have to be converted to this format. Several programs exist for doing this.

**latex** Starts LaTeX in interactive mode; this is obsolete and not used anymore in practice.

```
voss@shania:~> latex
This is pdfTeX, Version 3.1415926-1.40.11 (TeX Live 2010)
**
```

**latex** *file.tex*  Starts LATEX with the file *file.tex*; you don't have to specify the file extension (cf. Appendix A.3 on page 203) here.

> LATEX itself is **not** interested in the format of a graphics file, but only in the *bounding box* – the size of the figure. The DVI file therefore just contains a link to the location of the figure. Only the corresponding driver, which converts the DVI file into a PostScript or PDF file, restricts the format. LATEX **only** accepts .ps and .eps files.

## 1.2  pdfTEX and pdfLATEX

pdftex is a stand-alone program, but it uses the TEX kernel to format the document. The current version 1.40 doesn't distinguish between pdfTEX and pdfeTEX, and can create both DVI and PDF output. The syntax is:

| pdftex *options* & *format* *file | command(s)* |
| pdflatex *options* & *format* *file | command(s)* |

pdflatex is, like latex, not a stand-alone program, but a special format which is read by pdftex. pdftex can only process external .pdf, .png and .jpg graphics files when creating pdf files; you must convert other files into one of these formats, for example by using the ps2pdf and epstopdf programs, among others. At the TEX level, only the bounding box is of interest. In addition to the options given on page 4, there are special ones relating to the output format, as pdftex can create DVI as well as PDF.

**-draftmode**  Creates no PDF output.

**-output-format** *format*  Sets the output format to *format*, which can be either PDF or DVI. This selection affects the supported graphics formats:

*pdf* ⇒ .pdf, .png and .jpg (Note that .tiff is not supported anymore)     *graphics*
*dvi* ⇒ .ps and .eps.                                                        *formats*

**-8bit**  Always use the 8-Bit representation of characters.

## 1.3  XƎTEX and XƎLATEX

XƎTEX and XƎLATEX can both use TrueType and OpenType fonts directly, which isn't true of other programs. They are available in TEX Live as well as MiKTEX and can also be selected or at least set up in the graphic environments. The result is always a DVI or PDF file. XƎTEX is only needed to convert files that contain PostScript code to PDF through dvipdfmx. The encoding is always UTF-8 so you don't need to load the inputenc package. Using the fontspec package by Will Robertson makes loading fonts significantly easier.

| \setmainfont [*settings*] {*font family*} |
| \setsansfont [*settings*] {*font family*} |
| \setmonofont [*settings*] {*font family*} |
| \setmathfont [*settings*] {*font family*} |

Minion **bold** and *italic*
Biolinum **bold** and SMALL CAPS
Consolas **bold** and *italic*

```
\usepackage{fontspec}
\setmainfont[Mapping=tex-text]{Minion Pro}
\setsansfont[Mapping=tex-text]{Linux Biolinum O}
\setmonofont[Scale=0.9]{Consolas}

Minion \textbf{bold} and \textit{italic}\par
\sffamily Biolinum \textbf{bold} and \textsc{small caps}
\par\ttfamily Consolas \textbf{bold} and \emph{italic}
```

01-03-1

Minion ff ffi **bold** and *italic* 01234567
Myriad ff ffi **bold** and small caps
Vera Mono True Type, **mono bold**
and *mono italic 0123*
$(\alpha; R) \ne (\beta; R)$  012345

$$\int\limits_{1}^{\infty} \frac{1}{x}\,\mathrm{d}x = 1$$

```
\usepackage{amsmath}
\usepackage{mathspec}
\setmainfont[
  SizeFeatures = {
    {Size =      -8.41, OpticalSize = 8},
    {Size = 8.41-13.1, OpticalSize = 11},
    {Size = 13.1-20.0, OpticalSize = 19},
    {Size = 20.0-,     OpticalSize = 72}},
  Ligatures        = {Required, Common, Contextual, TeX},
  Numbers          = {OldStyle, Proportional},
  RawFeature       = {expansion  = default},
  UprightFeatures  = {RawFeature = {protrusion = mnr}},
  BoldFeatures     = {RawFeature = {protrusion = mnrb}},
  ItalicFeatures   = {RawFeature = {protrusion = mni}},
  BoldItalicFeatures = {RawFeature = {protrusion = mnib}}
]{Minion Pro}
\setmathfont(Digits,Latin,Greek){Minion Pro}
\setsansfont[Mapping=tex-text]{Myriad Pro}
\setmonofont[Scale=0.9]{Bitstream Vera Sans Mono}
\usepackage{MnSymbol}

Minion ff ffi \textbf{bold} and \textit{italic} 01234567\par
\sffamily Myriad ff ffi \textbf{bold} and \textsc{small caps}
\par\ttfamily Vera Mono True Type, \textbf{mono bold} and
\emph{mono italic 0123}\par$(\alpha;R)\ne(\beta;R)$ $012345$
\[ \int\limits_1^\infty\frac{1}{x}\mathrm{d}x=1 \]
```

01-03-2

## 1.4  LuaTeX and LuaLaTeX

The advantage of LuaTeX over the current pdfTeX is that it enables you to use the Lua
scripting language (http://www.lua.org).

$\pi/2 = 1.5707963267949$

```
$\pi/2=\directlua{tex.print(math.pi/2)}$
```

01-04-1

The following example could also be generated with normal TeX, but that would require
significantly more effort – either you'd need the fp package or you'd have to emulate the
calculations with TeX lengths.

<table><tr><td>01-04-2</td></tr></table>

The point $A(4,1)$ and the point $B(3.2,5.5)$ are 4.5705579528106 length units apart.

```
\usepackage[utf8]{luainputenc}
\def\Length(#1,#2)(#3,#4){%
   \directlua{%
      tex.print(math.sqrt((#4-#2)^2+
                        (#3-#1)^2))}}

The point $A(4,1)$ and the point $B(3.2,5.5)$ are
\Length(4,1)(3.2,5.5) length units apart.
```

## 1.5  Error messages

If errors occur during the compilation process, latex gives error messages such as in the following example where the name of the \textbf command was deliberately misspelt:

```
! Undefined control sequence.
l.7 \textf
          {foo}
?
```

There are several ways of proceeding now, as indicated by the question mark.

**<return>** Continue.

**S** Continue, but stop if a fatal error occurs, which would cause an *emergency stop* with R.

**R** Continue without stopping. TEX tries to correct the error as well as possible. Only stops on unknown file names.

**Q** Continue in any case without messages.

**I** Go to insert mode and enter the correct command (in the example above \textbf).

**E** Terminate the compilation pass, start an editor with the source file and jump to the line containing the error.

**1...9** Ignore the following 1...9 input tokens of the file.

**H** Output help, if possible.

**X** Terminate the compilation pass and write the state to the log file. The current page is not output.

## 1.6  DVIPS

The compilation of the TEX source file to DVI format (device independent) is the default for TEX and LATEX and also possible with pdftex and pdflatex. The call to dvips with the DVI file can be done with or without file extension.

dvips *options file*.dvi

The most important of the many options are listed below; you can obtain a complete list through dvips --help or the complete documentation through texdoc dvips or texdoctk, the graphical interface.

**j** *⟨file⟩* Loads only the required files of the Type 1 fonts; this is the default in the current version 5.98 of dvips. The psfonts.map map file offers further control over the fonts.

**o** *⟨file⟩* Outputs file. Required on some operating systems if the configuration would otherwise send the file to the printer.

**r⟨*digit*⟩** r1 reverses the order of the pages, which is important when printing two-sided on a printer without a duplex unit. r0 deactivates this option.

**t ⟨*format*⟩** Specifies the paper format; this can be important if the specification on the TEX side is wrong or missing.

**A** Outputs only the odd pages.

**B** Outputs only the even pages.

**P ⟨*Ext*⟩** Loads the config.EXT configuration file, for example P pdf to load the config.pdf file. The default is config.ps. The location of this configuration file can be found through kpsewhich (cf. Section 1.8.1 on the next page):

```
voss@shania:~> kpsewhich -format="dvips config" config.ps
/usr/local/texlive/2010/texmf/dvips/config/config.ps
```

**R⟨*digit*⟩** R1 means that file names of figures and other included files are *not* searched for in parent directories for security reasons; this corresponds to the z option in the config.ps configuration file. R0 deactivates this option.


## 1.7 From PostScript to PDF

After creating a .ps file, you can then use the ps2pdf script to create a .pdf file. Depending on the version and type of the operating system, this script may call another script that has the PDF version in its name – currently ps2pdf14. This script in turn calls another script named ps2pdfwr, which finally calls ghostscript.

```
#!/bin/sh
# $Id: ch01-prog-en.tex 59 2011-09-16 10:25:27Z herbert $
# Convert PostScript to PDF.
# Currently, we produce PDF 1.4 by default, but we can't guarantee that
# this won't change in the future.
version=14
ps2pdf="'dirname $0'/ps2pdf$version"
if test ! -x "$ps2pdf"; then
        ps2pdf="ps2pdf$version"
fi
exec "$ps2pdf" "$@"
```

```
#!/bin/sh
# $Id: ch01-prog-en.tex 59 2011-09-16 10:25:27Z herbert $
# Convert PostScript to PDF 1.4 (Acrobat 5-and-later compatible).
ps2pdfwr="'dirname $0'/ps2pdfwr"
if test ! -x "$ps2pdfwr"; then
        ps2pdfwr="ps2pdfwr"
fi
exec "$ps2pdfwr" -dCompatibilityLevel=1.4 "$@"
```

In the ps2pdfwr script, the -dSAFER option should either be commented in local systems if
-*dSAFER* active or renamed to -dNOSAFER. Otherwise, if the -dSAFER option is active, it will prevent the
-*dNOSAFER* loading of external files if the PostScript file isn't loaded directly and cause problems when trying to view a created PostScript file from a GUI (graphical user interface).

# 1.8   Auxiliary programs

Several useful auxiliary programs developed by Karl Berry come with every TeX distribution. If you have a TeX Live installation, you can find them in the .../texlive/<year>/bin/<platform>/ directory. For a default installation of MiKTeX, they are located in (for example) C:\Program Files\MiKTeX 2.9\miktex\bin.

TeX Live 2010 further restricts the execution of external programs from TeX for security reasons. To call a program from within TeX you must specify it explicitly in the local texmf.cnf configuration file. You can use kpsewhich (cf. Section 1.8.1) to find the location of texmf.cnf. It might contain the following list of programs, for example:

```
shell_escape_commands = \
bibtex,bibtex8,epstopdf,epspdf,fc-match,\
kpsewhich,makeindex,ps2pdf,pstopdf,pygmentize,\
pdfcrop,gnuplot,gs,asy,\
```

You can edit this list in the file to allow more or fewer external programs.

## 1.8.1   kpsewhich

kpsewhich lets you check for programs and paths, and is particularly useful for checking for the existence and path of a package or style file.

```
voss@shania:~> kpsewhich latex.ltx
/usr/local/texlive/2010/texmf-dist/tex/latex/base/latex.ltx
```

The syntax of the program is:

kpsewhich   *options*   *file name* ...

The following options are possible:

| | |
|---|---|
| -debug=NUM | sets debugging flags |
| -D, -dpi=NUM | uses a base resolution of NUM; default 600 |
| -engine=STRING | sets engine name to STRING |
| -expand-braces=STRING | outputs variable and brace expansion of STRING |
| -expand-path=STRING | outputs complete path expansion of STRING |
| -expand-var=STRING | outputs variable expansion of STRING |
| -format=NAME | uses file type NAME (see list below, when running kpsewhich -help) |
| -help | prints this message and exits |
| -interactive | asks for additional filenames to look up |
| [-no]-mktex=FMT | disables/enables mktexFMT generation (FMT=pk/mf/tex/tfm) |
| -mode=STRING | sets device name for $MAKETEX_MODE to STRING |
| -must-exist | searches the disk as well as the ls-R file if necessary |
| -path=STRING | searches in the path STRING |
| -progname=STRING | sets program name to STRING |
| -show-path=NAME | outputs search path for file type NAME |
| -var-value=STRING | outputs the value of variable $STRING |
| -version | prints the version number and exits |

## 1.8.2 kpsexpand

With kpsexpand, you can expand the individual environment variables:

```
voss@shania:~> kpsexpand '$TEXMF'
{/home/voss/.texlive2010/texmf-config,/home/voss/.texlive2010/texmf-var,/home/voss/texmf,!!/
↪usr/local/texlive/2010/texmf-config,!!/usr/local/texlive/2010/texmf-var,!!/usr/local/
↪texlive/2010/texmf,!!/usr/local/texlive/2010/../texmf-local,!!/usr/local/texlive/2010/
↪texmf-dist}
```

The paths starting with !! must contain an ls-R file list – then only this is searched and not the file system.

## 1.8.3 kpsepath

kpsepath lets you output the complete paths that TeX searches to find files. The syntax is:

kpsepath *options* path type

```
voss@shania:~> kpsepath bib
.:/home/voss/.texlive2010/texmf-config/bibtex/bib//:/home/voss/.texlive2010/texmf-var/bibtex/
↪bib//:/home/voss/texmf/bibtex/bib//:!!/usr/local/texlive/2010/texmf-config/bibtex/bib
↪//:!!/usr/local/texlive/2010/texmf-var/bibtex/bib//:!!/usr/local/texlive/2010/texmf
↪/bib//:!!/usr/local/texlive/2010/../texmf-local/bibtex/bib//:!!/usr/local/texlive/2010/
↪texmf-dist/bibtex/bib//
```

Possible path types are:

| | | | |
|---|---|---|---|
| gf | generic font bitmap | pk | packed bitmap font |
| base | Metafont memory dump | bib | BibTeX bibliography source |
| bst | BibTeX style files | cnf | Kpathsea runtime configuration files |
| fmt | TeX memory dump | mem | MetaPost memory dump |
| mf | Metafont source | mfpool | Metafont program strings |
| mp | MetaPost source | mppool | MetaPost program strings |
| mpsupport | MetaPost support files | pict | other kinds of figures |
| tex | TeX source | texpool | TeX program strings |
| tfm | TeX font metrics | vf | virtual font |
| dvips_config | dvips config files | dvips_header | dvips header files |
| troff_font | troff fonts | | |

## 1.8.4 Finding package documentation

Finding package documentation can usually be left to texdoc, which searches for a corresponding file in the specified TeX directories and displays it. The syntax is:

texdoc *options* package name

Possible options are:

```
-v        outputs the viewer command
-l        lists all relevant files and doesn't start the viewer
-s        searches the files; arguments are passed as patterns to egrep
```

## 1.8.5  Cropping PDF files

The pdfcrop program by Heiko Oberdiek is particularly useful for removing the white margin from a figure. The syntax is:

```
pdfcrop  options  file
```

The *file* must be in PDF format; the output file will have the suffix -crop after the file name. Page numbers in *file* prevent the cropping of the bottom margin because they are part of the text; they should only be used if they are explicitly required. The possible options are:

```
 --help                 print usage
 --version              print version number
 --(no)verbose          verbose printing                  (false)
 --(no)debug            debug information                  (false)
 --gscmd <name>         call of ghostscript                (gs)

 --pdftex | --xetex  use pdfTeX | use XeTeX               (pdftex)
 --pdftexcmd <name>  call of pdfTeX                        (pdftex)
 --xetexcmd <name>   call of XeTeX                         (xetex)
 --margins "<left> <top> <right> <bottom>"   (0 0 0 0)
                        add extra margins, unit is bp. If only one number is
                        given, then it is used for all margins, in the case
                        of two numbers they are also used for right and bottom.
 --(no)clip             clipping support, if margins are set  (false)
                        (not available for --xetex)
 --(no)hires            using '%%HiResBoundingBox'          (false)
                        instead of '%%BoundingBox'
Advanced options:
 --restricted           turn on restricted mode             (false)
 --papersize <foo>      parameter for ghostscript's -sPAPERSIZE=<foo>,
                        use only with older ghostscript versions <7.32 ()
 --resolution <res>     pass argument to ghostscript's option -r,
                        for example --resolution 72
 --resolution <xres>x<yres>  as above                     ()
 --bbox "<left> <top> <right> <bottom>"                   ()
                        override bounding box found by ghostscript
```

## 1.8.6  Converting between EPS and PDF

The epstopdf program lets you convert .eps figures to .pdf format without losing the vector properties of the figure. This program should be part of every TeX distribution. The syntax is:

```
epstopdf  options  file
```

The reverse conversion, from .pdf to .eps, is more difficult if the size of the bounding box of the original figure is not given as a parameter. The following script (pdf2eps) lets you convert any page of a PDF file to a single .eps figure; the white margin is cropped automatically.

```
#!/bin/sh
# $Id: ch01-prog-en.tex 59 2011-09-16 10:25:27Z herbert $
# Convert PDF to encapsulated PostScript.
```

```
# usage:
# pdf2eps <page number> <pdf file without ext>

pdfcrop $2.pdf
pdftops -f $1 -l $1 -eps "$2-crop.pdf"
rm  "$2-crop.pdf"
mv  "$2-crop.eps" $2.eps
```

## 1.8.7 Converting from PS to EPS

Although LaTeX is able to read pure PostScript files, it is advisable to use .eps files in some cases and the epstopdf program lets you convert them. The syntax is:

ps2eps *options* *file*

The options can be listed through ps2eps -*h*.

Chapter **2**

# The document

## 2.1 The structure

Formally, a document is composed of the preamble and the text body.

```
...
\documentclass [settings] {name} [version]    ⎫
...                                            ⎬  preamble
\begin{document}                               ⎭
...                                            ⎫
\end{document}                                 ⎬  text body
                                               ⎭
```

All formal definitions should or must be given in the preamble. The following list shows all commands and environments that must appear there if in use. In practice, the preamble commands also include the document keyword, which on the other hand contains the text body and is therefore not listed explicitly here.

| | | |
|---|---|---|
| \addtoversion | \AtBeginDocument | \AtEndOfClass |
| \AtEndOfPackage | \CheckCommand | \DeclareErrorFont |
| \DeclareFontEncoding | \DeclareFontEncodingDefaults | \DeclareFontSubstitution |
| \DeclareMathAccent | \DeclareMathAlphabet | \DeclareMathDelimiter |
| \DeclareMathRadical | \DeclareMathSizes | \DeclareMathSymbol |
| \DeclareMathVersion | \DeclareOldFontCommand | \DeclareOption |
| \DeclarePreloadSizes | \DeclareSizeFunction | \DeclareSymbolFont |
| \DeclareSymbolFontAlphabet | \DeclareTextAccent | \DeclareTextAccentDefault |
| \DeclareTextCommand | \DeclareTextCommandDefault | \DeclareTextComposite |
| \DeclareTextCompositeCommand | \DeclareTextFontCommand | \DeclareTextSymbol |
| \DeclareTextSymbolDefault | \documentclass | \documentstyle |

continued . . .

| | | |
|---|---|---|
| \ExecuteOptions | \includeonly | \listfiles |
| \LoadClass | \LoadClassWithOptions | \makeglossary |
| \makeindex | \NeedsTeXFormat | \newmathalphabet |
| \nofiles | \OptionNotUsed | \PassOptionsToClass |
| \PassOptionsToPackage | \ProcessOptions | \ProvidesClass |
| \ProvidesPackage | \RequirePackage | \RequirePackageWithOptions |
| \SetMathAlphabet | \SetSymbolFont | \UndeclareTextCommand |
| \usepackage | filecontents | |

## 2.2 The document class

The document class is usually chosen through the \documentclass command (rather than the document creating a new one for itself). You can pass options to the class as part of this command. The options are evaluated by the chosen document class as well as the included packages (cf. Chapter 8 on page 129).

\documentclass *[settings]* {*name*} *[version]*

The second optional argument isn't usually needed, as generally you want the most recent version, which is assumed by default. However, if you don't want the latest version, you can specify a date in the form yyyy/mm/dd. If the class is older than that date, the log file contains a warning such as the one produced by the following declaration:

```
\documentclass{book}[2009/01/01]
```

```
LaTeX Warning: You have requested, on input line 1, version
               '2009/01/01' of document class article,
               but only version
               '2007/10/19 v1.4h Standard LaTeX document class'
               is available.
```

### 2.2.1 Available classes

The standard distributions of TeX, like TeX Live or MiKTeX, usually provide the following classes:

| .cls name | description |
|---|---|
| a0poster | poster class DIN-A0 |
| aastex | American Astronomical Society Journal |
| abstbook | class for a book of abstracts |
| achemso | American Chemical Society |
| acmconf | Association for Computing Machinery (conferences) |
| acmtrans2e | ditto (transactions) |
| actawex | Acta Wexionensia |
| active-conf | Active conferences |
| afthesis | Air Force Institute of Technology |
| agecon | Agricultural Economics |

continued ...

| .cls name | description |
| --- | --- |
| aguplus | American Geophysical Union |
| aiaa-tc | American Institute of Aeronautics and Astronautics |
| ajae | American Journal of Agricultural Economics |
| akklecture | for lecture notes |
| akkscript | for scripts |
| akktecdoc | for technical documents |
| akletter | letter class |
| amsart | American Math Society (article) |
| amsbook | American Math Society (book) |
| amsdtx | American Math Society (LaTeXdoc) |
| amsldoc | American Math Society – documentations |
| amsproc | American Math Society – proceedings |
| aomart | The Annals of Mathematics |
| apa | American Psychological Association |
| apecon | Applied Economics |
| arabart | article class for ArabTeX |
| arabbook | book class for ArabTeX |
| arabrep | report class for ArabTeX |
| arabrep1 | ditto |
| article | article class (default) |
| articoletteracdp | article class for the University of Padua |
| artikel1 | NTG article class |
| artikel2 | ditto |
| artikel3 | ditto |
| asaetr | American Society for Agricultural Engineers |
| ascelike | American Society of Civil Engineers |
| assignment | homework assignments |
| barticle | article class for Bangla and Assamese |
| bbook | book class for Bangla and Assamese |
| beamer | presentations |
| beletter | Belgian letter class |
| bidibeamer | presentations for left and right font |
| bidimodernv | Curriculum Vitae for left and right font |
| bidipresentation | presentations for left and right font |
| bletter | letter class for Bangla and Assamese |
| boek | NTG book class |
| boek3 | ditto |
| book | book class (default) |
| bookest | extensions for the book class |
| brief | NTG letter class |
| cassete | labels for audio cassettes |
| cc | special class for complexity theory |
| cd-cover | CD covers |
| cd | ditto |
| chletter | letter class for Switzerland |
| cjw-env | class for envelopes |

continued …

| .cls name | description |
| --- | --- |
| cjw-ltr | letter class |
| cnx | for documents describing Connexions Modules |
| codedoc | code and documentation in one file |
| ConcProg | concert programmes |
| confproc | conference proceedings |
| combine | combine several complete documents |
| cours | modified article class with \chapter* |
| courseoutline | course documents |
| coursepaper | ditto |
| csbulletin | CSTUG bulletin class |
| ctexart | adaptation of the article class to ctex |
| ctexartutf8 | ditto with UTF-8 |
| ctexbook | adaptation of the book class to ctex |
| ctexbookutf8 | ditto with UTF-8 |
| ctexrep | adaptation of the report class to ctex |
| ctexrepkutf8 | ditto with UTF-8 |
| cweb | LaTeX markup in CWEB sources |
| curve | Curriculum Vitae |
| dinbrief | letter class according to DIN |
| disser | dissertations |
| dvdcoll | DVD archives |
| ebsthesis | European Business School (Gabler) |
| ecca | Economica |
| ecv | European Curriculum Vitae |
| elpres | presentations |
| elsart | Elsevier article class |
| elsart1p | ditto |
| elsart3p | ditto |
| elsart5p | ditto |
| elsarticle | ditto |
| emulateapj | emulation of the layout of the Astrophysical Journal |
| erae | European Review of Agricultural Economics |
| erdc | Engineer Research and Development Center (ERDC) |
| eskd | special Russian class |
| eskdgraph | graphical documentation |
| eskdtab | tabular documentation |
| eskdtext | text documentation |
| estcpmm | ESTCP MM report |
| etiketka | herbarium labels |
| euproposal | EU proposals |
| europecv | Curriculum Vitae |
| exam | multiple choice questions and similar |
| examdesign | exam questions |
| extarticle | bigger default fonts |
| extbook | ditto |
| extletter | ditto |

continued ...

| .cls name | description |
|---|---|
| extproc | ditto |
| extreport | ditto |
| facsimile | fax class |
| faltblat | leaflets |
| fiche | "fiches d'exercices" |
| flacards | flash cards |
| flashcard | business cards |
| flashcards | double-sided business cards |
| fribrief | letter class |
| frletter | French letter class |
| FUbeamer | presentation class with FU Berlin layout |
| FUpowerdot | ditto |
| g-brief | letter class |
| g-brief2 | ditto |
| gaceta | La Gaceta de la Real Sociedad Matematica Espanola |
| gatech-thesis | Georgia Institute of Technology |
| gmdocc | for gmdoc driver files |
| gost732 | special adaptation of the disser class |
| hepclass | thesis class for High Energy Physics |
| hcart | article class |
| hcletter | letter class |
| hcreport | report class |
| hcslides | presentation |
| hitec | article class technical documents |
| hpsdiss | doctoral dissertation |
| hssvita | Curriculum Vitae |
| iagproc | International Association of Geodesy |
| icsv | International Congress on Sound and Vibration |
| IEEEconf | IEEE conference paper |
| IEEEtran | IEEE transactions |
| ijmart | The Israel Journal of Mathematics |
| image-gallery | arrange pictures |
| IMTEKda | IMTEK diploma thesis template |
| isodoc | letter and invoice class |
| isov2 | International Standard Documents |
| itaxpf | International Tax and Public Finance |
| jhep | Journal of High Energy Physics |
| journal | article class derived from article |
| jpsj2 | Journal of the Physical Society of Japan |
| jrurstud | Journal of Rural Studies |
| jura | juristic homework |
| jurabook | juristic books |
| juraovw | juristic overviews |
| juraurtl | juristic decisions |
| k_fribri | letter class derived from KOMA script |

continued ...

| .cls name | description |
|---|---|
| kerntest | show kerning pairs of a font |
| kluwer | manuscript for Kluwer |
| l3doc | LaTeX3 project |
| labbook | book class for lab reports |
| leaflet | leaflets |
| lettcdpadi | letter class for the University of Padua |
| letter | letter class |
| letteracdp | class for the University of Padua |
| lettre | French letter class |
| limap | Information Mapping |
| lps | Logic and Philosophy of Science |
| ltnews | LaTeX news (default) |
| ltugboat | TUGboat (TeX Users Group) |
| ltugproc | ditto (proceedings) |
| ltxdoc | LaTeX documentation |
| ltxdockit | LaTeX documentation kit |
| ltxguide | ditto (guides) |
| macqassign | Macquarie University, Sydney |
| memoir | universal class |
| mentis | manuscripts for Mentis |
| minimal | minimal class (for testing) |
| moderncv | Curriculum Vitae |
| movie | DVI animations |
| mtn | Maple Technical Newsletter |
| muthesis | University of Manchester |
| mwart | special article class for Polish typography |
| mwbk | ditto (book class) |
| mwrep | ditto (report class) |
| my-thesis | derived from ua-thesis (University of Arizona) |
| nature | Nature journal |
| ncc | universal class for ncclatex |
| nccproc | ditto for proceedings |
| nddiss2e | University of Notre Dame |
| newlfm | letter, fax and memo class |
| nih | National Institutes of Health |
| nostarch | No Starch Press |
| nrc1 | National Research Council (Research Press) |
| nrc2 | ditto |
| octavo | special book class |
| oegatb | Austrian Society of Agricultural Economics |
| omdoc | open mathematical documents |
| paper | derived article class |
| papertex | class for magazines |
| pbsheet | special class for mathematical and computer science sheets |
| pecha | special class for Tibetan texts |

continued ...

| .cls name | description |
| --- | --- |
| pittetd | University of Pittsburgh |
| petiteannonce | small advertisements |
| philosophersimprint | article for "Philosophers' Imprint" |
| plari | class for plays |
| play | ditto |
| pocoec | Post-Communist Economies |
| postcards | print postcards with the envlab and mailing classes |
| powerdot | presentations |
| powersem | presentations with TEXpower |
| ppr-prv | printing for presentations with prosper |
| pracjourn | PracTEX journal class |
| proc | special article class |
| prosper | presentations (obsolete) |
| protocol | meeting minutes (protocols) |
| pst-doc | documentation class for PSTricks |
| ptptex | Progress of Theoretical Physics |
| qcm | multiple choice |
| rapport1 | NTG report class |
| rapport3 | ditto |
| recipe | cooking recipes |
| recipecard | ditto |
| refart | article class with special referencing facilities |
| refrep | ditto (report class) |
| regstud | regional studies |
| report | report class (default) |
| revtex4-1 | American Physical Society |
| rtklage | petitions |
| sageep | Environmental and Engineering Geophysical Society |
| sciposter | poster class |
| scrartcl | KOMA script article class (default) |
| scrbook | KOMA script book class (default) |
| scrdoc | KOMA script documentation class |
| screenplay | plays |
| scrreprt | KOMA script report class (default) |
| scrlettr | KOMA script letter class |
| scrlttr2 | KOMA script letter class (default) |
| script | predecessor of KOMA script |
| script_l | ditto |
| script_s | ditto |
| seminar | presentations (obsolete) |
| sffms | science fiction |
| sibjnm | Siberian Journal of Numerical Mathematics (SJNM) |
| sides | plays |
| siggraph | Siggraph conference proceedings (ACM) |
| simplecv | simple Curriculum Vitae |
| slides | presentations (obsolete) |

continued ...

| .cls name | description |
|---|---|
| spie | www.SPIE.org |
| stage | plays |
| sugconf | SAS(R) Users Group conference papers |
| talk | presentations (obsolete) |
| tcldoc | literate programming for the Tool Command Language (TCL) |
| tclldoc | ditto |
| third-rep | UMCSD third-year project reports (University of Manchester) |
| thuthesis | Tsinghua University thesis template |
| timesht | timesheet generator |
| tkz-doc | documentation class for tikz |
| toptesi | scientific articles |
| tufte-book | Tufte book class |
| tufte-handout | Tufte handout class |
| ua-thesis | University of Arizona |
| ucthesis | University of California |
| ucdavisthesis | University of California (Davis) |
| uebungsblatt | exercise sheets |
| uiucthesis | University of Illinois at Urbana-Champaign |
| umich-thesis | University of Michigan |
| umthesis | ditto |
| upmethodology-document | Unified Process Methodology |
| uwthesis | University of Washington |
| usthesis | University of Stellenbosch |
| ut-thesis | University of Toronto |
| vxulicentiate | Vaxjo University |
| vita | Curriculum Vitae |
| weekly | weekly calendar |
| worlddev | World Development |
| xepersian-magazine | Persian articles in XƎLaTeX |
| xepersian-thesis | Persian theses in XƎLaTeX |
| york-thesis | York University, Toronto |

### 2.2.2 Options

All options that can be passed to a document class (class options) have global scope within the document and are evaluated by the document class itself and by all packages included through \usepackage.

```
\documentclass[fontsize=11pt,paper=a4,british,parskip=half]{scrbook}
\usepackage[...]{babel}
...
```

**fontsize=11pt** class option
**paper=a4** class and package option (e.g. geometry package)
**british** class and package option (e.g. babel package)
**parskip=half** class option

Both the scrbook and babel classes evaluate the british option. If there is an option clash, where conflicting definitions are given, you can use either the \PassOptionsToClass command or the \PassOptionsToPackage command to ensure that the options are passed to the class or package nevertheless (cf. page 61).

### 2.2.3  Memoir

The memoir class is the brain child of Peter Wilson and is now maintained by Lars Madsen. Over the years Peter Wilson has written many packages to extend the functionality of the standard classes. However, the extensions can only improve things up to a certain point, so the memoir class was created. The functionality of other packages was tightly integrated and extended into a class that can be seen as a replacement of the book class. Give it the openany class option, and you have the look and feel of the report class. Memoir can even 'emulate' the article class (with \chapter playing the role of \section).

The memoir class provides

- flexible ways of laying out the page, for example either by setting the margins explicitly, or by deciding on the size of the text block and then placing it on the page, or a combination
- a comprehensive system for handling headers and footers (much more tighty integrated than any add-on package can ever achieve)
- interfaces for configuring the look and feel of the various *lists of* (aka TOC and friends), as well as interfaces to creating new ones
- methods to adapt the appearance of chapter titles and its sectional cousins
- plus other configurable features and interesting tools.

Besides the standard class options, memoir also supports extra font sizes (both 9pt and several sizes above 12pt). In addition, it extends the number of predefined paper sizes.

Among the more interesting class options are

**article**  as mentioned above, this will emulate the look of the article class (can be done even more tighty if combined with the reparticle chapter style).

**showtrims**  if using a trimmed document size on a larger stock, this will show the borders of the trimmed size. There are several different looks for these trim marks.

**oldfontcommands**  is a bit special. The memoir class honours the recommendation not to use the TeX commands \bf, \it, \sc, etc. in a document. They are instead replaced with errors. This particular class option bring back the original meaning, but will still issue a warning to the log file. Some old BibTeX .bst files still use \bf internally, so in that case you will need this option.

The last thing to mention about the memoir class is its manual, rather extensive, explaining how to use the class and how to configure it.

### A few memoir examples

Set up a B5 document to be typed on A4 (and trimmed after printing), additionally print trimmarks:

```
\documentclass[a4paper,showtrims,...]{memoir}
\pagebv % short for \settrimmedsize{176mm}{125mm}{*}
\setpagecc{\paperheight}{\paperwidth}{*} % reorient on stock
\settypeblocksize{8in}{5in}{*} % size of the type block
```

```
\setlrmargins{*}{*}{1.3}          % place the type block, h-dir
\setulmargins{*}{*}{1.3}          % place the type block, z-dir
\checkandfixthelayout[nearest]    % verify the layout, and reset
                                  % type block such that the height matches
                                  % an integral number of lines, nearest
                                  % to the required text height
\quarkmarks % Quark style trimmarks
```

In general, when using the memoir interface for margins, remember to use \checkandfixthelayout to setup the layout. In the example above an algorithm is specified for this command, the manual mentions more of these including the default.

Getting rid of the uppercasing headers in:

```
\nouppercaseheads
\pagestyle{headings} % default style in memoir
```

Remove the word \Chapter from the headers, and repeat chapter title in both headers if there are no sectional titles (yet):

```
\addtopsmarks{headings}{}{
  \createmark{chapter}{both}{shownumber}{}{. \ }}
\pagestyle{headings}
```

Add a line to the *headings* style header:

```
\makeheadrule{headings}{\textwidth}{\normalrulethickness}
\pagestyle{headings}
```

Change the page style of all pages with a chapter-like heading (incl. ToC, Bibliography and Index):

```
\aliaspagestyle{chapter}{otherstyle}
```

Show the size of the text block and the placement of the header and footer areas:

```
\pagestyle{showlocs}
```

Memoir keeps track of the last page number and also the total number of sheets used in the document. This can be used to automatically remove headers and footers in a document if it is only one page long (require at least two compilations):

```
\AtEndDocument{%
  \ifnum\value{lastsheet}=1\thispagestyle{empty}\fi}
```

Set the ToC depth and the sectional numbering depth to the subsubsection level:

```
\settocdepth{subsubsection}
\setsecnumdepth{subsubsection}
\maxsecnumdepth{subsubsection}
```

\maxsecnumdepth is important if you use \mainmatter in the document (the mainmatter will restore the value to that depth). To disable sectional numbering completely replace \subsubsection with the word none.

Make the space above chapter entries in the ToC stretchable:

```
\setlength{\cftbeforechapterskip}{1.0em plus 0.2em minus 0.1em}
```

Remove dots for section entries in the ToC:

```
\renewcommand{\cftsectiondotsep}{\cftnodots}
```

By default `memoir` will include the ToC in the ToC(!). Use

```
\tableofcontents*
```

to remove it. Or issue the `\KeepFromToc` command which will set the same flag. Use a different styling for `\chapter` titles. This particular one require little extra code:

```
\usepackage{color,graphicx}
\definecolor{ared}{rgb}{.647,.129,.149}
\renewcommand\colorchapnum{\color{ared}}
\renewcommand\colorchaptitle{\color{ared}}
\chapterstyle{pedersen}
```

## 2.2.4 KOMA-Script

KOMA-Script is a collection of classes and packages that give specific consideration to typographical particulars of a European layout (http://www.komascript.de). All options are also valid for the different KOMA-Script classes. This does not mean that all options make sense for all classes; for example a binding correction would not make sense for the `scrlettr2` letter class. Some typical examples for the KOMA-Script classes `scrartcl`, `scrreprt` and `scrbook` are shown in the following list.

```
\documentclass[paper=a4, BCOR=8.25mm]{scrreprt}
\documentclass[twoside, DIV=15, BCOR=12mm]{scrartcl}
\documentclass[BCOR12mm, DIV=calc, twoside=on]{scrbook}
\documentclass[fontsize=12pt, BCOR=7mm, DIV=calc, headings=small,
    headsepline=on]{scrreprt}
\documentclass[a4paper, fontsize=8pt, headings=small, twocolumn=on]{scrartcl}
\documentclass[fontsize=11pt, paper=a4, fleqn, listof=totoc]{scrbook}
\documentclass[paper=a4, fontsize=10pt, DIV=19, twoside=on, twocolumn=on,
    listof=totoc, open=any, parskip=false, titlepage=on, headings=small,
    BCOR=12mm]{scrbook}
```

Since version 3 of KOMA-Script, the parameters have been specified through a key-value interface, for example `parskip=half+`. You can also specify the options at any point later using the `\KOMAoptions` command. A summary of all the available options is given below. For more details, see the documentation that comes with KOMA script or [9].

KOMA-Script comes with several other packages that are not only suitable for the KOMA classes but work particularly well with them, so we recommend that you use these in preference to others. These packages include, for example, `typearea` for adjusting the document layout and `scrpage2` for headers and footers.

| meaning | option=value | example |
|---|---|---|
| paper format | paper=letter, legal, executive, aX[1], bX[1], cX[1], dX[1], or landscape | paper=a4 |
| binding adjustment | BCOR=<length>[2] | BCOR=12mm |
| separation ratio | DIV=4, 5, ..., calc, classic, areaset, last or default | DIV=15 |
| headers | headlines=<number of lines> | headlines=2.4 |
| print pages | oneside=on or off | oneside=on |
| print pages | twoside=on or off | twoside=on |
| columns | onecolumn=on or off | onecolumn=on |
| columns | twocolumn=on or off | twocolumn=on |
| chapter start[3] | open=any or right | open=any |
| page feed | cleardoublepage=empty, plain, headings, scrheading or current | cleardoublepage=empty |
| title page | titlepage=on or off | titlepage=off |
| paragraph spacing | parskip=full, full*, full+, full-, half, half*, half-, half+ or false | parskip=half |
| paragraph indentation | parskip=false | parskip=false |
| header line | headsepline=on or off | headsepline=off |
| footer line | footsepline=on or off | footsepline=on |
| chapter[4] | chapterprefix=on or off | chapterprefix=off |
| appendix[5] | appendixprefix=on or off | appendixprefix=off |
| figure captions | captions=oneline or nooneline | captions=nooneline |
| table captions | captions=tableheading or tablesignature | captions=tableheading |

continued ...

1. Replace X by 0, 1, ..., 8. All ISO formats are supported.
2. Specify the length as an absolute value with a valid unit; relative values like 3em aren't allowed.
3. Only makes sense in conjunction with the twoside option.
4. Chapter number with or without prefix "chapter".
5. Appendix with or without prefix "appendix".

| meaning | option=value | example |
|---|---|---|
| font size | fontsize=8pt[6], 9pt[7], 10pt, 11pt, 12pt, 14pt[8], 17pt[9], 20pt[10], Xpt[11] | fontsize=11pt |
| heading | headings=small, normal or big | headings=big |
| catalogues | listof=totoc, numbered, flat and/or graduated | listof=totoc,flat |
| | index=totoc | index=totoc |
| | bibliography=totoc or totocnumbered | index=totocnumbered |
| table of contents | toc=flat and/or graduated | toc=graduated |
| summary[12] | abstract=on and/or off | abstract=on |
| numbering[13] | numbers=enddot or noenddot | numbers=noenddot |

6. Requires the file size8.clo of the extsizes package.
7. The same for size9.clo.
8. The same for size14.clo.
9. The same for size17.clo.
10. The same for size20.clo.
11. X can be replaced by an arbitrary number; a corresponding X.clo file must be provided.
12. Summary with or without title.
13. This option refers to all numbered captions.

## 2.3 The layout of the document

When determining the layout of a document, the first thing that you have to specify is whether it is one-sided or two-sided. For two-sided documents, you should set the inner margin to be about the same width as the two outer margins (Figure 2.1). A detailed explanation of the historic reasons and different ways of partitioning and arranging margins and text area is given in [8].

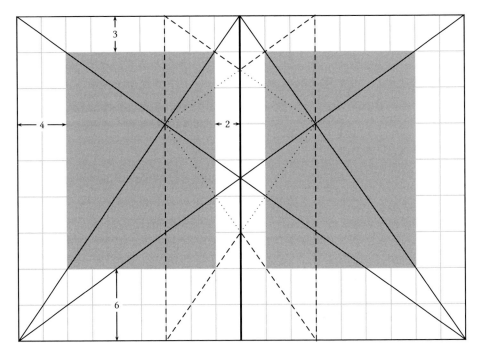

02-03-1

**Figure 2.1:** The type area – a double page for a typical "nine-fold separation" (corresponds to DIV=9 for a KOMA class)

Paragraphs usually either begin with an indentation (\parindent) or are separated with additional vertical space (\parskip). Both at the same time is rare; we show it in Figure 2.3 on page 30 only for the sake of completeness.

Without any additional specifications, the page layout for DIN A4 is the one shown in Figure 2.2 on the facing page with the listed values. To change this layout, use the geometry package or, if one of the KOMA-script classes is specified, use the scrpage2 package.

```
\documentclass[paper=a4,10pt]{scrbook}
\usepackage[paperheight=240mm,paperwidth=170mm,tmargin=5mm,
  textwidth=125mm,textheight=195mm,rmargin=22mm,heightrounded,includeheadfoot,
  headheight=5mm,headsep=8mm,foot=18mm,marginparsep=2mm,marginparwidth=19mm]{geometry}
\usepackage{layout}  \def\notshown{}
\layout* \clearpage \layout*
```

02-03-2

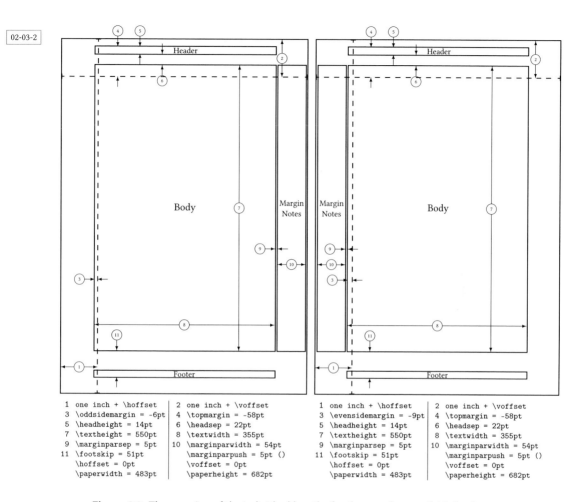

| 1 one inch + \hoffset | 2 one inch + \voffset | 1 one inch + \hoffset | 2 one inch + \voffset |
|---|---|---|---|
| 3 \oddsidemargin = -6pt | 4 \topmargin = -58pt | 3 \evensidemargin = -9pt | 4 \topmargin = -58pt |
| 5 \headheight = 14pt | 6 \headsep = 22pt | 5 \headheight = 14pt | 6 \headsep = 22pt |
| 7 \textheight = 550pt | 8 \textwidth = 355pt | 7 \textheight = 550pt | 8 \textwidth = 355pt |
| 9 \marginparsep = 5pt | 10 \marginparwidth = 54pt | 9 \marginparsep = 5pt | 10 \marginparwidth = 54pt |
| 11 \footskip = 51pt | \marginparpush = 5pt () | 11 \footskip = 51pt | \marginparpush = 5pt () |
| \hoffset = 0pt | \voffset = 0pt | \hoffset = 0pt | \voffset = 0pt |
| \paperwidth = 483pt | \paperheight = 682pt | \paperwidth = 483pt | \paperheight = 682pt |

**Figure 2.2:** The meaning of the individual lengths for the page layout of this book

Headers and footers are best changed through the fancyhdr package or, if one of the KOMA-script classes is specified, use the scrpage2 package. The meanings of the lengths for the individual list environments are shown in Figure 2.4 on the next page. They are also illustrated with example values on page 76. Changes are possible through the list environment (cf. page 43) or through the paralist or mdwlist packages, which let you change the default values easily. You can also make local changes immediately after the start of a list environment, but this isn't recommended, especially if you have a lot of lists.

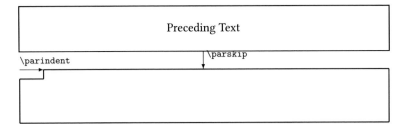

02-03-3

**Figure 2.3:** Parameters of a paragraph

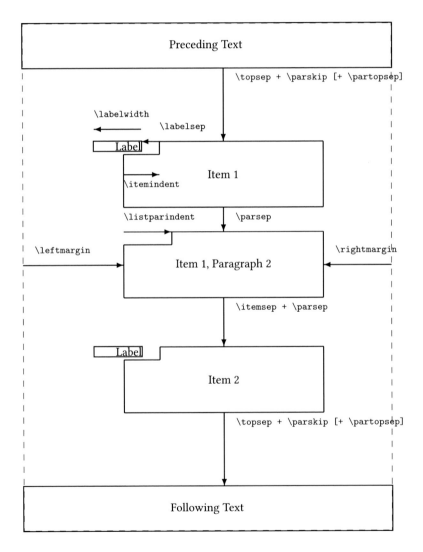

02-03-4

**Figure 2.4:** General layout of a list environment

# Typographical subtleties

## 3.1  Ligatures

A ligature (from the Latin *ligare* meaning "to tie up") in typography is the connection of two or more letters as a single optical unit that corresponds to *one* character. Ligatures are used nowadays mainly for two consecutive letters with ascenders, such as f, i, l or t. Without correction of the horizontal spacing, there is either a gap between the letters or a pairwise kerning. Table 3.1 shows a selection of ligatures in the character set used here; sometimes the difference is obvious while in some cases it is less so. All other ligatures consist of two characters with a smaller space in between them.

**Table 3.1:** Selection of some ligatures

| without | with | without | with |
|---------|------|---------|------|
| ff | ff | fi | fi |
| fl | fl | ffi | ffi |
| ffl | ffl | | |
| -- | – | --- | — |

Ligatures are always language-dependent. You can make manual corrections, i.e. breaking a ligature, either through the character combination `"|` if using the `babel` package with such a defined shortcut (e. g. for `ngerman`) or otherwise through `\/`.

## 3.2 Emphasis

**majuscules** The use of capital letters for emphasis is usually not recommended because they stand out a lot from the surrounding text. To make them appear less dense, they should be spaced out through the `\textls` command from the `microtype` package – `\textls{MAJUSCULE}` ⇒ M A J U S C U L E. Alternatively, you can use the `soul` package.

**small capitals** As with majuscules, words typeset in small capitals can appear very intrusive and should be spaced out – SMALL CAPITALS – S M A L L  C A P I T A L S.

**spacing out** The s p a c i n g  o u t, or increasing of the letter spacing, is problematic in typography, so avoid using this as a means of emphasis. In preference add emphasis through *italic* font.

**bold font** Only use emphasis through **bold font** in captions because words in bold usually stand out too much from the surrounding text.

**italic font** Emphasis through *italic font* is much the best method; the emphasized word doesn't stand out too much from the surrounding text.

## 3.3 Hyphenation and hyphens

The hyphenation algorithm of TeX is usually good enough for manual intervention to be required only in exceptional cases. The Example 03-03-1 on the next page uses the shorthands which are defined with the german language, the reason why we load this language, too. The last one in the list is the default one, in this case *english*. The shorcuts are defined as:

```
\declare@shorthand{ngerman}{"-}{\nobreak\-\bbl@allowhyphens}
\declare@shorthand{ngerman}{"|}{%
  \textormath{\penalty\@M\discretionary{-}{}{\kern.03em}\allowhyphens}{}}
\declare@shorthand{ngerman}{""}{\hskip\z@skip}
\declare@shorthand{ngerman}{"~}{\textormath{\leavevmode\hbox{-}}{-}}
\declare@shorthand{ngerman}{"=}{\penalty\@M-\hskip\z@skip}
```

Example 03-03-1 on the facing page shows how to force hyphenation points through `\-` (others in the word are not valid anymore) and the use of protected ( `"~` no hyphenation) and unprotected ( `"=` other hyphenation possible) hyphens. In addition, there is the invisible hyphen (`""`), which allows for hyphenations without a hyphen. You can specify document-wide hyphenation rules in the preamble through `\hyphenation` (cf. Section 4.2 on page 54).

03-03-1

1 This is a completely normal hyphenation point.
2 This is a completely normal hyphenation point.
3 This is a completely normal-hyphenation point.
4 This is a completely normal-hyphenation point.
5 This is a completely normal-hy-phenation point.
6 This is a completely normal-hyphe-nation point.
7 This is a completely useless line/curve-hyphenation point.
8 This is a completely useless line/curve-hyphenation point.
9 This is a completely useless line/curve-hyphenation point.

```
\usepackage[ngerman,english]{babel}% english is default
\usepackage{paralist}

\extrasngerman% enable german shortcuts
\begin{compactenum}
\item[1] This is a completely normal hyphenation point.
\item[2] This is a completely normal hyphe\-nation point.
\item[3] This is a completely normal-hyphenation point.
\item[4] This is a completely normal-hy"=phenation point.
\item[5] This is a completely normal-hy"~phenation
         point.
\item[6] This is a completely normal-hy\-phe"~nation
         point.
\item[7] This is a completely useless
         line/curve-hyphenation point.
\item[8] This is a completely useless
         line/""curve-hyphenation point.
\item[9] This is a completely useless
         line\slash{}curve-hyphenation point.
\end{compactenum}
```

General problems with hyphenation, especially with compound nouns, occur because of the hyphenation algorithm in use. Nevertheless the number of errors is limited compared to other hyphenation algorithms. You can find the data with the hyphenation points in the $TEXMF/tex/generic/hyphen file, and this can be activated through a corresponding entry in the $TEXMF/tex/generic/config/language.dat file such that they are available for documents.

LaTeX knows various types of hyphens to separate words:

| input | output | description |
|---|---|---|
| A-B | A-B | hyphen (divis) |
| A -- B | A – B | rule (half em dash with word spacing) |
| A--B | A–B | dash (half em dash without word spacing) |
| A---B | A—B | em dash (long dash) |
| $A-B$ | $A-B$ | minus sign |

## 3.4 Abbreviations

Always typeset abbreviations with a \thinspace. Some common examples are shown in Table 3.2. If the abbreviation occurs at the start of a sentence, use the full version, i.e. *not* "…end. E. g. …", but "…end. For example, …".

*start of sentence*

| long form | input | output |
|---|---|---|
| for example | foo, e.\, b. bar | foo, e. g. bar |
| that is | foo, i.\, e. bar | foo, i. e. bar |
| and others | foo et~al bar | foo et al bar |

**Table 3.2:** Summary of some abbreviations

It's a good idea to use the xspace package (CTAN: `latex/contrib/tools/xspace.sty/`) when defining abbreviations. This takes care of a potential subsequent space character as \xspace tests the following character to decide whether to insert a space or not, as illustrated in the following example:

03-04-1

This is, e. g. nothing but …
This is, e. g., nothing but …

```
\usepackage{xspace}
\newcommand*\eg{e.\,g.\xspace}

This is, \eg nothing but \ldots\\
This is, \eg, nothing but \dots
```

Join name affixes to the preceding word with \, to prevent line breaks between the parts.

| normal line break | no break at ~ | keep together |
|---|---|---|
| `Friedrich Wilhelm\,I.` | `Friedrich~Wilhelm\,I.` | `\mbox{Friedrich Wilhelm\,I.}` |
| `F.\,W. King\,I.` | `F.\,W.~King\,I.` | `\mbox{F.\,W. King\,I.}` |
| `Prof.\,Dr.\,med. John Doe` | `Prof.\,Dr.\,med.~John~Doe` | `\mbox{Prof.\,Dr.\,med. John Doe}` |

- With normal line breaks, a line can be broken between words as well as through hyphenation of the words.
- If two parts of a word are connected by a tilde, they appear as one word and hyphenation is only allowed as normal hyphenation within the two parts.
- If you want all parts of a word kept together, enclose it in an \mbox; hyphenation or line breaks aren't allowed in the box.
- A tilde only symbolically keeps parts of a word together; for line breaks, this space can be stretched, which is shown here exaggerated for demonstration purposes:
  foo ''two~words'' bar ⇒ foo      "two          words"          bar.

## 3.5 Physical units

Always typeset measurement units in normal upright font and separated from the measurements themselves by a \thinspace. We recommend using the siunitx package by Joseph Wright (CTAN: `latex/contrib/siunitx/`) and nicefrac (CTAN: `latex/contrib/units/`) for compound units.

The following example shows a selection of the possibilities for formatting measurements and units with the siunitx package. It automatically inserts a \, (thinspace) space between measurement and unit.

03-05-1

$10\,\mathrm{g}\ 23.4\,\mathrm{g\,cm}^3$

$1\times10^{34}\ 1°2'3''$

$16.7\,\mathrm{m\,s}^{-1}$

$30\times10^3\,\mathrm{Hz}$

$1.2\,\mathrm{mm}\times3.56\,\mathrm{mm}\times9.2\,\mathrm{mm}$

$\mathbf{-4.5\,cm}$

$\mathrm{J\,mol^{-1}\,K^{-1}}$

$\frac{\mathrm{J}}{\mathrm{mol\,K}}$

1.2346 9.8000

| Heading |
|---|
| 1.3 |
| 134.2 |
| 3.56 |
| 74.7 |

```
\usepackage{siunitx,booktabs}
\sisetup{expproduct=times}

\SI{10}{\gram}      \SI{23.4}{g.cm^3}\\
\num{1e34}          \ang{1;2;3}\\
\emph{\SI{16,7}{\metre\per\second}}\\
\textbf{\SI{30e3}{\Hz}}\\
\SI{1.2 x 3.56 x 9.2}{\milli\metre}\\
\sisetup{obeyall} \textbf{\SI{-4.5}{\cm}}\\
\si{\joule\per\mole\per\kelvin}\\
\si[per=frac]{\joule\per\mole\per\kelvin}\\
\num[dp=4]{1.23456} \num[dp=4]{9.8}\\
\begin{tabular}{S[tabformat=3.2]}\toprule
{Heading}\\\midrule
1.3 \\ 134.2 \\ 3.56 \\ 74,7 \\\bottomrule
\end{tabular}
```

## 3.6  Quotation marks

Table 3.3 on the next page gives a summary of different quotation marks and inverted commas. The csquotes package is also helpful.

```
\usepackage[ngerman,french,english]{babel}
\usepackage[autostyle,german=guillemets,english=british]{csquotes}
\MakeAutoQuote{>}{<}
\subsection*{A ''quotation mark'' test}
\enquote{english \enquote{inner} text} \quad
''english 'inner' text'' \quad 'english 'inner' text' \quad >english >inner< text< \par
\selectlanguage{ngerman}
\enquote{german \enquote{inner} text} \quad ''german 'inner' text''\quad
'german 'inner' text' \quad >german >inner< text<         \par
\selectlanguage{french}
\enquote{french \enquote{inner} text} \quad ''french 'inner' text'' \quad
'french 'inner' text' \quad  >french >inner< text<         \par
\foreignquote{ngerman}{Hans sagte, >das ist ok< und dann \ldots}
\foreignquote{french}{Jean dit, <d'accord>, et en plus \ldots}
```

03-06-1

### A "quotation mark" test

'english "inner" text'    "english 'inner' text"    'english 'inner' text'    'english "inner" text'
»german ›inner‹ text«    "german 'inner' text"    'german 'inner' text'    »german ›inner‹ text«

« french "inner" text »    "french 'inner' text"    'french 'inner' text'    « french "inner" text »
»Hans sagte, ›das ist ok‹ und dann …« « Jean dit, »d'accord« , et en plus … »

**Table 3.3:** Summary of the different quotation marks and inverted commas

| output | input |
|--------|-------|
| »German«, „German", „German" | "'German"', ,,German'', \glqq German\grqq{} |
| ,German', ,German' | ,German', \glq German\grq{} |
| »yes, ,German' it is« | "'yes, ,German' it is"' |
| „yes, ,German' it is" | \glqq yes, \glq German\grq{} it is\grqq{} |
| "English" | ''English'' |
| "yes, 'English' it is" | ''yes, 'English' it is'' |
| «French» « French » | \flqq French\frqq{} \og French\fg |
| «French» | <<French>> |
| ‹ French › | \flq French\frq{} |
| « yes, ‹French› it is » | \og yes, \flq French\frq{} it is\fg{} |

## 3.7 Special characters

Almost all fonts have their own version of the Euro sign, which doesn't necessarily correspond to the "official" version, for example \texteuro (cf. Table 3.4 on the facing page) or € (\geneuro) in contrast to € (cf. http://en.wikipedia.org/wiki/Euro) and the construction blueprint:

```
\usepackage{eurosym}

\euro\quad
\fontsize{50}{50}
\usefont{U}{eurosym}{m}{n}
\symbol{0}
```

03-07-1

For the degree symbol, you should use \textdegree (cf. Table 3.4 on the next page) to avoid conflicts with other input encodings. The gensymb package also defines a degree symbol. Table 3.4 on the facing page shows two additional versions and a summary of the frequently used \textXXXX commands of the textcomp package. Not all characters are necessarily available in every font though.

## 3.8 Float parameters

The positioning of a floating environment depends on several parameters, which don't always default to the optimal values. The prefix dbl for *double* distinguishes the parameters for *two-column* mode. The default of the individual values depends on the document class and may therefore be different to the values given here.

**Table 3.4:** Summary of some special characters and the `textcomp` characters

| input | output | input | output | input | output |
|---|---|---|---|---|---|
| 5\textsuperscript{°} | 5° | 5$\circ$ | 5° | \S\,9 | §9 |
| 5\,\% | 5 % | \copyright{} | © | | |
| \textquotestraightbase | ‚ | \textquotestraightdblbase | „ | \texttwelveudash | — |
| \textthreequartersemdash | — | \textdollar | $ | \textquotesingle | ' |
| \textasteriskcentered | ∗ | \textfractionsolidus | / | \textminus | − |
| \textlbrackdbl | ⟦ | \textrbrackdbl | ⟧ | \textasciigrave | ` |
| \texttildelow | ˷ | \textasciibreve | ˘ | \textasciicaron | ˇ |
| \textgravedbl | ˵ | \textacutedbl | ″ | \textdagger | † |
| \textdaggerdbl | ‡ | \textbardbl | ‖ | \textperthousand | ‰ |
| \textbullet | • | \textcelsius | ℃ | \textflorin | ƒ |
| \texttrademark | ™ | \textcent | ¢ | \textsterling | £ |
| \textyen | ¥ | \textbrokenbar | ¦ | \textsection | § |
| \textasciidieresis | ¨ | \textcopyright | © | \textordfeminine | ª |
| \textlnot | ¬ | \textregistered | ® | \textasciimacron | ¯ |
| \textdegree | ° | \textpm | ± | \texttwosuperior | ² |
| \textthreesuperior | ³ | \textasciiacute | ´ | \textmu | µ |
| \textparagraph | ¶ | \textperiodcentered | · | \textonesuperior | ¹ |
| \textordmasculine | º | \textonequarter | ¼ | \textonehalf | ½ |
| \textthreequarters | ¾ | \texttimes | × | \textdiv | ÷ |
| \texteuro | € | \textohm | Ω | \textestimated | ℮ |
| \textcurrency | ¤ | \textleftarrow | ← | \textrightarrow | → |
| \textblank | ␢ | \textdblhyphen | = | \textzerooldstyle | 0 |
| \textoneoldstyle | 1 | \texttwooldstyle | 2 | \textthreeoldstyle | 3 |
| \textfouroldstyle | 4 | \textfiveoldstyle | 5 | \textsixoldstyle | 6 |
| \textsevenoldstyle | 7 | \texteightoldstyle | 8 | \textnineoldstyle | 9 |
| \textlangle | ⟨ | \textrangle | ⟩ | \textmho | ℧ |
| \textbigcircle | ◯ | \textuparrow | ↑ | \textdownarrow | ↓ |
| \textborn | ⋆ | \textdivorced | ⚮ | \textdied | † |
| \textleaf | ☙ | \textmarried | ⚭ | \textmusicalnote | ♪ |
| \textdblhyphenchar | = | \textdollaroldstyle | $ | \textcentoldstyle | ¢ |
| \textcolonmonetary | ₡ | \textwon | ₩ | \textnaira | ₦ |
| \textguarani | ₲ | \textpeso | ₱ | \textlira | ₤ |
| \textrecipe | ℞ | \textinterrobang | ‽ | \textinterrobangdown | ⸘ |
| \textdong | ₫ | \textpertenthousand | ‱ | \textpilcrow | ¶ |
| \textbaht | ฿ | \textnumero | № | \textdiscount | ⁒ |
| \textopenbullet | ◦ | \textservicemark | ℠ | \textlquill | ⁅ |
| \textrquill | ⁆ | \textcopyleft | 🄯 | \textcircledP | ℗ |
| \textreferencemark | ※ | \textsurd | √ | \textcircled{digit} | ⑦ |

| name | description | current value |
|---|---|---|
| *counter* – change value through \setcounter{*counter*}{*value*} | | |
| topnumber | Maximum number of floats for position t per page. | 2 |
| dbltopnumber | The same for two-column mode. | 2 |
| bottomnumber | The same for position b. | 1 |
| totalnumber | Maximum number per page. | 3 |
| *fraction* – change value through \renewcommand\⟨*name*⟩{0.0...1.0} | | |
| \topfraction | Maximum fraction of a page of floats of type t. | .9 |
| \dbltopfraction | The same for two-column mode. | .8 |
| \bottomfraction | The same for type b. | .9 |
| \floatpagefraction | Maximum fraction of floats on a page. | .9 |
| \dblfloatpagefraction | The same for two-column mode. | .6 |
| \textfraction | Minimum fraction of text. | .05 |
| *length* – change value through \setlength\⟨*name*⟩{*value*} | | |
| \floatsep | Space between floats of type t and b. | 12.0pt plus 2.0pt minus 2.0pt |
| \dblfloatsep | The same for two-column mode. | 12.0pt plus 2.0pt minus 2.0pt |
| \textfloatsep | Space between float of type t or b and text. | 20.0pt plus 2.0pt minus 4.0pt |
| \dbltextfloatsep | The same for two-column mode. | 20.0pt plus 2.0pt minus 4.0pt |
| \intextsep | Space between float of type h and text. | 12.0pt plus 2.0pt minus 2.0pt |
| \@fptop | Upper page spacing for float of type p. | 0.0pt |
| \@fpbot | Lower page spacing for float of type p. | 0.0pt plus 1.0fil |
| \@fpsep | Space between two floats of type p. | 8.0pt plus 2.0fil |
| *commands* | | |
| \suppressfloats [*value*] | Do not output any further floats on the page after this command. The optional argument can be t or b and restricts this to floats of the respective type. | |
| \clearpage | Output all open floats before starting a new page. | |
| \cleardoublepage | The same for two-page mode. | |

You can change the default values for the individual parameters as follows:

**\floatpagefraction** \renewcommand\floatpagefraction{0.6}

A value between 0.5 and 0.8 (50% and 80%) is recommended, depending on how many figures and tables exist, how big they are and how different the sizes are. One or more figures only appear on a separate page, the "float page", if they take up at least 60% of the page. This reduces the number of float pages, which are often partly empty.

**\textfraction** \renewcommand\textfraction{0.15}

This value should not be chosen too small in order to avoid creating pages with very little text on them. If there are many figures, it is better to choose a small value for

\floatpagefraction. A value between 0.1 and 0.3 (10% and 30%) is recommended.

**\topfraction, \bottomfraction** \renewcommand\topfraction{0.8}
\renewcommand\bottomfraction{0.5}

These values should not be too large. If there are many figures, it is better to choose a small value for \floatpagefraction. \bottomfraction in particular should be small because figures usually appear at the top of a page. Values between 0.5 and 0.85 (50% and 85%) for \topfraction and 0.2 to 0.5 (20% to 50%) for \bottomfraction are recommended.

- One of these two values should always be larger than \floatpagefraction.
- \topfraction should never be 1.
- \bottomfraction should never be 0.

**topnumber, totalnumber** \setcounter{topnumber}{3}
\setcounter{totalnumber}{5}

If there are many small figures, these values should be increased. If figures should always appear on a separate float page, topnumber and bottomnumber should be set to 0 and \floatpagefraction decreased to 0.01.

**\dbltopfraction,\dblfloatpagefraction**
\renewcommand\dbltopfraction{0.8}
\renewcommand\dblfloatpagefraction{0.6}

The following summary shows the decision flow of where to place the figure depending on the placement specifier.

1. If ! is specified, ignore the restrictions above.
2. If h is specified, try to place the floating environment at the current position. If this is not possible because of the restrictions, replace h by t; the float will appear at the earliest available position on the following page.
3. If t is specified, try to place the floating environment at the top of the current or the next page.
4. If b is specified, try to place the floating environment at the bottom of the current or the next page.
5. If p is specified, place the floating environment on the following page without any text.

The default placement is specified by the \fps@<*name*> (float placement specifier) command. The definitions can be found in the respective document classes if they support floating environments.

\fps@figure{*placement*}      \fps@table{*placement*}

Usually they are set to default to tbp, but you can change this globally through \renewcommand.

\makeatletter
\renewcommand\fps@figure{tb}  \renewcommand\fps@table{t}
\makeatother

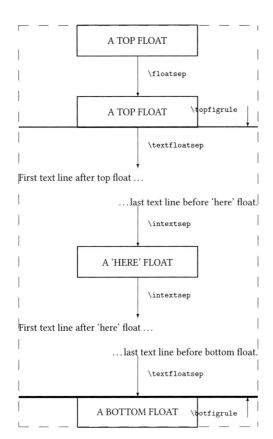

```
\usepackage{layouts}

\setlayoutscale{1}
\floatdiagram
```

03-08-1

The caption package by Axel Sommerfeld is worth using. It provides many ways of formatting figure and table descriptions (cf. Section 8.4 on page 132). If a figure or table should *not* float but does have a caption, use the \captionof command (capt-of or caption packages), which typesets the caption and the figure or table in a minipage. Some floating environments can be defined through the caption package. The floatrow package by Olga Lapko provides further support for placing figures/tables with captions (cf. Section 8.5 on page 138).

# Command list

The tables in this chapter contain all the more or less LaTeX-specific commands and environments. If the name is self-explanatory, no further description is provided. *Optional* arguments and characters have a `grey` background. It's often hard to distinguish between these LaTeX commands and the pure TeX commands, unless the command in question is a TeX primitive. LaTeX is backward compatible; i.e. all TeX commands usually also work in LaTeX, unless they have been redefined to have a different meaning.

## 4.1 Environments

| name | description |
|---|---|
| `$...$` | Robust math environment for inline mode. Equivalent to the `math` environment. |
| `\( ...\)` | Non-robust math environment for inline mode. If the `fixltx2e` package is loaded, `\(...\)` becomes robust, and is then equivalent to `math` and `$...$`. |
| `\[ ...\]` | Short form of the non-numbered `displaymath` environment. |
| `\begin{`**abstract**`}` ... `\end{abstract}` | For the `article` and `report` document classes, an abstract can be given, which is typeset narrower than the current line width. |
| `\begin{`**array**`}` `[`*position*`]` `{`*column definition*`}` ... `\end{array}` | Creates a tabular arrangement. The vertical position can be b (*bottom*), t (*top*) or c (*centre*, default). The environment can only be used in math mode and is extended significantly by the `array` package (cf. Section 8.7 on page 150). |
| `\begin{`**center**`}` ... `\end{center}` | Corresponds to a `trivlist` with `\centering`. Additional whitespace typical for a list (cf. Figure 2.4 on page 30) is inserted before and after the environment, so it should *not* be used in conjunction with floating environments and `\caption`; in those cases it is better to use `\centering`. |

*continued . . .*

| *name* | *description* |
|---|---|

`\begin{`**description**`}` `\item[`*label*`]` *text* `\item[`*label*`]`...`\end{description}`    The labels are all indented and typeset right-aligned and in bold. The exact behaviour depends on the document class.

`\begin{`**displaymath**`}` ...`\end{displaymath}`    Creates a displayed formula without numbering:
$$\sin^2 x + \cos^2 x = 1$$

`\begin{`**document**`}` ...`\end{document}`    Starts and terminates the body of the text; for most document classes, it appears only once.

`\begin{`**enumerate**`}` `\item` [#] *text* `\item` [#] *text*...`\end{enumerate}`    Creates a numbered list that can be nested up to a depth of four. The optional argument can be used to ignore the default numbering. Without the optional argument, one of the counters enumi, enumii, enumiii and enumiv is used, depending on which level is active. The output style of these counters is determined by `\labelenumi`, `\labelenumii`, ..., which you can overwrite, e.g.
`\renewcommand*\labelenumi{\Roman{`*enumi*`}}`.

`\begin{`**eqnarray***`}` ...&...&...\\...&...&...\\...`\end{eqnarray` * `}`    Creates a multi-line displayed formula, with line-by-line numbering, as an array with column definition rcl and the math font style `\scriptstyle` for the central column. The number of lines is formally unlimited. The starred version suppresses the numbering. However, eqnarray can result in poor horizontal and vertical spacing, so it's better to use one of the align environments from the amsmath package (cf. Section 6.3 on page 82).

$$\sin x \quad = \quad \cos x \times \tan x \tag{4.1}$$
$$\sin^2 x + \cos^2 x \quad = \quad 1 \tag{4.2}$$

`\begin{`**equation**`}` ...`\end{equation}`    Creates a single-line displayed formula with numbering.
$$\sin^2 x + \cos^2 x = 1 \tag{4.3}$$

`\begin{`**figure***`}` [*pos*] ...`\end{figure` * `}`    Creates a floating environment, whose content is positioned freely within the current section by LaTeX. The content can be arbitrary and does not have to be a figure. LaTeX only distinguishes between the individual figure and table floating environments when the `\caption` command is used. The environment can't contain page breaks. The optional argument gives you a degree of control over the figure's position: h, here; t, top; b, bottom; p, page (own page). The standard article and book classes have a default of *tbp*; if only h is given, it is amended to ht. A leading exclamation mark ! (e.g. !htb) instructs LaTeX to minimize all length parameters that affect the position of floating environments. The order of the position parameters does not matter. The starred version is useful in `\twocolumn` mode, as it lets you create a floating environment that spans both columns (though not on the first page).

`\begin{`**filecontents***`}{`*file name*`}` ...`\end{filecontents` * `}`    Creates the file *file name* and writes the content of the environment into it. The starred ver-

*continued*...

| name | description |
|---|---|

sion suppresses the first three comment lines. If the file exists already, nothing happens. Using the `filecontents` package, it is possible to overwrite files.

`\begin{`**`flushleft`**`}` ... `\end{flushleft}`    Switches to left-aligned ragged margin without hyphenation by typesetting the content of the environment with `\raggedright` in a `trivlist`. The `ragged2e` package provides the `FlushLeft` environment, which supports hyphenation.

`\begin{`**`flushright`**`}` ... `\end{flushright}`    Switches to right-aligned ragged margin without hyphenation by typesetting the content of the environment with `\raggedleft` in a `trivlist`. The `ragged2e` package provides the `FlushRight` environment, which supports hyphenation.

`\begin{`**`itemize`**`}` `\item` [*symbol*] *text* `\item` [*symbol*] *text* ... `\end{itemize}`    Creates a marked list that can be nested up to a depth of four. By default, the list uses one of the output styles `\labelitemi`, `\labelitemii`, ... as defined by the document class. You can alter the symbol to be used either by using the optional argument or by redefining the styles, e. g. `\renewcommand\labelitemiii{$\Box$}`.

  - item 1
    - item 1.1
    - item 1.2
      □ item 1.1.1
        ⇒ item 1.1.1.1
      □ item 1.1.2
    - item 1.3
  - item 2

`\begin{`**`list`**`}{`*label*`}{`*parameters*`}` `\item` [...] *text* `\item` [...] *text* ... `\end{list}`    You can use this environment to define arbitrary list environments. The optional argument of `\item` overwrites the marks defined by *label*. Most of the *parameters* let you set lengths:

| | |
|---|---|
| `\topsep` | additional vertical space before the list |
| `\partopsep` | additional vertical space before the list if it is preceded by an empty line (should be defined as a dynamic length) |
| `\itemsep` | additional vertical space between `\item` |
| `\parsep` | additional vertical space between paragraphs within an `\item` |
| `\leftmargin` | horizontal space between the left edge of the environment and `\item` |
| `\rightmargin` | horizontal space between the right edge of the environment and the list text |
| `\listparindent` | paragraph indentation of an `\item` (may be negative) |
| `\itemindent` | line indentation of the first line of an `\item` (may be negative) |
| `\labelsep` | horizontal space between label and text |
| `\labelwidth` | minimum box width of the label; wider labels will have a wider box |

*continued* ...

| name | description |
|---|---|

\makelabel{*label*}     generates the label

\usecounter{*counter*}   activates the counter to be used in the list

\begin{**lrbox**}{\⟨*box name*⟩} ...\end{lrbox}     Saves the content of the environment into the to-be-defined box register \⟨*box name*⟩ (corresponds to \sbox). Line breaks are only possible if you use a \parbox or minipage.

\begin{**math**} ...\end{math}     A less-used notation for a math environment for inline mode. Equivalent to the \(...\) environment; neither environment is robust.

\begin{**minipage**} [*vPos*] [*height*] [*iPos*] {*width*} ...\end{minipage}

Typesets the content of the environment in a box of the specified {*width*}. The environment may not contain page breaks. The first optional parameter specifies the vertical position relative to the line: c for centred, b for base line of the previous box line and surrounding base line are the same and t for base line of the first box line and surrounding base line are the same. The second optional parameter gives the box a specific height, and the third optional parameter affects the inner vertical alignment (default is c):

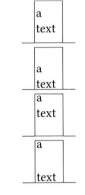

    c:   \begin{minipage}[b][6ex][c]{2em}
         a\\text
         \end{minipage}

    b:   \begin{minipage}[b][6ex][b]{2em}
         a\\text
         \end{minipage}

    t:   \begin{minipage}[b][6ex][t]{2em}
         a\\text
         \end{minipage}

    s:   \begin{minipage}[b][6ex][s]{2em}
         a\par\vfill text
         \end{minipage}

s is only effective if the content contains vertical rubber (stretchable) space, for example \vfill. The valid combinations of optional parameters are: only [*vPos*]; only [*vPos*]height; or all three. Footnotes in a minipage environment are counted with lowercase letters and are part of the minipage themselves, i.e. they don't necessarily appear at the bottom of the page (cf. \fnsymbol command on page 52).

\begin{**picture**}(*x,y*) (*dx,dy*) ...\end{picture}     The specifications for the size do not take a unit; \unitlength is assumed. The optional offset (*dx,dy*) specifies the coordinates of the lower left corner and is assumed to be (0,0) if not specified.

\begin{**quotation**} ...\end{quotation}     Starts a new paragraph with additional left and right margin. \parindent is taken into account, in contrast to the quote environment.

\begin{**quote**} ...\end{quote}     Starts a new paragraph with additional left and right margin. Does not take \parindent into account, in contrast to quotation.

*continued* ...

| name | description |
|------|-------------|

\begin{**sloppypar**} ...\end{sloppypar}    Starts and terminates a paragraph; similar to \sloppy (cf. page 64).

\begin{**tabbing**} ...\end{tabbing}    Creates a tabular arrangement, even in two-column mode and potentially across several pages. The following commands are available within the environment:

| | |
|---|---|
| \= | Puts a tab at the current position. |
| \> | Jumps to the next tab. |
| \< | Typesets something left of the left margin without changing the margin. |
| \+ | The left margin is moved to the right by a tab. |
| \- | The left margin is moved to the left by a tab. |
| \' | The text before the \' command is typeset right-aligned and the text after left-aligned. |
| \` | The text after the \` command is typeset right-aligned. |
| \a | To add accents within the tabbing environment; for example \a 'e⇒é. |
| \kill | Deletes the current (template) line but keeps the tabs defined in it. |
| \pushtabs | Saves or sets all current tabs. |
| \poptabs | Deletes all current tabs such that the previous ones become active again. |

\begin{**table∗**} [*Pos*] ...\end{table ∗ }    Creates a floating environment whose content is positioned freely within the current section by LaTeX. The content can be arbitrary and does not have to be a table. The same conditions apply as for the figure environment (cf. page 42).

\begin{**tabular**} [*position*] {*column definition*} ...\end{tabular}    Creates a tabular arrangement. The vertical *position* can be b (*bottom*), t (*top*) and c (*centre*, default). The following parameters are possible for the column definitions:

| | |
|---|---|
| l | left-aligned column |
| r | right-aligned column |
| c | centred column |
| p{*width*} | \parbox with vertical position t (top) (cf. page 60) |
| \| | vertical line |
| @{*text*} | suppresses the specified inter-column space and inserts *text* instead. You can insert additional inter-column space through \extracolsep{*length*} instead of *text*. |

\begin{**tabular∗**}{*width*} [*position*] {*column definition*} ...\end{tabular∗}    The starred version extends the *right* column until the whole table has the specified width. The vertical position can be b (*bottom*), t (*top*) or c (*centre*, default).

\begin{**thebibliography**}{*labelwidth*} \bibitem [*label*] {*key*} text \bibitem [*label*] {*key*} text ...    \end{thebibliography}
Creates the bibliography as a non-numbered chapter with default caption "Bibliography" or "References" for the article class. The *label width* is specified as an arbitrary string, e. g. *999*.

*continued ...*

| name | description |
|---|---|
| | |

`\begin{theindex}` `\item`...`\subitem`...`\subsubitem`...`\end{theindex}`    Creates the index as a non-numbered chapter with the default caption "Index". If the makeindex program is used, the index is created automatically and saved in the file `\jobname.ind`. Then you can insert this file into the document with the `\printindex` command.

`\begin{titlepage}`...`\end{titlepage}`    Within this environment, a title can be created.

`\begin{trivlist}`...`\end{trivlist}`    Corresponds to a list without labels and list description. The lengths `\listparindent`=`\parindent` and `\parsep`=`\parskip` are set; all other lengths are equal to 0 pt.

`\begin{verbatim*}`...`\end{verbatim * }`    Typesets the content of the environment with `\verbatim@font` font style (usually `\normalfont\ttfamily`) in a separate paragraph as input; commands are not interpreted. The starred version outputs spaces as ␣.

```
The␣verbatim*␣environment␣...
```

`\begin{verse}`...`\end{verse}`    Environment for verses of a poem; you can create line breaks through \\.

## 4.2 Commands

| name | description |
|---|---|
| `{` | Corresponds to `\bgroup`. Starts a local group and must be terminated by `}` or `\egroup`. |
| `}` | Corresponds to `\egroup` and terminates a local group. |
| `~` | Adds a `\nobreakspace`; no line break may occur after this character, for example figure~`\ref{\ldots}`. |
| `\⟨space⟩` | Adds a normal space character. Important after a dot that is not at the end of a sentence or a command. |
| `\@` | If placed in front of a dot, `\@` makes sure that the dot is always treated as a full stop. If placed after a dot, it makes sure that the dot is *never* treated as a full stop (e. g. for abbreviations). |
| `\\` * *[length]* | Starts a new line within a paragraph. The starred version prevents a page break afterwards. The optional *length* changes the line feed, which may be negative. |
| `\"⟨character⟩` | Umlauts: `\"U`⇒Ü; not necessary if an input encoding is specified (cf. Section 8.2 on page 129). |
| `\*` | Allows a line break at this position in math mode and replaces the `\*` command by a multiplication character (`\times`). |
| `\,` | Adds a `\thinspace` in text mode and `\thinmuskip` in math mode. |
| `\;` | Adds a `\thickmuskip` in math mode. |
| `\:` | Adds a `\medmuskip` in math mode. |

*continued ...*

| name | description |
|------|-------------|
| | |

*name   description*

`\!`       Adds a *negative* `\thinmuskip` in math mode.

`\-`       Marks hyphenation points in normal text. Moves the left margin one tab to the left in a `tabbing` environment.

`\=`       Sets a tab (in a `tabbing` environment).

`\=`⟨*character*⟩       Puts a bar (Macron accent) above the *character*. `\=o`⇒ō.

`\>`       Jumps to the next tab (in a `tabbing` environment).

`\<`       Lets you place something left of the margin without changing the margin.

`\+`       Moves the left margin one tab to the right in a `tabbing` environment.

`\'`⟨*character*⟩       Adds an *acute* accent to the *character*. `\'e`⇒é.

`\'`       In a `tabbing` environment, the text before the `\'` command is typeset right-aligned and the text after it left-aligned.

`\`⟨*character*⟩       Adds a *grave* accent to the *character*. `` \`a ``⇒à.

`\``       In a `tabbing` environment, the text after the `\`` command is typeset right-aligned.

`\.`⟨*character*⟩       Adds an accent to the *character*. `\.o`⇒ȯ.

`\|`       ‖, only in math mode.

`\(`       Starts math inline mode.

`\)`       Terminates math inline mode.

`\[`       Starts math display mode.

`\]`       Terminates math display mode.

`\/`       Italic correction, for example [*f*]⇒[*f*] [{\itshape f}\/].

`\#`       Outputs the # character.

`\$`       Outputs the $ character, alternatively `\textdollar`⇒$.

`\%`       Outputs the % character.

`\&`       Outputs the & character.

`\~`⟨*character*⟩       Puts a tilde above the *character*. `\~a`⇒ã. The tilde alone can be output with `\~{}`⇒˜, or alternatively lower with `\textasciitilde`⇒~.

`\_`       Outputs the _ (textunderscore) character.

`\^`       Outputs the ^ character, alternatively `\textasciicircum`⇒^.

`\}`       Outputs the } character.

`\{`       Outputs the { character.

`\aa`     Identical to command `\r{a}`⇒å

`\AA`     Identical to command `\r{A}`⇒Å

`\active`       Used to mark individual characters as active (category 13).

`\addpenalty`{*value*}       Usually used to mark positions as particularly suitable for a page break.

`\addcontentsline`{*file type*}{*level*}{*entry*}       Adds *entry* as caption level *level* to the file with extension *file type*. The default file types are `.toc` (*table of contents*), `.lof` (*list of figures*) and `.lot` (*list of tables*). The *level* depends on the document class and must be a valid name like *chapter, section, ....*

`\addtocontents`{*file type*}{*entry*}       Adds *entry* to the file with extension *file type*. The default file types are `.toc` (*table of contents*), `.lof` (*list of figures*) and `.lot` (*list of tables*).

`\addtocounter`{*counter*}{*value*}       Adds the positive or negative *value* to the existing *counter*.

*continued ...*

| | |
|---|---|
| *name* | *description* |

**\addtolength**\⟨*length command*⟩{*length*}     Adds *length* to \⟨*length command*⟩; *length* must have a unit. The value may be negative or part of a given length command: \addtolength\topskip{-0.3\normalbaselineskip} ⇒ 6.39996pt.

**\addvspace**{*length*}     Adds additional vertical space *length*. If \addvspace has been called before, *length* is only inserted if it is longer than the previous one and even then only the difference between the two.

**\ae**     Outputs the æ character.

**\AE**     Outputs the Æ character.

**\alph**{*counter*}     Outputs the value of *counter* in lowercase letters: \alph{*chapter*}⇒d.

**\and**     Language-independent command to list authors.

**\appendix**     Changes the numbering of captions, equations, . . . as suitable for an appendix; for example for the standard book class: \gdef\thechapter{\@Alph\c@chapter}.

**\arabic**{*counter*}     Outputs the value of *counter* in Arabic numerals: \arabic{*chapter*}⇒4.

**\arraystretch**     Specifies the stretch of array and tabular lines where the text size is unchanged (default is 1). Can be changed through \renewcommand\arraystretch{*factor*}.

**\AtBeginDocument**{*argument*}     Executes *argument* at the beginning of the document.

**\AtBeginDvi**{*argument*}     Places the expanded text of *argument* at the beginning of the DVI file.

**\AtEndDocument**{*argument*}     Executes *argument* at the end of the document.

**\AtEndOfPackage**{*argument*}     Executes *argument* at the end of the package.

**\AtEndOfClass**{*argument*}     Executes *argument* at the end of the document class.

**\author**{*name*}     Defines the author name for the title page; multiple authors should be separated by \and. Remarks in the form of footnotes are possible through the \thanks command. *name* is only output through \maketitle.

**\b**{*character*}     Puts a bar below the *character*: \b{o}⇒o̱.

**\backslash**     Outputs the \ character in math mode: ⇒ \.

**\baselinestretch**     Specifies the scaling factor for \baselineskip. You can change it through \renewcommand\baselinestretch{*value*}, but it's better to use the setspace package to change the line spacing.

**\bf**     Obsolete form for bold font (LaTeX2.09). Replaced by \textbf{*text*}.

**\bfdefault**     Specifies the font series for *bold* (default bx).

**\bfseries**     Switches to the bold font series specified by \bfdefault for the current text character set (like \textbf).

**\bgroup**     Same as {; starts a local group and must be terminated with \egroup or }.

**\bibitem** [*label*] {*key*}     Within thebibliography, \bibitem makes an entry. If no *label* is specified, the value of the enumivcounter is taken. The *key* may contain any alphanumeric and punctuation characters except the comma.

**\bibliography**{*file name*}     Specifies the literature database(s) to be used for BibTeX.

**\bibliographystyle**{*style*}     Specifies the *style* to be used for the bibliography. Usual values are plain, unsrt, alpha and abbrv. Not valid for biblatex.

*continued . . .*

| name | description |
|---|---|

**\bibname**     Caption for the bibliography of the book and report classes (cf. \refname).

**\bigskip**     Adds a vertical space: \vspace{\bigskipamount}. The value depends on the size of the base font.

**\boldmath**     Mathematical expressions after this command are typeset in bold font if the current character set provides the appropriate characters and symbols. \boldmath can only be used outside math mode, so if you are in math mode you can insert it, for example, in an \mbox: $w\mbox{\boldmath$xy$}z$⇒ $wxyz$.

**\c{*character*}**     Adds a cedilla accent below the *character*. \c{c}⇒ç.

**\cal**     Obsolete form for calligraphic uppercase letters (LATEX2.09).     Replaced by \mathcal{*TEXT*}⇒ $\mathcal{TEXT}$.

**\caption** [*TOC*] {*entry*}     The optional *TOC* argument is added to the *table of contents*, *list of figures*, or *list of tables*, depending to the environment, in which \caption is used. If *TOC* is not specified, the normal caption is added to contents list. Further parameters are available if you use the caption package.

**\cdots**     Outputs three continuation dots in math mode that are on the *mathematical* centre line: ⋯.

**\centering**     In contrast to the center environment, \centering does not start a new paragraph with additional vertical space and should therefore be used primarily in floating environments and table columns.

**\chapter** [*TOC*] {*title*}     Starts a new chapter. The optional argument adds *TOC* instead of *title* to the table of contents.

**\chapter\***{*title*}     Starts a new non-numbered chapter, which is not added to the table of contents.

**\chaptermark**{*argument*}     Specifies the page column title for the structuring command \chapter. Executed at each \chapter command.

**\CheckCommand** \* \⟨*command name*⟩ [*N*] [*default*] {*definition*}     Tests     whether     the \⟨*command name*⟩ command is already present in the system with the *identical* definition. If so, an error message is produced. For details of the optional arguments and starred version, see \newcommand.

**\circle** \* {*diameter*}     Creates a circle with the specified *diameter*. The starred version fills it with the current line colour. Only specific diameters are possible; for arbitrary diameters, use the pict2e package.

**\cite** [*Text*] {*key0,key1,...*}     Outputs the labels that correspond to the *keys*. The optional text is added after the reference. Numerous packages change the behaviour and form of \cite.

**\cleardoublepage**     Triggers the output of all open floating environments, ends the page and adds an empty page in two-sided documents unless the following page has an odd page number.

**\clearpage**     The same for one-sided documents.

**\cline**{*i–j*}     In a tabular, array or similar environment (for example longtable), \cline creates a horizontal line starting at the *i*th column and ending at the *j*th column inclusive. Multiple \cline only have an effect if you are using a corresponding package (e. g. hhline).

*continued ...*

| | |
|---|---|
| *name* | *description* |

**\copyright**     Outputs the copyright symbol ©.

**\dag**     Outputs the dagger symbol †.

**\ddag**     Outputs the double dagger symbol ‡.

**\dashbox**{*dash length*}(*w,h*) [pos] {*content*}     Creates a dashed frame of width *w* and height *h* around *content*, which is centred horizontally. Width and height should be a multiple of *dash length*. The position *pos* specifies the vertical position of *content* within the frame: c for centred (default), t for top and b for bottom.

**\date**{*text*}     Specifies the date for the title. If not specified, the date of the current day is assumed; identical to \date{\today}.

**\ddots**     Outputs three continuation dots arranged diagonally from top to bottom: ⋱; the opposite direction is possible with the \reflectbox command from the graphicx package: ⋰ (\reflectbox{$\ddots$}).

**\DeclareErrorFont**{*encoding*}{*family*}{*series*}{*shape*}{*size*}     If the normal font or a replacement can't be used, the error font is chosen: \DeclareErrorFont{OT1}{cmr}{m}{n}{10}.

**\DeclareFixedFont**{\⟨*name*⟩}{*encoding*}{*family*}{*series*}{*shape*}{*size*}     Defines a new (fixed) font that can be referenced directly through \⟨*name*⟩: \DeclareFixedFont{\RM}{T1}{ptm}{b}{n}{2cm}.

**\DeclareFontEncoding**{*name*}{*text*}{*math*}     Specifies the encoding of *name*, where the argument *text* is executed on activation in text mode and *math* on activation in math mode: \DeclareFontEncoding{U}{}{\noaccents@}.

**\DeclareFontEncodingDefaults**{*text*}{*math*}     Specifies the default values, where the argument *text* is executed on activation in text mode and *math* on activation in math mode.

**\DeclareFontFamily**{*encoding*}{*family*}{*options*}     Declares the font family *family*: \DeclareFontFamily{T1}{cmtt}{\hyphenchar \font\m@ne}.

**\DeclareFontShape**{*encoding*}{*family*}{*series*}{*shape*}{*list*}{*options*}     Specifies the grouping of character sets in a specific family: \DeclareFontShape{T1}{cmss}{m}{sc}{<->sub*cmr/m/sc}{}.

**\DeclareFontSubstitution**{*encoding*}{*family*}{*series*}{*shape*}     Specifies the replacement for missing fonts: \DeclareFontSubstitution{OML}{cmm}{m}{it}.

**\DeclareMathAccent**{\⟨*name*⟩}{\⟨*type*⟩}{*font*}{*number*} Defines a new mathematical symbol as an accent: \DeclareMathAccent{\vec}{\mathord}{letters}{"7E}.

**\DeclareMathAlphabet**{\⟨*name*⟩}{*encoding*}{*family*}{*series*}{*shape*}     Defines the font command \⟨*name*⟩: \DeclareMathAlphabet{\mathbf}{OT1}{cmr}{bx}{n}.

**\DeclareMathDelimiter**{\⟨*name*⟩}{*type*}{*standard*}{*number*}{*big*}{*number*}     Defines a new mathematical symbol as a parenthesis (delimiter): \DeclareMathDelimiter{\Vert}{\mathord}{symbols}{"6B}{largesymbols}{"0D}.

*continued* ...

| name | description |
|------|-------------|

**\DeclareMathRadical**{\⟨*name*⟩}{*standard*}{*number*}{*big*}{*number*}

   Defines a new mathematical symbol as an accent:
   \DeclareMathRadical{\sqrtsign}{symbols}{"70}{largesymbols}{"70}.

**\DeclareMathSizes**{*textsize*}{*displaysize*}{*scriptsize*}{*scriptscriptsize*}    Specifies the font sizes for the current math font of size *textsize*:
   \DeclareMathSizes{\@xivpt}{\@xivpt}{\@xpt}{7}.

**\DeclareMathSymbol**{*name*}{*type*}{*font*}{*number*}    Defines a new mathematical symbol: \DeclareMathSymbol{<}{\mathrel}{letters}{"3C}.

**\DeclareMathVersion**{*version*}    Specifies *version* as a new mathematical type: \DeclareMathVersion{bold}.

**\DeclareOption** * {*name*}{*code*}    Defines a new class option *name* that executes *code* if specified when the document class is loaded. The starred version only handles known options.

**\DeclareRobustCommand**\⟨*command name*⟩{*definition*}    Defines a robust command, which may then be passed as an argument to another command.

**\DeclareSymbolFont**{*name*}{*encoding*}{*family*}{*series*}{*shape*}    Defines a new font for symbols: \DeclareSymbolFont{letters}{OML}{cmm}{m}{it}

**\DeclareSymbolFontAlphabet**{\⟨*command name*⟩}{*font*}

   Defines a mapping from font command to font, for example from \matheug to font type EulerGreek:
   \DeclareSymbolFontAlphabet\matheug{EulerGreek}.

**\displaystyle**    Main style in math mode for displayed formulae.

**\documentclass** [*options*] {*class name*} [*release date*]    The *options* are evaluated by the document class and all other packages. Some of the options that are valid for almost all document classes are listed below, with the *default* in italics:
   - *10pt*, 11pt, 12pt – default font size
   - a4paper, a5paper, *letterpaper* – default paper size
   - *portrait*, landscape – orientation
   - *titlepage*, notitlepage – title page
   - leqno – equation numbers on the left
   - fleqn – left-aligned formulae
   - draft, *final* – draft or final version; in the draft version, overfull boxes are marked and figures replaced by a frame
   - openbib – open bibliography format where author, title, etc. are each placed on individual lines
   - *oneside*, twoside – one- or two-sided; twoside is the default for book
   - *openright*, openany – chapters start on either side or only on the right-hand side (only for book)
   - *onecolumn*, twocolumn – one or two columns

**\dotfill**    Fills the line horizontally with a line of dots . . . . . . . . . . . . . . . . . . . . . . . . . . . . .

**\downbracefill**    \makebox[3cm]{\downbracefill}⇒

**\egroup**    Corresponds to } and terminates a local group.

*continued ...*

| name | description |
|---|---|

*name   description*

**\em**      Obsolete command for emphasized font (LaTeX2.09). Replaced by the \emph{*text*} command.

**\emph{*text*}**      *text* is output with emphasis in the current text character set; usually as *italic*. If you use \emph again within its argument, it changes back to normal font.

**\encodingdefault**      The default font encoding (default OT1).

**\endgraf**      The same as \par.

**\endline**      The same as the TeX command \cr (carriage return).

**\enlargethispage** * {*length*}      Extends or shortens (via a negative length) the current page by *length*. The starred version shortens all other dynamic vertical spaces to their minimal values.

**\enspace**      Adds a fixed horizontal space of 0.5 em; equivalent to "\kern{0.5em}␣". Starts a new paragraph if called in vertical mode.

**\enskip**      In principle the same as \enspace, but does not start a new paragraph in vertical mode.

**\ensuremath{*expression*}**      Always typesets the argument *expression* in math mode, regardless of whether it is currently active or not. \newcommand*\al{\ensuremath{\alpha}} means that \al ($\alpha$) as well as $\al$ ($\alpha$) are correct expressions.

**\ExecuteOptions{*options*}**      Executes the corresponding code for the comma-separated list of options, where the order of the options is kept; used for default settings of document options.

**\familydefault**      The default font family; for a sans-serif font for example \renewcommand\familydefault{\sfdefault}.

**\fbox{*text*}**      Puts a frame around *text* with spacing \fboxsep (default 3.0pt) and a line width of \fboxrule (default 0.4 pt).

**\flushbottom**      The text on each page ends before the footer; additional vertical space is inserted all over the page if necessary.

**\fmtname**      Outputs the format name; here ⇒ LaTeX2e.

**\fmtversion**      Outputs the version of the used format; here ⇒ 2011/06/27.

**\fnsymbol{*counter*}**      Depending on the given *counter*, one of nine different symbols can be used as a footnote, where counting starts at one. *, †, ‡, §, ¶, ‖, **, ††, ‡‡, named *asterisk, dagger, double dagger, section mark, paragraph mark, double vertical lines, double asterisks, double daggers, double double daggers*. *counter* must be a valid counter and \fnsymbol can only be used in math mode.

**\fontencoding{*encoding*}**      Specifies the font *encoding*, for example OT1 or T1. Only takes effect after the \selectfont command. \fontencoding{OT1}\selectfont ?<>äöü ⇒ ?¡¿äöü.

**\fontfamily{*family*}**      Specifies the font *family*, for example cmr, lm or pmx. Only takes effect after the \selectfont command. \fontfamily{cmss}\selectfont family cmss⇒ family cmss.

*continued ...*

| name | description |
|---|---|

**\fontseries**{*series*}    Specifies the font *series m* for medium (default), *b* for bold, *c* for condensed, *bc* for bold condensed, *bx* for bold extended. Not all versions are always available. Only takes effect after the \selectfont command. \fontseries{b}\selectfont series b⇒**series b.**

**\fontshape**{*shape*}    *shape* corresponds to *n* for normal (default), *it* for italic, *sl* for slanted, *sc* for small caps, *ui* for upright italics, *ol* for outline. Not all versions are available in every font. Only takes effect after the command \selectfont. \fontshape{sc}\selectfont shape sc⇒ SHAPE SC.

**\fontsize**{*size*}{*line spacing*}    Both parameters must be given without unit and always refer to pt. The line spacing corresponds to \baselineskip, which should be about 1.2 times the font size. Only takes effect after the \selectfont command. \fontsize{6}{7.2}\selectfont size {6}{7.2}⇒ size {6}{7.2}.

**\footnote** [*number*] {*text*}    Increments the footnote counter and puts the footnote number as well as the *text* as a footnote. If you use the optional argument, the footnote counter is not changed and *number* is assumed to be the footnote number. It must always be given as a positive number, regardless of whether the actual footnote is output as number, letter or Roman numeral.

**\footnotemark** [*number*]    Increments the footnote counter but only inserts the footnote number; it is mainly used where \footnote is not possible, such as in a table. If you use the optional argument, the footnote counter is not changed and *number* is assumed to be the footnote number. It must always be given as a positive number, regardless of whether the actual footnote is output as number, letter or Roman numeral.

**\footnoterule**    Creates a footnote line of width 2 inches and height 0.4pt.

**\footnotesize**    Switches the current font size to *footnotesize*. Valid until another font command specifies something else.

**\footnotetext** [*number*] {*text*}    Puts only the footnote text without incrementing the footnote counter and without footnote mark in the text. If you use the optional argument, it is assumed to be the footnote number. It must always be given as a positive number, regardless of whether the actual footnote is output as number, letter or Roman numeral.

**\frac**{*numerator*}{*denominator*}    Creates a fraction in math mode with *numerator* and *denominator*.

**\frame**{*text*}    Creates a ⬛frame⬛ for *text*, but in contrast to \fbox it does not add additional space.

**\framebox** [*width*] [*position*] {*text*}    Creates a frame in normal text mode; if you don't use the optional arguments of *width* and *position*, the frame is similar to \fbox. You can change it by specifying the horizontal *width*: a frame . *position* specifies the horizontal alignment of the *text* within the box:

*continued ...*

| *name* | *description* | |
|---|---|---|

| c | a frame | default |

| l | a frame | |

| r | a frame | |

| s | a | frame | only effective if *text* contains rubber space, which does not

include the normal space between characters.

**\framebox**(*width,height*) [position] {*text*}    Similar to the previous command but only makes sense inside a `picture` environment. (*width,height*) are required; only *position* is optional with possible values c centred (default); t top; b bottom; l left; r right.

**\frenchspacing**    LaTeX does not add additional space after the end of a sentence after this command (default for non-English languages).

**\fussy**    Sets the default values for the paragraph break (cf. `\sloppy` on page 64).

**\H**{*character*}    Puts an umlaut with long ticks over the *character.* \H{o}⇒ő.

**\hfill**    Fills the current line with whitespace as far as possible until the next character. Corresponds to \hspace\fill⇒                                                                                                                 !.

**\hline**    Draws a horizontal like across the width of a table; it must be used after a line feed (\\) except for the top line. Multiple \hline draw multiple offset lines that will not be interrupted by any vertical lines.

**\hphantom**{*text*}    Inserts a space of zero height with equivalent to the width of *text*.

**\hrulefill**    Fills the current line as far as possible with a horizontal line at base line level.

**\hspace** * {*length*}    Adds horizontal space of *length*. The starred version also adds this space at the beginning of a line, which would be ignored otherwise.

**\huge**    Switches the current font size to *huge* (bigger). Valid until another font command is given.

**\Huge**    Switches the current font size to *Huge* (still bigger). Valid until another font command is given.

**\hyphenation**{*word list*}    *word list* is a space separated list of words and their hyphenation points, for example \hyphenation{*su-per-cal-ifrag-ilis-tic-ex-pi-ali-do-cious DANTE*}, where *DANTE* will not be hyphenated. Within normal text, hyphenation points can be defined through \-.

**\i**    Outputs an ı without a dot.

**\IfFileExists**{*file name*}{*true action*}{*false action*}    If the file exists, the code in *true action* is executed, otherwise the code in *false action* is executed.

**\include**{*file*}    Includes an external TeX file and starts a new page (in contrast to \input). Therefore \include is primarily suitable for chapters or paragraphs and is usually used in conjunction with \includeonly. \include may not occur in the preamble or be part of a file that is being \included. In these cases, \input must be used, which may be nested arbitrarily.

**\includeonly**{*file1,file2,...*}    Only the files listed (separated by comma) may be included using an \include command. For all others, only the .aux file is used such that links, references and page numbers correspond to the entire document.

*continued ...*

| name | description |
|------|-------------|

**\includegraphics** * [*options*] {*file name*}    Includes a graphic (requires either the graphics or graphicx packages). For further explanation, see Section 8.3.1 on page 130.

**\indent**    Horizontal indention which corresponds to the current value of \parindent.

**\input**{*file*}    Includes an external TeX file exactly where the \input command occurs (in contrast to \include). \input may occur in the preamble and in files being \input and can be nested arbitrarily.

**\InputIfFileExists**{*file*}{*true action*}{*false action*}    If *file* exists, the code in *true action* is executed and the *file* is included and added to the list of files (which can be output through \listfiles afterwards). Otherwise the code in *false action* is executed.

**\it**    Obsolete form for italic text (LaTeX2.09). Replaced by \textit{*text*}.

**\itdefault**    Specifies the font form for *italic* (default it).

**\item** [*label*]    Starts a new entry within lists. The optional argument can be used to specify a custom symbol or text label.

**\itshape**    Switches to the font form specified by \itdefault within the current text character set (similar to \textit).

**\j**    Outputs a ȷ without a dot.

**\kill**    Deletes the current line. Primarily used when defining tabs as they are retained after the prototype line is deleted.

**\l**    Outputs the ł character.

**\L**    Outputs the Ł character.

**\label**{*key*}    Assigns *key* to a countable object like section title, figure caption, equation number, ... \label must therefore appear *after* the command that creates the object being counted.

**\large**    Switches the current font size to the next bigger size. Valid until another font command is given.

**\Large**    Switches the current font size to the size after \large. Valid until another font command is given.

**\LARGE**    Switches the current font size to \Large; note that this is not available in all document classes. Valid until another font command is given.

**\LaTeX**    Outputs LaTeX in the current font.

**\LaTeXe**    Outputs LaTeX $2_\varepsilon$ in the current font.

**\lbrack**    Outputs an opening square bracket ([).

**\ldots**    Outputs three horizontal continuation dots ...; works in either math mode or text mode. Equivalent to \dots

**\left**{*parenthesis*}    Marks the left parenthesis in math mode. *parenthesis* can take one of the following values: (, ), [, ], \{, \}, |,\vert, \|, \Vert, /, \backslash, \langle, \rangle, \uparrow, \downarrow, \updownarrow.

**\leftmark**    Contains the content of the last \markboth command of the current page for the header.

*continued* ...

| name | description |
|---|---|

**\let**\⟨*commandA*⟩=\⟨*commandB*⟩    \let assigns the *current* meaning of \⟨*commandB*⟩ to \⟨*commandA*⟩, which does not behave like a normal command, i.e. it is not expandable. If you change the definition of \⟨*commandB*⟩ after the assignment, this doesn't affect \⟨*commandA*⟩.

**\limits**    Lets you set limits above and below the symbol for mathematical operations.

**\line**(*dx,dy*){*length*}    A line of *length* is drawn. The two integer numbers *dx,dy* specify a fraction (which must be less than 6 and completely cancelled down) that gives the gradient of the line. Depending on whether *dx* or *dy* is greater, *length* refers to the horizontal or vertical length, respectively. Negative gradients are possible as well. Because of the restrictions on the gradient, it's better to use the pict2e package.

**\linebreak** [*value*]    Terminates the current line and formats it in the same way as the preceding one. If that line is justified, this line would be justified as well. The optional argument *value* takes integer values between 0 and 4 inclusive to specify the urgency of the line break; 4 means it *must* occur.

**\linethickness**{*thickness*}    Defines the line width of horizontal and vertical lines.

**\listfiles**    LATEX adds a list of all loaded files (usually with version numbers) at the end of the log file.

**\llap**{*text*}    Writes *text* into a box of width zero such that *text* does not move the current point while the text is moved to the left. Can be used to overwrite text: ABC\llap{DEF}GHI⇒ABCGHI (cf. \rlap on page 63).

**\LoadClass** [*options*] {*document class*} [*date*]    Loads *document class* with the specified *options*.

**\LoadClassWithOptions**{*document class*} [*date*]    Loads *document class* with the options that are valid for the current document class.

**\loop**{*loop arguments*}    Starts a loop that can be terminated through \exit. The end of the loop is marked by \repeat.

**\lq**    Outputs the opening (left) single quote mark '.

**\makeatletter**    Changes the catcode of the @ character to 11, which corresponds to a normal character (letter).

**\makeatother**    Changes the catcode of the @ character to 12, which corresponds to no normal character.

**\makebox** [*width*] [*position*] {*text*}    Puts the *text* argument into a box in normal text mode; if you don't use the optional *width* and *position* arguments, the box is similar to \mbox. The *width* argument changes the horizontal width of the box (the frames in these examples are only for illustration purposes): ⎍ some text ⎍. The *position* argument controls the horizontal alignment within the box: c ⎍ some text ⎍ (default), l ⎍some text ⎍, r ⎍ some text⎍ and s ⎍some      text⎍. s is only effective if *text* contains rubber space, which doesn't include the normal spacing between characters. The \makebox command is useful if a line or paragraph needs to be wider than \linewidth and centred: \makebox[1.2\linewidth]{*text*}.

*continued* ...

| name | description |
|------|-------------|

*name description*

**\makebox** (*width,height*) [position] {*text*}    Similar to the previous command, but you can use this form within a `picture` environment. You must specify (*width,height*) with units, and can also specify *position*, with the possible values c centred (default); t top; b bottom; l left; r right.

**\makeindex**    Creates the \jobname.idx index file for the \index commands.

**\MakeLowercase**{*text*}    Converts {*text*} to lowercase letters: \MakeLowercase{BIG}⇒ big.

**\MakeRobust**\⟨*command*⟩    Declares the \⟨*command*⟩ retroactively as not fragile. Requires the fixltx2e package.

**\maketitle**    Creates the title according to the specifications in \author, \date, \thanks and \title, which, depending on the document class, may appear on its own page. For customization, you can use the titlepage environment.

**\MakeUppercase**{*text*}    Converts    {*text*}    to    uppercase    letters: \MakeUppercase{small}⇒SMALL.

**\marginpar** [left] {*right*}    Creates a margin note; usually the first line of the note will appear at the same height as the command itself. Use the optional argument for two-sided documents.

**\markboth**{*left head*}{*right head*}    Sets the header for two-sided documents. Usually used in conjunction with the *myheadings* page style, but you can also use it to overwrite the current header definition. Evaluated by LaTeX only when the page ends.

**\markright**{*right head*}    Sets the header for one-sided documents; otherwise the same as \markboth.

**\mathbf**{*math*}    Typesets (just) the normal variables of the *math* expression in boldface and upright: $\mathbf{f(x)=2+x+x^2}$⇒ $f(x) = 2 + x + x^2$.

**\mathcal**{*math*}    Outputs the *math* expression with calligraphic letters; only uppercase letters are possible: $\mathcal{math}$⇒ $\mathcal{MATH}$.

**\mathit**{*math*}    Outputs the *math* expression in italic: $\mathit{f(x)=2+x+x^2}$⇒ $f(x) = 2 + x + x^2$.

**\mathnormal**{*math*}    Outputs the *math* expression in the default math font: \mathnormal{$f(x)=2+x+x^2$} ⇒ $f(x) = 2 + x + x^2$.

**\mathop**{*operator*}    Declares *operator* to be of mathematical type, which means that it can have limits; you can only use this command in math mode:

$$f(x) = A(x) \cdot B_{i=1}^{n}(x_i) \qquad f(x) = A(x) \cdot \overset{n}{\underset{i=1}{B}}(x_i)$$

**\mathrm**{*math*}    Outputs the *math* expression in roman: $\mathrm{f(x)=2+x+x^2}$⇒ $f(x) = 2 + x + x^2$.

**\mathsf**{*math*}    Outputs the *math* expression in sans serif: $\mathsf{f(x)=2+x+x^2}$⇒ $f(x) = 2 + x + x^2$.

**\mathtt**{*math*}    Outputs    the    {*math*}    expression    in    typewriter: $\mathtt{f(x)=2+x+x^2}$⇒ $f(x) = 2 + x + x^2$.

**\mathversion**{*version*}    Switches the math character set to *version*.

*continued* ...

| name | description |
| --- | --- |

**\mbox**{*text*}    Puts *text* into a LR box. Uses the current text font even when in math mode: compare $A\_\mbox{big}$ ⇒ $A_{\mathrm{big}}$ and $A\_{big}$ ⇒ $A_{big}$

**\mddefault**    Specifies the font series for *medium* (default m).

**\mdseries**    Switches to the font series defined by \mddefault within the current character set (similar to \textmd).

**\medskip**    Vertical feed; the same as \vspace{\medskipamount}.

**\multicolumn**{*number of columns*}{*position*}{*text*}    Used in tabular and array environments to merge multiple columns, for example for captions. All three arguments are required, but the last one can be empty. *number of columns* specifies the number of columns to be merged, *position* the alignment of the columns: either c for centred, l for left, r for right or p for a fixed width. \multicolumn must be used at the beginning of a row or immediately after a column separator.

**\multiput**$(x,y)(dx,dy)${*N*}{*object*}    Starting at $(x,y)$, *object* is output *N* times in $(dx,dy)$ steps.

**\narrower**    Increases the left (\leftskip) and the right (\rightskip) margin by the value of \parindent.

**\NeedsTeXFormat**{*format*} [*date*]    Checks you are using a suitable file format. *format* is usually *LaTeX2e* and *date* a specific publication date that must be at least reached with the current version; if not, a message is output to the log file.

**\negthinspace**    A negative horizontal space of $2/3$ em.

**\newcommand** * \⟨*command name*⟩ [*N*] [*default*] {*definition*}    Defines a new command, where *N* is only mandatory if the command has at least one parameter. The optional *default* can be the definition of an optional argument if it is not used by the user. LaTeX only allows one optional parameter in the definition, which is always called #1 (however, the twoopt package allows two optional parameters). By default, the command is defined as *long* version, and the parameter may contain text with paragraphs. However, the starred version creates an error message if one of the arguments contains a \par command or an empty line for a new paragraph.

**\newcounter**{*name*} [*reset counter*]    Defines the counter *name*. The optional *reset counter* resets the defined counter when it is incremented.

**\newenvironment**{*name*} [*N*] [*default*] {*startDef*}{*endDef*}    Defines a new environment *name*, where *N* is only mandatory if the environment has at least one parameter. The optional specification of the default value requires *N* to be at least 1. LaTeX only allows one optional parameter in the definition, which is always called #1. *startDef* specifies the commands to be executed on \begin{*name*} and *endDef* those to be executed on \end{*name*}.

**\newfont**\⟨*command name*⟩{*font name*}    Assigns the font *font name* to \⟨*command name*⟩, which you can then use to change the current font.

**\newif**\if⟨*name*⟩    Defines a new if variable, which you can use as \if⟨*name*⟩ ... \else ... \fi and set through \⟨*name*⟩false and \⟨*name*⟩true.

**\newlength**\⟨*name*⟩    Defines the length \⟨*name*⟩, with default value 0 pt.

*continued . . .*

| name | description |
|------|-------------|

**\newline** Terminates the line at the current position and starts a new one. You can also use this within a table cell if line breaks are allowed here.

**\newpage** Terminates the current page at the current position and starts a new one.

**\newsavebox\**⟨*box name*⟩ Defines \⟨*box name*⟩ as a box. You must not use the name otherwise, and it has global scope.

**\newtheorem**{*name*} [*counter*] {*title*} [*environment*] *name* specifies the environment (must not be used as environment or counter) and *title* the preamble of the theorem environment in front of the running number. Only one of the two optional arguments can be used at a time: either an existing counter is given, for example *section*, or an environment defined with a counter.

**\nobreakspace** Disallows line breaks at that position; equivalent to ~.

**\nocite**{*key list*} Lets you output a reference in the bibliography that was not cited explicitly in the text. \nocite{*} outputs all entries in the literature database specified through \bibliography.

**\noindent** Prevents a new paragraph from being indented if it would be indented otherwise; no effect in other places.

**\nointerlineskip** Suppresses the additional spacing between two lines; you can only use this after \par.

**\nolinebreak** [*value*] Instructs LaTeX not to insert a line break at this position. The optional argument *value* takes integer values between 0 and 4 inclusive to specify the importance of there being no line break; the value 4 means *definitely* no line break.

**\nonfrenchspacing** Switches to the non-European layout at the end of a sentence.

**\nonumber** Skips the numbering of an equation:

$$y' = xy$$
$$y'' = y \tag{1}$$

```
\usepackage{amsmath}

\begin{align}
y'  &= xy\nonumber\\
y'' &= y
\end{align}
```

**\nopagebreak** [*value*] Instructs LaTeX not to insert a page break at this position. The optional argument *value* takes integer values between 0 and 4 inclusive to specify the importance of there being no page break; the value 4 means *definitely* no page break.

**\normalbaselines** Resets the line skips to their default values.

**\normalmarginpar** Resets the default left/right alignment of margin notes.

**\normalsize** Switches to default font size.

**\not\**⟨*command*⟩ \not, which can only be used in math mode, negates the majority of symbols, e.g. $\in$ and $\notin$ ($\in$ and $\not\in$).

**\null** The command is the same as \hbox{} and formally does nothing but counts as input for LaTeX. An empty page can be achieved through the \newpage\null\newpage sequence.

**\o** Outputs the ø character.

*continued ...*

04-02-1

| name | description |
|---|---|

**\O**     Outputs the Ø character.

**\obeyspaces**     Makes the space active so that consecutive ones are no longer ignored by LaTeX; compare foo␣␣␣␣bar⇒ foo bar and \obeyspaces␣foo␣␣␣␣bar⇒ foo bar.

**\oe**     Outputs the œ character.

**\OE**     Outputs the Œ character.

**\offinterlineskip**     Switches off the additional space between lines.

**\onecolumn**     Starts a new page and changes to one-column mode.

**\oval**(*width,height*) [*selection*]     \oval creates a rectangle with rounded corners. You can use the optional argument to select only parts of it: *t* top, *b* bottom, *r* right and *l* left. Only specific radii are possible.

**\overbrace**{*equation*}^{*label*}     Puts a brace on top of the *equation*, which you can label in the usual fashion through ^: $\overbrace{a^2+b^2}^{c^2}$ ⇒ $\overbrace{a^2 + b^2}^{c^2}$

**\overline**{*equation*}     Puts a line on top of the *equation*: $\overline{a^2+b^2}$ ⇒ $\overline{a^2 + b^2}$

**\P**     Outputs the pilcrow character (or paragraph mark) ¶.

**\pagebreak** [*value*]     \pagebreak terminates the current page *after* the current line – in contrast to \newpage, which breaks the page immediately and doesn't do any vertical formatting. The optional argument *value* takes integer values between 0 and 4 inclusive to specify the urgency of the page break; the value 4 means it *must* occur.

**\pagenumbering**{*style*}     Specifies the style for the output of the page numbers. *arabic* for Arabic numerals, *roman* for lowercase Roman numerals, *Roman* for uppercase Roman numerals, *alph* for lowercase letters and *Alph* for uppercase letters.

**\pageref**{*mark*}     Outputs the page number that has been labelled with *mark*; for example, this section of the command definitions starts on page 46.

**\pagestyle**{*type*}     Defines the page style with one of the standard values:
- plain (only a page number)
- empty (no headers and footers, no page numbers)
- headings (running titles and page numbers in the footer)
- myheadings (evaluates the user-set values of \markboth and \markright)

**\par**     Terminates a paragraph; equivalent to an empty line in the source text.

**\paragraph**{*title*}     Starts a new paragraph that is not numbered and whose title is inserted into the normal line of text using \textbf.

**\paragraphmark**{*argument*}     Specifies the page column title for the structuring type paragraph.

**\parbox** [*vPos*] [*height*] [*iPos*] {*width*}{*content*}     Puts *content* into a paragraph box of width {*width*}. The optional parameter *vPos* specifies the vertical position within the surrounding line:

*continued* ...

| name | description |
|---|---|

c: centred

b: base line of the last line of the box and base line of the surrounding text are the same

t: base line of the first line of the box and base line of the surrounding text are the same

The second optional parameter gives the box a certain height. The third optional parameter specifies the vertical alignment within the box:

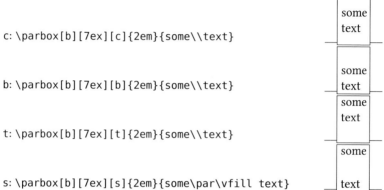

c: `\parbox[b][7ex][c]{2em}{some\\text}`

b: `\parbox[b][7ex][b]{2em}{some\\text}`

t: `\parbox[b][7ex][t]{2em}{some\\text}`

s: `\parbox[b][7ex][s]{2em}{some\par\vfill text}`

s is only effective if the *text* contains rubber space, e. g. `\vfill`. The valid combinations of optional parameters are: just [ *vPos*], [ *vPos*] [ *height*], or all three.

`\PassOptionsToPackage`{*options*}{*package*}    Passes the options (comma-separated list) to the specified package. You can use this to avoid option clashes.

`\PassOptionsToClass`{*options*}{*class*}    Passes the options (comma-separated list) to the specified class.

`\poptabs`    Restores the last tab positions saved through `\pushtabs` for the `tabbing` environment.

`\ProcessOptions` *    All document class and package options that have not been processed so far are processed after this command. The starred version makes sure that the options are processed in the order in which they were specified.

`\protect`\⟨*command*⟩    Protects \⟨*command*⟩ from being broken (expanded) as the argument of another command, for example `\protect\cite{...}` if it is part of the argument to `\caption`.

`\providecommand` * \⟨*command name*⟩ [*N*] [*default*] {*definition*}    Identical syntax and effect to `\newcommand`, except that it has no effect if \[*command name*] is defined already.

`\ProvidesClass`{*name*} [*version dates*]    Specifies the class file *name* through version dates:    `\ProvidesClass{`*article*`}[2005/09/16 v1.4f Standard LaTeX document class]`.

`\ProvidesFile`{*name*} [*version dates*]    Specifies the file *name* through version dates:    `\ProvidesFile{`*utf8.def*`}[2006/03/30 v1.1i UTF-8 support for inputenc]`.

*continued* ...

| name | description |
| --- | --- |

**\ProvidesPackage**{*name*} [*version dates*]  Specifies the package file *name* through version dates: \ProvidesPackage{alltt} [ *1997/06/16 v2.0g defines alltt environment*].

**\pushtabs**  Saves the current tab positions in a `tabbing` environment.

**\put**(*x*,*y*){*object*}  Puts the *object* at the position specified by the coordinates. The coordinates are specified without a unit and refer to the defined \unitlength. The main application of the \put command is the placement of the \line, \vector, \circle and \oval picture objects.

| | | |
| --- | --- | --- |
| **\quad** | Adds a horizontal space of 1em: | A\quad B⇒A   B. |
| **\qquad** | Adds a horizontal space of 2em: | A\qquad B⇒ A   B. |

**\raggedbottom**  Vertical equivalent to \raggedright. Instructs LaTeX not to insert additional vertical space to make the last line of text appear at the foot of the page. This formatting is the default for the `article`, `report` and `letter` document classes.

**\raggedleft**  Outputs lines right-aligned. This command corresponds to the `flushright` environment.

**\raggedright**  Output lines left-aligned. This command corresponds to the `flushleft` environment.

**\raisebox**{*length*} [*upper length*] [*lower length*] {*text*}  Shifts *text* up or down, depending on *length*. The optional parameters let you specify the upper and lower length of the box independent of *text*. If only one optional argument is specified, it is assumed to be the upper length:

\fbox{\raisebox{1ex}[1ex][1ex]{box}} ⇒ $\boxed{\text{box}}$

\fbox{\raisebox{\height}{box}} ⇒ $\boxed{\text{box}}$

**\rbrack**  Outputs the closing right square bracket (]).

**\ref**{*mark*}  Creates a reference to *mark*, which must be defined through the command \label after a "countable" command, for example \section, somewhere in the text.

**\refname**  Caption for the bibliography of the `article` class (cf. \bibname).

**\renewcommand** * \⟨command name⟩ [*N*] [*default*] {*definition*}  Same syntax and effect as \newcommand except that ⟨command name⟩ must be defined already.

**\repeat**  Marks the end of a loop started by \loop.

**\RequirePackage** [*settings*] {*package name*} [*release date*]  Corresponds to \usepackage for classes and packages. The command is ignored if the package has already been loaded; if not, the package is loaded with the options specified, given through \PassOptionsToPackage and the class options. You can use the optional *release date* to require a particular package date.

**\RequirePackageWithOptions**{*package name*} [*release date*]  If the package has not been loaded already, it is loaded with the options of the active document class and/or those of an active package.

**\reversemarginpar**  Switches left/right alignment of the margin notes.

*continued . . .*

| name | description |
|---|---|

**\right**{*parenthesis*}     Marks the right parenthesis in math mode. *parenthesis* can take one of the following values: (, ), [, ], \{, \}, |, \vert, \|, \Vert, /, \backslash, \langle, \rangle, \uparrow, \downarrow, \updownarrow.

**\rightmark**     Contains the lower mark for the header that was defined through the first \markboth or \markright command on the current page. If this does not exist, the previous mark is assumed.

**\rlap**{*text*}     Puts *text* into a box of zero width such that *text* does not move the current point to the right. You can use this to overwrite text:
\rlap{ABCDEF}GHI⇒G̶H̶IDEF                                        (cf. \llap on page 56).

**\rm**     Obsolete form for Roman font (LATEX2.09). Replaced by \textrm{*text*}.

**\rmdefault**     Specifies the font family for Roman (default cmr).

**\rmfamily**     Switches to the font family defined through \rmdefault (similar to \textrm).

**\roman**{*counter*}     Outputs the value of *counter* in lowercase Roman numerals, e. g. \roman{*chapter*}⇒iv.

**\Roman**{*counter*}     Outputs the value of *counter* in uppercase Roman numerals, e. g. \Roman{chapter}⇒IV.

**\rq**     Outputs the closing (right) single quote mark '.

**\rule** [*shift*] {*width*}{*height*}     Creates a rectangle of size *width* and *height* filled with the current line colour. The optional *shift* argument shifts the rectangle vertically; negative values are also possible.                      ▆

▆     (\rule{30pt}{12pt}  –  \rule[6pt]{30pt}{12pt}  – \rule[-6pt]{30pt}{12pt}).     Values of 0 pt for either *width* or *height* yield invisible lines, which can be useful for formatting.

**\S**     Outputs the section sign §.

**\samepage**     Obsolete command.

**\savebox**\⟨box name⟩ [*width*] [*position*] {*text*}     In principle the same as \sbox, but \savebox is not robust and has two optional parameters, similar to \makebox.

**\sb**{*text*}     Corresponds to the _ character for subscript in math mode.

**\sbox**\⟨box name⟩{*text*}     Saves *text* in \⟨box name⟩, which can then be used with \usebox. The box must have been defined before through \newsavebox. \sbox corresponds to \mbox, in principle.

**\sc**     Obsolete form for SMALL CAPS (LATEX2.09). Replaced by \textsc{*text*}.

**\scdefault**     Specifies the font form for SMALL CAPS (default sc).

**\scriptsize**     Switches the current font size to a very small size scriptsize. Valid until another font command is given.

**\scshape**     Switches to the font form defined by the \scdefault command within the current TEXT CHARACTER SET (similar to \textsc).

**\scriptstyle**     Style for sub- and superscripts in math mode.

**\scriptscriptstyle**     Style for second-level sub- and superscripts in math mode.

**\section** [*TOC*] {*title*}     Starts a new section. The optional argument specifies the entry in the table of contents; if not given, *title* is assumed.

*continued . . .*

| name | description |
| --- | --- |

**\section**∗{*title*}    Starts a new non-numbered section that is not added to the table of contents.

**\sectionmark**{*argument*}    The same as \chaptermark for \section.

**\selectfont**    Activates the settings specified by previous \fontxxx commands.

**\seriesdefault**    The specified standard font series (default \mddefault).

**\setcounter**{*counter*}{*value*}    Sets *counter* to *value*.

**\setlength**\⟨*length*⟩{*value*}    Sets \⟨*length*⟩ to *value*, which must have been specified in the valid units (cf. Section 5.1 on page 71).

**\SetMathAlphabet**\⟨*name*⟩{*math version*}{*encoding*}{*family*}{*series*}{*shape*}
Defines the font \⟨*name*⟩ of version *math version*:
\SetMathAlphabet\mathsf{bold}{OT1}{cmss}{bx}{n}.

**\SetSymbolFont**{*name*}{*math version*}{*encoding*}{*family*}{*series*}{*shape*}
Defines the font *name* of version *math version*:
\SetSymbolFont{letters}{bold}{OML}{cmm}{b}{it}.

**\settodepth**\⟨*length*⟩{*text*}    Sets \⟨*length*⟩ to the depth of *text*.

**\settoheight**\⟨*length*⟩{*text*}    Sets \⟨*length*⟩ to the height of *text*.

**\settowidth**\⟨*length*⟩{*text*}    Sets \⟨*length*⟩ to the width of *text*.

**\sf**    Obsolete form for sans serif (LaTeX2.09). Replaced by \textsf{*text*}.

**\sfdefault**    Specifies the font family for sans serif (default cmss).

**\sffamily**    Switches to the font family specified by \sfdefault (similar to \textsf).

**\shapedefault**    The specified standard font form (default \updefault).

**\shortstack** [*position*] {... \\... \\... }    Creates a table with a single column and an arbitrary number of rows. The optional parameter passes the horizontal alignment of all rows and can have the usual values *c* (default), *l* or *r*.

**\showhyphens**{*word1 word2*}    Outputs the hyphenation points of *word1 word2* ... in the log file. Must appear *after* \begin{document} if the babel package was loaded.

**\sl**    Obsolete form for *slanted* (LaTeX2.09). Replaced by \textsl{*text*}.

**\sldefault**    Specifies the font form for *slanted* (default sl).

**\slash**    Outputs /, which behaves like a hyphen when it comes to hyphenation.

**\slshape**    Switches to the font form defined by \sldefault within the current text character set (similar to \textsl).

**\sloppy**    Sets the values for tolerant paragraph breaks, which allow larger inter-word spacing (cf. \fussy on page 54).

**\small**    Switches the current font size to a smaller size: small. Valid until another font command is given.

**\smallskip**    Vertical feed; the same as \vspace{\smallskipamount}.

**\space**    Outputs a space that is not "swallowed" by TeX.

**\sp**{*text*}    Corresponds to the ^ character for superscript in math mode.

**\sqrt** [*root*] {*radicand*}    The optional *root* argument is not necessary for square roots, only for higher roots. The root sign is adapted to the size of the radicand
$\sqrt[3]{2}$⇒ $\sqrt[3]{2}$.

**\ss**    The ß character (\ss⇒ß); important for BibTeX databases in 7 bit mode.

*continued* ...

| *name  description* |
| --- |

**\stackrel**{*top*}{*normal*}    Can be used to created stacked symbols in math mode; for example ∧ and = to ≜ ($\stackrel{\wedge}{=}$). The *normal* parameter is always typeset at the same height as normal characters.

**\stretch**{*value*}    Lets you achieve certain ratios of the otherwise dynamic spacings \hspace and \vspace. In the following example, the spacings between the vertical lines have a ratio of 3 to 10: |\hspace{\stretch{3}}|\hspace{\stretch{10}}|

|      |              |                              | |

**\strut**    Outputs the contents of the \strutbox, which consists of a vertical line of height 0,7 \baselineskip and depth 0,3 \baselineskip. The width of the box is zero.

**\subparagraphmark**{*argument*}    The same as \chaptermark for \subparagraph.

**\subsection** [*TOC*] {*title*}    Starts a new subsection. The optional argument specifies the entry to be added to the table of contents instead of *title*.

**\subsection**∗{*title*}    Starts a new non-numbered subsection that is not added to the table of contents.

**\subsectionmark**{*argument*}    The same as \chaptermark for \subsection.

**\subsubsection** [*TOC*] {*title*}    Starts a new subsubsection. The optional argument specifies the entry to be added to the table of contents instead of *title*.

**\subsubsection**∗{*title*}    Starts a new subsubsection that is not numbered and not added to the table of contents.

**\subsubsectionmark**{*argument*}    The same as \chaptermark for \subsubsection.

**\suppressfloats** [*position*]    Suppresses the output of any floating environments after the command on the current page. The optional *position* parameter can be t or b and restricts the command to these options.

**\symbol**{*character number*}    Outputs the character that is assigned the given number: \symbol{64}⇒@.

**\t**{*characters*}    Adds an arc on top of *two* characters: \t{oo}⇒o͡o.

**\tableofcontents**    Inserts the table of contents at the current position.

**\TeX**    Outputs TEX in the current standard font.

**\textbf**{*text*}    Puts *text* in bold face: \textbf{*boldface*}⇒**boldface**.

**\textit**{*text*}    Puts *text* in italic: \textit{*italic*}⇒ *italic*.

**\textmd**{*text*}    Puts *text* in medium bold: \textmd{*medium*}⇒medium.

**\textnormal**{*text*}    Puts *text* in standard font: {\itshape\textnormal{itshape}}⇒itshape.

**\textrm**{*text*}    Puts *text* in roman font: \textrm{*roman*}⇒roman.

**\textsc**{*text*}    Puts *text* in small caps: \textsc{*Small Caps*}⇒Sᴍᴀʟʟ Cᴀᴘs.

**\textsf**{*text*}    Puts *text* in sans serif font: \textsf{*sans serif*}⇒sans serif.

**\textsl**{*text*}    Puts *text* in slanted: \textsl{*slanted*}⇒ *slanted*.

**\textstyle**    Main math style in the normal text.

**\textsubscript**{*argument*}    Puts *argument* as index: H\textsubscript{2}O⇒$H_2O$. Requires the fixltx2e package.

**\textsuperscript**{*argument*}    Puts *argument* as exponent: 4\textsuperscript{th}⇒$4^{th}$.

**\texttt**{*text*}    Puts *text* in typewriter font: \texttt{*typewriter*}⇒typewriter.

*continued . . .*

| name | description |
| --- | --- |

\textup{*text*}   Puts *text* upright: \itshape\textup{*upright*}⇒upright.

\thanks{*text*}   Used as a replacement for \footnote in titles and author names because usually a symbol is used instead of the footnote number.

\the⟨*counter*⟩   Outputs the current representation (*not* the value) of ⟨*counter*⟩, a LATEX counter: \thepage⇒64; \thesection⇒4.2.

\the\⟨*length*⟩   Outputs the current value of the length or skip register \⟨*length*⟩, for example \the\bigskipamount⇒12.0pt plus 4.0pt minus 4.0pt.

\thinspace   Outputs a horizontal space of 2/3 em.

\thispagestyle{*page style*}   The same as \pagestyle except that the definition only applies to the page where it appears.

\tiny   Switches the current font size to the smallest font ₜᵢₙᵧ. Valid until another font command is given.

\title{*text*}   Specifies the title. Line breaks are possible with \\. Footnotes are possible through \thanks

\today   Outputs today's date in the form chosen through a language option.

\tt   Obsolete form for ttfamily (LATEX2.09). Replaced by \texttt{*text*}.

\ttdefault   Specifies the font family for typewriter (default cmtt).

\ttfamily   Switches to the font family \ttdefault (similar to \texttt).

\twocolumn [*caption*]   Starts a *new page* in two-column mode. The optional argument lets you specify a caption that will span both columns. This command is not available in all document classes.

\typein [\⟨command name⟩] {*text*}   Outputs *text* on the terminal and interprets the input until the next enter as normal TEX source code. If a \⟨*command name*⟩ is specified through the optional argument, the input is assigned to this command.

\typeout{*argument*}   Outputs *argument* on standard output (screen).

\u{*character*}   Adds a breve accent on top of the *character*: \u{o}⇒ŏ.

\underbar{*argument*}   Similar to \underline except that no <u>descenders</u> are taken into account.

\underbrace{*equation*}_{*Label*}   An underbrace is added to the *equation*. You can add a label in the usual manner through _: $\underbrace{a^2+b^2}_{c^2}$ ⇒ $\underbrace{a^2 + b^2}_{c^2}$

\underline{*argument*}   Underlines the *argument*; works in both math mode and text mode. The words in *argument* can't be hyphenated however, though this is fixed by loading the soul package.

\upbracefill   \makebox[3cm]{\upbracefill}⇒⏞

\updefault   Specifies the font form for *upright* (default n).

\upshape   Switches to the font form defined by \updefault within the current text character set (similar to \textup).

\usebox\⟨*box name*⟩   Outputs the content of \⟨*box name*⟩.

\usecounter{*counter*}   Assigns the counter to be used in the second argument of a list environment (cf. page 43).

*continued ...*

| name | description |
|---|---|
| \usefont{*encoding*}{*family*}{*series*}{*shape*} | Easier switching of fonts when all parameters are changed:\usefont{T1}{futs}{b}{it} ⇒ ***T1-Utopia-Bold-Italic.*** |
| \usepackage [*options*] {*name(s)*} | Includes the packages *name(s)* in a comma-separated list, with options *options*. |
| \v{*character*} | Adds a háček accent on top of the *character.* \v{o}⇒ŏ. |
| \value{*counter*} | Outputs the value of *counter* as a number, which you can use wherever LaTeX expects a number as input. |
| \vdots | Outputs three vertical dots in math mode $\vdots$ |
| \vector(*dx,dy*){*length*} | The same as \line except that an arrow is added at the end of the line. |
| \verb * ⟨*character*⟩ *text* ⟨*character*⟩ | The *character*s must be the same and must not occur in *text*, which is output verbatim. Usually \verb can't be used in the argument of another command. The starred version outputs all spaces as ␣. |
| \vfill | \vfill creates a dynamic length (rubber length), which expands and shrinks at will. The command is equivalent to an empty line with \vspace\fill. |
| \vline | Creates a vertical line \vline⇒\|that expands to the full height and depth of a line (the \totalheight). You can also use \vline within an @ expression in table headers. |
| \vphantom{*text*} | Creates a box of zero width but of the same height as *text*. |
| \vspace * {*length*} | Adds vertical space of *length*; you must specify the value with a valid unit. If this command is used in the middle of a paragraph, it only takes effect after the current line. The starred version allows space immediately at the beginning of a page. |

## 4.3  Special commands

These special commands usually contain the @ character so you have to enclose them in \makeatletter / \makeatother to use them in a normal document.

| name | description |
|---|---|
| \@backslashchar | Outputs the \ character; useful if you need a backslash as part of an argument to a command. |
| \@cclvi | Number 256 or 256th character in the current math font: $\@cclvi$ ⇒ $\Gamma$; $\the\@cclvi$ ⇒ $256$. |
| \@depth | Outputs the word *depth*. |
| \@dottedtocline{*level*}{*indentation*}{*S-width*}{*text*}{*page*} | Lets you format an entry in the table of contents. *Level* determines the usual *chapter–section* . . . hierarchy, *indentation* is the space between the left margin and the entry, *S-width* is the width of the box that contains the number of the entry, *text* is the string to be output and *page* is the page number. |

*continued* . . .

| name | description |
| --- | --- |

**\@firstofone**{*argument*}     Expands *argument* and returns it.

**\@firstoftwo**{*arg1*}{*arg2*}     Expands the first of the two arguments and returns it; the second one is discarded.

**\@fnsymbol**{*number*}     Defines the symbols for the footnotes on the title page; it can be redefined.

**\@for** \⟨*loopVar*⟩:=$i_1, i_2, \ldots, i_n$ \do {*argument*}     The *argument* is executed $n$ times, with \⟨*loopVar*⟩ taking the next value from the comma-separated list on each loop for use in the *argument*.

**\@gobble**{*argument*}     Discards *argument* and replaces it with {}.

**\@gobbletwo**{*arg1*}{*arg2*}     Discards both *arg1 and arg2* and replaces them with {}.

**\@gobblefour**{*arg1*}{*arg2*}{*arg3*}{*arg4*}     The same for four arguments.

**\@height**     Outputs the word *height*.

**\@ifdefinable**{\*command*}{*definition*}     If \*command* is definable, i.e. it does *not* already exist, it is set to *definition*.

**\@ifnextchar**{*character*}{*true*}{*false*}     If the next character in the list of parameters is equal to *character*, *true* is executed, otherwise *false* is executed.

**\@ixpt**     Number 9: \@ixpt $\Rightarrow$ 9.

**\@m**     Number 1000 in math mode: $\the\@m$ $\Rightarrow 1000$.

**\@M**     Number 10000 in math mode: $\the\@M$ $\Rightarrow 10000$.

**\@minus**     Outputs the word *minus*.

**\@MM**     Number 20000 in math mode: $\the\@MM$ $\Rightarrow 20000$.

**\m@ne**     Number -1: \the\m@ne $\Rightarrow$ -1.

**\@namedef**{*argument*}{*definition*}     Defines *argument* after expanding it as a command with *definition*; for example \@namedef{cp@#1}{foo} where the parameter #1 is substituted accordingly.

**\@nameuse**{*argument*}     In principle the same as \@namedef, but doesn't expand its argument.

**\@ne**     Number 1 or first character in the current font: \@ne $\Rightarrow$ ´; \the\@one $\Rightarrow$ 1.

**\@onlypreamble**\⟨*command*⟩     Adds \⟨*command*⟩ to the list of commands that may only appear in the preamble.

**\@percentchar**     Outputs the % character. Useful when you want to use a percentage sign as part of an argument for commands.

**\@plus**     Outputs the word *plus*.

**\@secondoftwo**{*arg1*}{*arg2*}     Expands the second of two arguments and returns it; the first one is discarded.

**\@spaces**     Outputs \space four times.

*continued ...*

| name | description |
| --- | --- |

**\@testopt**{\\⟨*command*⟩}{*argument*}     Tests whether the next character in the parameter list is an opening square bracket for an optional argument. If so, \\⟨*command*⟩ is called, otherwise \\⟨*command*⟩[*argument*].

**\@tfor** \\⟨*loopVar*⟩:=$t_1 t_2,\ldots,t_n$\do {*argument*}     Executes *argument* $n$ times, with \\⟨*loopVar*⟩ taking the next token from the comma-separated list on each loop for use in the *argument*.

**\@thirdofthree**{*arg1*}{*arg2*}{*arg3*}     Expands the third of three arguments and returns it; the first two are discarded.

**\@vpt**     Number 5: **\@vpt** ⇒ 5.

**\@vipt**     Number 6: **\@vipt** ⇒ 6.

**\@viipt**     Number 7: **\@viipt** ⇒ 7.

**\@viiipt**     Number 8: **\@viiipt** ⇒ 8.

**\@width**     Outputs the word *width*.

**\@whiledim** ⟨*test*⟩ \do {*argument*}     Executes *argument* repeatedly until *test* returns false. *test* must compare two dimensions, e. g. \linewidth>15cm.

**\@whilenum** ⟨*test*⟩ \do {*argument*}     Same as above, but *test* compares two counters, e. g. \thechapter>5.

**\@whilesw** \if⟨*name*⟩ \fi {*argument*}     Executes *argument* repeatedly while \if*name* returns true.

**\@xdblarg**{*arg1*}{*arg2*}     Returns the two arguments in the form #1[{#2}]{#2}.

**\@xpt**     Number 10: \@xpt ⇒ 10.

**\@xipt**     Number 10.95: \@xipt ⇒ 10.95.

**\@xiipt**     Number 12: \@xiipt ⇒ 12.

**\@xivpt**     Number 14.4: \@xivpt ⇒ 14.4.

**\@xviipt**     Number 17.28: \@xviipt ⇒ 17.28.

**\@xxpt**     Number 20.74: \@xxpt ⇒ 20.74.

**\@xxvpt**     Number 24.88: \@xxvpt ⇒ 24.88.

**\csname**     Starts a new command; in practice the same as the backslash. For example, \csname⟨*name*⟩\endcsname executes the command \⟨*name*⟩.

**\endcsname**     Terminates a command. For example \csname#1\endcsname executes the command \#1, where #1 represents the given argument.

**\f@size**     The size of the current font without unit: \f@size ⇒ 10.

**\g@addto@macro**{\*name*}{*Code*}     Globally adds the given code to the existing command \name.

**\hexnumber@**{*counter*}     Outputs the value of *counter* (0...15) as a hexadecimal number: $\hexnumber@{\value{chapter}}$ ⇒ 4.

*continued ...*

| name | description |
|---|---|

**\sixt@@n**     Number 16 or 16th character in the font: \sixt@@n ⇒ "; \the\sixt@@n ⇒ 16.

**\strip@prefix**{*argument*}     Removes everything up to a ">" character inclusive from *argument*. You can use this to output command definitions: \expandafter\strip@prefix\meaning\newpage⇒\noalign {\break }

**\strip@pt**\⟨*length*⟩     Removes the unit pt from \⟨*length*⟩: \strip@pt\textwidth ⇒ 375.57637, in contrast to \the\textwidth ⇒ 375.57637pt.

**\thr@@**     Number 3 or third character in the current font: \thr@@ ⇒ ˜; \the\three@@ ⇒ 3.

**\toks@**     Temporary token register.

**\tw@**     Number 2 or second character in the current font: \tw@ ⇒ ˆ; \the\tw@ ⇒ 2.

**\two@digits**{*number*}     Outputs *number* with a leading zero if it only contains one digit: \two@digits{9} ⇒ 09.

**\verbatim@font**     Font style for the verbatim mode; usually defined as \normalfont\ttfamily by the document class.

Chapter 5

# Lengths and counters

In LaTeX, all lengths and counters are referenced by symbolic names. In TeX, this is done through *dimen*, *skip* and *count* registers, which are addressable through a register number. However, it's best not to use the corresponding TeX commands in LaTeX, as TeX and LaTeX treat counters differently. Apart from two lengths related to footnotes, the listing of all lengths uses only these symbolic names.

## 5.1 Lengths

A length in the physical sense is a measure and a unit of measurement, for example 3.14 cm. LaTeX accepts many units of measurement. Each unit can be prefixed by true such that they are not affected by different scales.

| name | description | current value |
|------|-------------|--------------:|
| bp | big point (72 bp/in) | 1.00374pt |
| cc | Cîcero (1 cc=12 dd) | 12.8401pt |
| cm | centimetre | 28.45274pt |
| dd | Didôt (1157 dd = 1238 pt) | 1.07pt |
| em | width of the letter "M" in the chosen font; usually different from the current font size: $\mathbb{M}\rightarrow$8.38998pt | 10.0pt |
| ex | height of the letter "x" in the chosen font, also usually different: $\boxtimes\rightarrow$4.165pt | 4.29pt |
| in | inch (correct value 72.27 pt) | 72.26999pt |
| mm | millimetre | 2.84526pt |
| mu | Mathematical unit (1 mu=$^1/_{18}$ em) | 0.05554pt |
| pc | Pica (12 pt/pc) | 12.0pt |
| pt | (TeX-)points ($^1/_{72.27}$ inch) | 1.0pt |

| name | description | current value |
|---|---|---|
| **px** | image point, 1 px=$^1/_{72}$ in (only in pdfTEX) | 1.00375pt |
| **sp** | scaled point (65536 sp/pt) | 0.00002pt |

em, ex, mu and px are *dynamic* units: they change automatically if the current font or screen resolution (px) are changed. You can only use mu in math mode, and it can't be combined with other units. The command to set the lengths is \mkern.

$$\int\limits_1^\infty \frac{1}{x^2}\,\mathrm{d}x = 1$$

```
\usepackage{amsmath}
\newcommand*\dx{\,\mathrm{d}x}
```

$$\int\limits_1^\infty \frac{1}{x^2}\,\mathrm{d}x = 1$$

```
\begin{align*}
  \int\limits_1^\infty\frac{1}{x^2}\dx &= 1\\
  \int\limits_1^\infty\mkern-7mu\frac{1}{x^2}
                        \mkern4mu\dx &= 1
\end{align*}
```

05-01-1

All lengths require a unit and may have positive as well as negative values. In LATEX you should only change a length's value through the \setlength and \addtolength commands. Apart from fixed lengths in *dimen registers*, TEX also provides *skip registers.* They may contain two additional values for shrinking and stretching apart from the main value. These additional values are marked by minus and plus respectively; for example 12pt plus 2pt minus .2ex. A third length is called *rubber length*' if it can be shrunk and stretched *arbitrarily*, such as \hfill. The table below gives some practical examples, but first here are a few key points to note:

- Lengths always require a unit of measurement.
- You can work with multiples or fractions of a length by prefixing it with a factor; for example 1.5\abovedisplayskip corresponds to 15.0pt.
- All length commands are robust so they never have to be prefixed with \protect.
- You can output a length through the \the command, for example \the\topskip→10.0pt.

| name | description |
|---|---|
| **\newlength**\⟨*name*⟩ | Defines a new length command of type skip, which is also able to process adjuncts like plus or minus. After the definition, the length has the value 0 pt:<br>\newlength\myLength \the\myLength⇒0.0pt. |
| **\setlength**\⟨*name*⟩ | Sets a length command to a specific value:<br>\setlength\myLength{5cm plus 5mm minus 3mm}<br>\the\myLength⇒142.26378pt plus 14.22636pt minus 8.53581pt. |
| **\addtolength**\⟨*name*⟩ | Adds the given length to a length command:<br>\addtolength\myLength{20pt minus 5pt}<br>\the\myLength⇒162.26378pt plus 14.22636pt minus 13.53581pt. |
| **\settolength**\⟨*name*⟩{*template*} | Sets \⟨*name*⟩ to the width of *template*, which can be text or another arbitrary object:<br>\settowidth\myLength{long word}<br>\the\myLength⇒41.80992pt. |

| name | description |
|------|-------------|
| **\settoheight**\⟨*name*⟩{*template*} | Sets \⟨*name*⟩ to the height of *template*, which can be text or another arbitrary object:<br>\settoheight\myLength{long word} \the\myLength⇒6.87pt. |
| **\settodepth**\⟨*name*⟩{*template*} | Sets \⟨*name*⟩ to the depth of *template*, which can be text or another arbitrary object:<br>\settodepth\myLength{long word} \the\myLength⇒2.36pt. |

The \hfill and \hspace commands affect horizontal lengths and the \addvspace, \smallskip, \medskip, \bigskip, \vfill and \vspace commands affect vertical lengths. Each length defined through \newlength is automatically a *skip register* and *may* have \skip additional plus or minus specifications. The following list contains all LaTeX-specific lengths with their default values, which are not necessarily the same for all classes. The list is partitioned into general, mathematical and list-specific lengths. The specified values refer to the used document class and therefore don't necessarily apply to LaTeX in general.

| name | description | current value |
|------|-------------|---------------|
| **\abovecaptionskip** | | 5.0pt |
| | Normal space between floating environment and caption. | |
| **\abovedisplayskip** | | 10.0pt plus 2.0pt minus 5.0pt |
| | Normal space between text and equation. | |
| **\abovedisplayshortskip** | | 0.0pt plus 3.0pt |
| | Normal space between text on a short line and equation. | |
| **\arraycolsep** | Space between columns of an array environment. | 5.0pt |
| **\arrayrulewidth** | | 0.4pt |
| | Line width for \hline in array and tabular environments. | |
| **\baselineskip** | Space between two lines in a paragraph (line feed). | 12.0pt |
| **\belowcaptionskip** | | 5.0pt |
| | Normal space between caption and floating environment. | |
| **\belowdisplayskip** | | 10.0pt plus 2.0pt minus 5.0pt |
| | Normal space between equation and text. | |
| **\belowdisplayshortskip** | | 6.0pt plus 3.0pt minus 3.0pt |
| | Normal space between equation and text on a short line. | |
| **\bigskipamount** | | 12.0pt plus 4.0pt minus 4.0pt |
| | Vertical space used for \bigskip. | |
| **\columnsep** | Space between the text columns in \twocolumn mode. | 10.0pt |
| **\columnseprule** | Width of the column separation line in \twocolumn mode. | 0.0pt |
| **\columnwidth** | Width of a column in the local environment. | 375.57637pt |
| **\dblfloatsep** | | 12.0pt plus 2.0pt minus 2.0pt |
| | Vertical space between two floating environments in \twocolumn mode. | |
| **\depth** | You can use this length as a parameter for boxes in order to refer to the internal depth of the contents of the box. | |
| **\doublerulesep** | | 2.0pt |
| | Spacing of a double line in an array or tabular environment. | |

continued . . .

| name | description | current value |
|---|---|---|
| `\dbltextfloatsep` | | 20.0pt plus 2.0pt minus 4.0pt |
| | Vertical space between a floating environment and text in `\twocolumn` mode. | |
| `\emergencystretch` | | 30.0pt |
| | The maximum possible space between two words, which is only taken into account in the third and last iteration of paragraph breaking. | |
| `\evensidemargin` | Left margin for even pages. | 63.21346pt |
| `\fboxrule` | Line width of the frame of an `\fbox`. | 0.4pt |
| `\fboxsep` | Space between text and frame of an `\fbox`. | 3.0pt |
| `\fill` | Arbitrarily stretchable length. | 0.0pt plus 1.0fill |
| `\floatsep` | | 12.0pt plus 2.0pt minus 2.0pt |
| | Vertical space between two floating environments. | |
| `\fontdimen1\font` | Gradient of a font in 1 pt height of the character. | 0.0pt |
| `\fontdimen2\font` | General space between words. | 2.5pt |
| `\fontdimen3\font` | Flexibility of the space between words. | 1.49998pt |
| `\fontdimen4\font` | | 0.59999pt |
| | Allowed value for the compression of the space between words. | |
| `\fontdimen5\font` | The height of an "x" in the current font (1 ex). | 4.29pt |
| `\fontdimen6\font` | The width of an "M" in the current font (1 em). | 10.0pt |
| `\fontdimen7\font` | | 0.59999pt |
| | Additional space after full stop. For `\nonfrenchspacing`. | |
| `\dimen\footins` | Maximum height of the footnote area (8 in). | 578.15999pt |
| `\skip\footins` | | 9.0pt plus 4.0pt minus 2.0pt |
| | Space between the text and the first footnote. | |
| `\footnotesep` | Space between two footnotes. | 6.65pt |
| `\footskip` | Space between the last line of text and the lower line of the footer. | 42.67912pt |
| `\hangindent` | Specifies the indentation from the second line and should therefore only be used at the beginning of the paragraph. | 0.0pt |
| `\headheight` | Height of the header. | 14.22636pt |
| `\headsep` | Space between the header and the text area. | 22.76219pt |
| `\height` | You can use this length as a parameter for boxes in order to refer to the internal height of the contents of the box. | |
| `\hoffset` | Horizontal space for the absolute page margin. | 0.0pt |
| `\intextsep` | Vertical space of a floating environment to the surrounding text. | 12.0pt plus 2.0pt minus 2.0pt |
| `\linewidth` | Width of a line in the current environment. | 375.57637pt |
| `\marginparsep` | Space between the text and a margin note. | 5.69054pt |
| `\marginparwidth` | Width of a margin note. | 51.21495pt |
| `\mathindent` | Indentation for left-aligned formulae. | 25.00003pt |
| `\maxdepth` | Specification for the maximum depth. | 5.0pt |
| `\maxdimen` | Maximum length that can be handled by TeX, ($\approx$5,7 m). | 16383.99998pt |
| `\medskipamount` | | 6.0pt plus 2.0pt minus 2.0pt |

continued . . .

| name | description | current value |
|------|-------------|--------------:|
| | Vertical space that is used for \medskip. | |
| \normalbaselineskip | | 12.0pt |
| | Normal space between the lines in a paragraph. | |
| \normallineskip | | 1.0pt |
| | Normal lead between two lines in a paragraph. | |
| \normallineskiplimit | | 0.0pt |
| | Minimum lead between two lines in a paragraph. | |
| \oddsidemargin | | 22.76219pt |
| | Left margin for odd pages if the twoside option is set. | |
| \overfullrule | Width of the "overfull" line in the margin if using the draft document class option. | 0.0pt |
| \paperheight | The total page height. | 662.9492pt |
| \paperwidth | The total page width. | 503.61377pt |
| \parindent | Normal indentation of a paragraph. | 18.0pt |
| \parskip | Vertical space between paragraphs. | 0.0pt |
| \smallskipamount | | 3.0pt plus 1.0pt minus 1.0pt |
| | Vertical space used for \smallskip. | |
| \tabbingsep | Space to the left of the tab moved through \'. | 5.0pt |
| \tabcolsep | Space between columns of a tabular environment. | 0.0pt |
| \textheight | Height of the text area on the page. | 550.0pt |
| \textfloatsep | | 20.0pt plus 2.0pt minus 4.0pt |
| | Vertical space of a text between two floating environments. | |
| \textwidth | Width of the text area of the page. | 375.57637pt |
| \topmargin | The space between the upper edge of the header and the upper edge of the page is \voffset+1inch+\topmargin (page 29). | -58.04362pt |
| \topskip | Space between the upper edge of the page and the base line of the first line of text. | 10.0pt |
| \totalheight | You can use this length as a parameter for boxes in order to refer to the internal height *and* depth of the contents of the box. | |
| \unitlength | Length unit of the picture environment; used by all commands like \line, \vector, \circle or \oval. | 1.0pt |
| \voffset | Vertical offset for the absolute page margin. | 0.0pt |
| \width | You can use this length as a parameter for boxes in order to refer to the internal width of the contents of the box. | |

| *Lengths (skips) in math mode.* | | |
|------|-------------|--------------:|
| \abovedisplayshortskip | Space above a short displayed formula. | 0.0pt plus 3.0pt |
| \abovedisplayskip | | 10.0pt plus 2.0pt minus 5.0pt |
| | Space above a displayed formula. | |
| \belowdisplayshortskip | | 6.0pt plus 3.0pt minus 3.0pt |
| | Space below a short displayed formula. | |
| \belowdisplayskip | | 10.0pt plus 2.0pt minus 5.0pt |
| | Space below a displayed formula. | |
| \medmuskip | Space before/after an operator. | 4.0mu plus 2.0mu minus 4.0mu |

continued …

| name | description | current value |
|---|---|---|
| \thickmuskip | Space before/after a comparison operator. | 5.0mu plus 5.0mu |
| \thinmuskip | Space between operator and variable. | 3.0mu |

*Lengths in lists (Figure 2.4 on page 30)*

| name | description | current value |
|---|---|---|
| \itemindent | Indentation of the first line of an \item; may be negative. | 0.0pt |
| \itemsep | Additional vertical space between the \items of a list. | 6.0 pt |
| \labelsep | Horizontal space between a label and the text. | 8.0 pt |
| \labelwidth | Minimum width of the box of a label. | 10.0 pt |
| \leftmargin | Horizontal space between the left margin of the environment and \item. | 18.0 pt |
| \listparindent | Paragraph indentation of an \item; may be negative. | 0.0 pt |
| \parsep | Vertical space between paragraphs within an \item. | 0.0 pt |
| \partopsep | Additional vertical space at the start of a list. | 0.0 pt |
| \rightmargin | Horizontal space between the right margin of the environment and the text. | 0.0 pt |
| \topsep | Additional vertical space at the start of a list. | 10.0pt plus 4.0pt |

**Special lengths**

These special lengths usually contain the @ character so you have to enclose them in the \makeatletter and \makeatother commands in order to use them within a normal document.

| name | description | current value |
|---|---|---|
| \dimen@ | Temporary dimension register. | 541.20004pt |
| \dimen@i | Ditto. | 0.0pt |
| \dimen@ii | Ditto. | 0.5pt |
| \p@ | TeX base unit. | 1.0pt |
| \skip@ | Temporary skip register. | 0.0pt |
| \z@ | Corresponds to 0 pt *and* 0. | 0.0pt |
| \z@skip | Ditto, as skip register. | 0.0pt |
| \@tempdima | Temporary register; therefore has a random value. | 8.39996pt |
| \@tempdimb | Ditto. | 10.0pt |
| \@tempdimc | Ditto. | 0.0pt |

## 5.2 Counters

The LaTeX-internal counters always have the same name as the corresponding environment or command, for example table. You can output a counter by prefixing its name with \the, for *output ≠ value* example \thepage→76. It's important to remember though that the *output* of a LaTeX counter is *not* the same as its *value*; to retrieve the value you must use one of the \arabic, \Roman, …commands (cf. \arabic). However, TeX counters are different: they don't distinguish between a counter's value and output, so the value of a TeX counter can be retrieved through \the⟨name⟩, for example \the\day⇒9.

## 5.2.1  Commands to create and change counters

Counters can take positive and negative values. You can define and change them using the commands listed below. \refstepcounter is particularly useful as only counters changed through \refstepcounter can be used for \labels and \references. As an example let's insert here a reference to the counter marked through \refstepcounter in the following listing. The value of the counter at that place is \ref{counter}⇒73 and that increment occurred on page \pageref{counter}⇒77.

*counter*
*reference*

| name | description |
|---|---|
| \newcounter{*name*} | Defines a new counter. After the definition, it has the value 0: \newcounter{Counter} \theCounter⇒0. |
| \setcounter{*name*}{*value*} | Sets the specified counter to a given value: \setcounter{Counter}{60} \theCounter⇒60. |
| \addtocounter{*name*}{*value*} | Adds a given value to a counter: \addtocounter{Counter}{11} \theCounter⇒71. |
| \stepcounter{*name*} | Increments the given counter by 1: \stepcounter{Counter}\theCounter⇒72. |
| \refstepcounter{*name*} | Increments the given counter by 1 and makes it possible to reference this counter in a label through \ref (cf. page on this page). \refstepcounter{Counter} \theCounter⇒73(\label{counter}). |
| \usecounter{*name*} | If a command expects a counter as an argument, it can be specified through \usecounter, for example in a list definition (cf. page 43). |
| \value{*name*} | If a counter is to be set depending on another one, the value can be passed through \value: \setcounter{Counter}{\value{section}}⇒2. This would not be possible with \thesection because it does not yield the value, but the representation of the counter: 5.2. |
| \arabic{*name*} | Outputs the counter in Arabic numerals: \arabic{Counter}⇒2. |
| \roman{*name*} | Outputs the counter in lowercase Roman numerals: \roman{Counter}⇒ii. |
| \Roman{*name*} | Outputs the counter in uppercase Roman numerals: \Roman{Counter}⇒II. |
| \alph{*name*} | Outputs the counter in lowercase letters: \alph{Counter}⇒b. |
| \Alph{*name*} | Outputs the counter in uppercase letters: \Alph{Counter}⇒B. |
| \fnsymbol{*name*} | Outputs the counter as a footnote symbol: \fnsymbol{Counter}⇒†. |

## 5.2.2  Defined counters

This section contains a list of the defined counters; if an output is missing, then the counter is a TeX counter that doesn't support the LaTeX syntax \value and \the⟨*name*⟩.

| name | description | current value | output |
|---|---|---|---|
| part | structuring | 0 | |
| chapter | structuring | 5 | 5 |
| section | structuring | 2 | 5.2 |
| subsection | structuring | 2 | 5.2.2 |
| subsubsection | structuring | 0 | 5.2.2.0 |
| paragraph | structuring | 0 | 5.2.2.0.0 |
| subparagraph | structuring | 0 | 5.2.2.0.0.0 |
| page | page counter | 77 | 77 |
| equation | equations | 0 | 5.0 |
| figure | floating environment | 0 | 5.0 |
| table | floating environment | 5 | 5.5 |
| footnote | footnote | 0 | 0 |
| mpfootnote | footnote in a minipage | 0 | |
| enumi | list counter, 1st level | 5 | 5 |
| enumii | list counter, 2nd level | 0 | |
| enumiii | list counter, 3rd level | 0 | |
| enumiv | list counter, 4th level | 0 | |
| \secnumdepth | depth of structure | 2 | — |
| \tocdepth | TOC levels | 1 | — |
| | (\part=-1, \chapter=0, \section=1, ...) | | |
| \day | today's day | 16 | — |
| \month | today's month | 9 | — |
| \year | today's year | 2011 | — |
| \lefthyphenmin | minimum number of characters to the left of a hyphen | 2 | — |
| \righthyphenmin | the same for the right side of a hyphen | 3 | — |

| | special counters | | |
|---|---|---|---|
| \errorcontextlines | number of lines of context for an error in the log file | -1 | — |
| \badness | \vbox/\hbox value when breaking paragraphs | 0 | — |
| \hbadness | \hbox value of a line | 1000 | — |
| \vbadness | \vbox value of a page | 1000 | — |
| \@tempcnta | temporary TeX counter | 2 | — |
| \@tempcntb | temporary TeX counter | 256 | — |
| \@multicnt | for \multiput and similar | 0 | — |
| \count@ | temporary counter register | | |
| \pretolerance | maximum badness when breaking paragraphs | 100 | — |
| \tolerance | final badness when breaking paragraphs | 9999 | — |

# Mathematics

The first two sections of this chapter look at the standard symbols and accents available for math in LaTeX, but for serious mathematical typesetting it is recommended that you load the amsmath package, developed by the American Mathematical Society. Some of the extensions provided by this package are discussed briefly in the final section of this chapter. For more information on typesetting math see [24].

## 6.1 Mathematical symbols

A list of all possible symbols in standard LaTeX and with additional packages can be found in [17]. Only the symbols available by default are given here.

**Table 6.1:** Mathematical symbols in standard LaTeX. b: binary symbol; r: relation symbol; d: delimiter symbol.

| command | output | type | command | output | type |
|---|---|---|---|---|---|
| \| | ‖ | | \aleph | ℵ | |
| \alpha | α | | \amalg | ⨿ | b |
| \angle | ∠ | | \approx | ≈ | r |
| \ast | ∗ | b | \asymp | ≍ | r |
| \backslash | \ | d | \beta | β | |
| \bigcap | ⋂ | | \bigcirc | ◯ | b |
| \bigcup | ⋃ | | \bigodot | ⨀ | |
| \bigoplus | ⨁ | | \bigotimes | ⨂ | |
| \bigtriangledown | ▽ | b | \bigtriangleup | △ | b |

*continued ...*

| command | output | type | command | output | type |
|---|---|---|---|---|---|
| \bigsqcup | ⊔ | | \biguplus | ⊎ | |
| \bigcap | ⋁ | | \bigwedge | ⋀ | |
| \bot | ⊥ | | \bowtie | ⋈ | r |
| \Box | □ | | \bullet | • | b |
| \cap | ∩ | b | \cdot | · | b |
| \chi | χ | | \circ | ∘ | b |
| \clubsuit | ♣ | | \cong | ≅ | r |
| \coprod | ∐ | | \cup | ∪ | b |
| \dagger | † | b | \dashv | ⊣ | r |
| \ddagger | ‡ | b | \Delta | Δ | |
| \delta | δ | | \Diamond | ◇ | |
| \diamond | ◇ | b | \diamondsuit | ◆ | |
| \div | ÷ | b | \doteq | ≐ | r |
| \downarrow | ↓ | d | \Downarrow | ⇓ | d |
| \ell | ℓ | | \emptyset | ∅ | |
| \epsilon | ϵ | | \equiv | ≡ | r |
| \eta | η | | \exists | ∃ | |
| \flat | ♭ | | \forall | ∀ | |
| \frown | ⌢ | r | \Gamma | Γ | |
| \gamma | γ | | \ge | ≥ | |
| \geq | ≥ | r | \gets | ← | |
| \gg | ≫ | r | \hbar | ℏ | |
| \heartsuit | ♥ | | \hookleftarrow | ↩ | |
| \hookrightarrow | ↪ | | \iff | ⟺ | |
| \Im | ℑ | | \in | ∈ | r |
| \infty | ∞ | | \int | ∫ | |
| \iota | ι | | \Join | ⋈ | |
| \kappa | κ | | \Lambda | Λ | |
| \lambda | λ | | \land | ∧ | |
| \langle | ⟨ | d | \lbrace | { | d |
| \lbrack | [ | d | \lceil | ⌈ | d |
| \le | ≤ | | \leadsto | ⤳ | |
| \Leftarrow | ⇐ | | \leftarrow | ← | |
| \leftharpoondown | ↽ | | \leftharpoonup | ↼ | |
| \Leftrightarrow | ⇔ | | \leftrightarrow | ↔ | |
| \leq | ≤ | r | \lfloor | ⌊ | d |
| \lhd | ◁ | | \ll | ≪ | r |
| \lnot | ¬ | | \longleftarrow | ⟵ | |
| \longleftrightarrow | ⟷ | | \longmapsto | ⟼ | |
| \longrightarrow | ⟶ | | \lor | ∨ | |
| \mapsto | ↦ | | \mho | ℧ | |
| \mid | | | r | \models | ⊨ | r |
| \mp | ∓ | b | \mu | μ | |

*continued ...*

| command | output | type | command | output | type |
|---------|--------|------|---------|--------|------|
| \nabla | ∇ | | \natural | ♮ | |
| \ne | ≠ | | \nearrow | ↗ | |
| \neg | ¬ | | \neq | ≠ | r |
| \ni | ∋ | r | \not | ≠. | |
| \notin | ∌ | | \nu | ν | |
| \nwarrow | ↖ | | \odot | ⊙ | b |
| \oint | ∮ | | \Omega | Ω | |
| \omega | ω | | \ominus | ⊖ | b |
| \oplus | ⊕ | b | \oslash | ⊘ | b |
| \otimes | ⊗ | b | \owns | ∋ | |
| \parallel | ∥ | r | \partial | ∂ | |
| \perp | ⊥ | r | \phi | φ | |
| \Pi | Π | | \pi | π | |
| \pm | ± | b | \prec | ≺ | r |
| \preceq | ⪯ | r | \prime | ′ | |
| \prod | ∏ | | \propto | ∝ | r |
| \Psi | Ψ | | \psi | ψ | |
| \rangle | ⟩ | d | \rbrace | } | d |
| \rbrack | ] | d | \rceil | ⌉ | d |
| \Re | ℜ | | \rfloor | ⌋ | |
| \rhd | ▷ | b | \rho | ρ | |
| \Rightarrow | ⇒ | | \rightarrow | → | |
| \rightharpoondown | ⇁ | | \rightharpoonup | ⇀ | |
| \rightleftharpoons | ⇌ | | \searrow | ↘ | |
| \setminus | \ | b | \sharp | ♯ | |
| \Sigma | Σ | | \sigma | σ | |
| \sim | ∼ | r | \simeq | ≃ | r |
| \smallint | ∫ | | \smile | ⌣ | r |
| \spadesuit | ♠ | | \sqcap | ⊓ | b |
| \sqcup | ⊔ | b | \sqsubset | ⊏ | r |
| \sqsubseteq | ⊑ | r | \sqsupset | ⊐ | r |
| \sqsupseteq | ⊒ | r | \star | ⋆ | b |
| \subset | ⊂ | r | \subseteq | ⊆ | r |
| \succ | ≻ | r | \succeq | ⪰ | r |
| \sum | ∑ | | \supset | ⊃ | r |
| \supseteq | ⊇ | r | \surd | √ | |
| \swarrow | ↙ | | \tau | τ | |
| \theta | θ | | \times | × | b |
| \to | → | | \top | ⊤ | |
| \triangle | △ | | \triangleleft | ◁ | b |
| \triangleright | ▷ | b | \unlhd | ⊴ | b |
| \unrhd | ⊵ | b | \Uparrow | ⇑ | d |
| \uparrow | ↑ | d | \Updownarrow | ⇕ | d |

*continued . . .*

| command | output | type | command | output | type |
|---------|--------|------|---------|--------|------|
| \updownarrow | ↕ | d | \uplus | ⊎ | b |
| \Upsilon | Υ | | \upsilon | υ | |
| \varepsilon | ε | | \varphi | φ | |
| \varpi | ϖ | | \varrho | ϱ | |
| \varsigma | ς | | \vartheta | ϑ | |
| \vdash | ⊢ | r | \vee | ∨ | b |
| \Vert | ‖ | d | \vert | │ | d |
| \wedge | ∧ | b | \wp | ℘ | |
| \wr | ≀ | b | \Xi | Ξ | |
| \xi | ξ | | \zeta | ζ | |

## 6.2 Mathematical accents

**Table 6.2:** Mathematical accents that differ from those in text mode.

| command | output | command | output | command | output |
|---------|--------|---------|--------|---------|--------|
| \acute{x} | $\acute{x}$ | \bar{x} | $\bar{o}$ | \breve{x} | $\breve{x}$ |
| \check{x} | $\check{x}$ | \ddot{x} | $\ddot{x}$ | \dot{x} | $\dot{x}$ |
| \grave{x} | $\grave{x}$ | \hat{x} | $\hat{x}$ | \imath | $\imath$ |
| \jmath | $\jmath$ | \tilde{x} | $\tilde{x}$ | \vec{x} | $\vec{x}$ |
| \widehat{x+y} | $\widehat{x+y}$ | \widetilde{x+y} | $\widetilde{x+y}$ | | |

## 6.3 The amsmath package

### 6.3.1 align environments

The graphical display of the following examples always follows the principle below; each expression is put into an \fbox for display purposes.

```
\begin{<name>}
   <name> & = x & x & = x\\    <name> & = x & x & = x
\end{<name>}
```

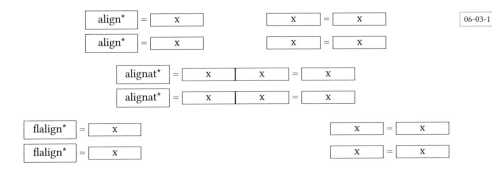

You should always put the separation character (&) *in front of* the mathematical symbol (y &= x); otherwise the wrong horizontal spacing may occur. The number of & characters on a line is formally not limited (cf. Section 6.3.9 on page 88). The separation character doesn't have to be followed by a mathematical symbol – it can be used as an ordinary column separator. The unstarred versions (used below) add the usual numbering to the equations. The number appears below the equation if there is not enough space on the line, in contrast to standard LaTeX.

06-03-2

$$\boxed{\text{align}} = \boxed{\phantom{x}} \quad \boxed{\phantom{x}} = \boxed{\phantom{x}} \tag{1}$$

$$\boxed{\text{alignat}} = \boxed{\phantom{x}} \quad \boxed{\phantom{x}} = \boxed{\phantom{x}} \tag{2}$$

$$\boxed{\text{flalign}} = \boxed{\phantom{x}} \quad \boxed{\phantom{x}} = \boxed{\phantom{x}} \tag{3}$$

The same equations with the same default `align` environment but with the `leqno` document class option result in a different arrangement. This is because the environment uses the entire horizontal width if there is more than one column separator and aligns itself with the equation number. The space is always the same and therefore the alignment changes with respect to other equations, which are always aligned with the centre of the line.

06-03-3

(1) $\boxed{\text{align}} = \boxed{\phantom{x}} \quad \boxed{\phantom{x}} = \boxed{\phantom{x}}$

(2) $\boxed{\text{alignat}} = \boxed{\phantom{x}} \quad \boxed{\phantom{x}} = \boxed{\phantom{x}}$

(3) $\boxed{\text{flalign}} = \boxed{\phantom{x}} \quad \boxed{\phantom{x}} = \boxed{\phantom{x}}$

You can suppress the equation numbers for individual lines as usual through the \nonumber command.

```
\usepackage{amsmath,empheq,xcolor}
\begin{empheq}[box=\fcolorbox{blue}{yellow!40}]{align}
y        &= d              & z &= 1          \nonumber\\
y        &= cx+d           & z &= x+1                    \\
y_{12} &= bx^{2}+cx+d      & z &= x^{2}+x+1\nonumber
\end{empheq}
```

06-03-4

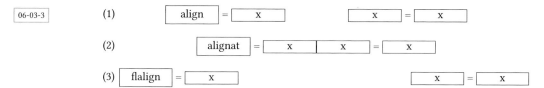

$$
\begin{array}{ll}
y = d & z = 1 \\
y = cx + d & z = x + 1 \\
y_{12} = bx^2 + cx + d & z = x^2 + x + 1
\end{array}
\tag{1}
$$

## 6.3.2 alignat environment

The name of the environment comes from "align at several places" and corresponds in principle to two individual `align` environments *next to each other* (side-by-side). The main difference, however, is the expected parameter, which specifies the number of side-by-side objects (blocks). Each of these objects must be separated by another & symbol: for a parameter value of $n$, $2n - 1$ column separators must be given altogether.

```
\begin{alignat}{number of blocks} ...\\...\\...\end{alignat}
```

```
\usepackage{amsmath}
\begin{alignat}{2}
y        &= d & z & =1                        \\
y        &= cx+d & z & =x+1                    \\
y_{12} &= bx^{2}+cx+d & z &=x^{2}+x+1\nonumber
\end{alignat}
```

$$y = d \qquad\qquad z = 1 \qquad\qquad (1)$$
$$y = cx + d \qquad\qquad z = x + 1 \qquad\qquad (2)$$
$$y_{12} = bx^2 + cx + dz = x^2 + x + 1$$

06-03-5

The advantage of the `alignat` environment is the possibility of aligning several equations vertically with several separators, which is also possible with subexpressions of significantly different sizes.

```
\usepackage{amsmath,empheq,xcolor}% \FBox->Praeambel
\begin{empheq}[{box=\FBox[an example]}]{alignat=3}
  abc &= xxx             &&= xxxxxxxxxxxx &&= aaaaaaaaa \\
  ab  &= yyyyyyyyyyyyyyy &&= yyyy         &&= ab
\end{empheq}
```

$$\boxed{\begin{aligned} &\qquad\qquad\qquad \textbf{an example} \\ abc &= xxx \qquad\qquad\quad = xxxxxxxxxxxx = aaaaaaaaa \qquad (1) \\ ab &= yyyyyyyyyyyyyyy = yyyy \qquad\qquad\quad = ab \qquad\qquad (2) \end{aligned}}$$

06-03-6

### 6.3.3 flalign environment

The `flalign` environment is the replacement for the obsolete `xalignat` and `xxalignat` environments.

$$x_{11} = 0.25$$
$$x_{21} = \frac{1}{3} x_{11} \qquad (1)$$

```
\usepackage{amsmath}
\begin{flalign}
  x_{11} &= 0.25           \nonumber\\
  x_{21} &= \frac{1}{3}\,x_{11}
\end{flalign}
```

06-03-7

If more than one column separator (&) appears, the equation becomes left-aligned. This provides an easy way of left-aligning the equations from the example above; an additional column separator is simply added to the end of the equation.

$$x_{11} = 0.25$$
$$x_{21} = \frac{1}{3} x_{11} \qquad (1)$$

```
\usepackage{amsmath}
\begin{flalign}
  x_{11} &= 0.25           &\nonumber\\
  x_{21} &= \frac{1}{3}\,x_{11} &
\end{flalign}
```

06-03-8

Several groups can be put next to each other without specifying the number of blocks, in contrast to the alignat environment – you just need to get the number of column separators right.

```
\usepackage{amsmath}
\begin{flalign}
i_{11}&= 0.25                     & i_{12} &= i_{21}         & i_{13} &= i_{23}\nonumber \\
i_{21}&= \frac{1}{3}\,i_{11}& i_{22} &= 0.5\,i_{12}   & i_{23} &= i_{31}
\end{flalign}
```

$$i_{11} = 0.25 \qquad i_{12} = i_{21} \qquad i_{13} = i_{23}$$
$$i_{21} = \frac{1}{3}\,i_{11} \qquad i_{22} = 0.5\,i_{12} \qquad i_{23} = i_{31} \quad (1)$$

In some cases, you might want to have both left-aligned and centred equations. Both can be achieved easily through the flalign environment if the global setting through the fleqn document option can't be used for some reason.

```
\usepackage{amsmath,xcolor} \newcommand*\dx{\mathrm{d}x}
\begin{flalign}   f(x) & = \int\frac{1}{x^2}\,\dx \end{flalign}
\begin{flalign}
  f(x) & = \color{magenta}\int\frac{1}{x^2}\,\dx & % <-- dummy &
\end{flalign}
```

$$f(x) = \int \frac{1}{x^2}\,\mathrm{d}x \qquad\qquad (1)$$

$$f(x) = \int \frac{1}{x^2}\,\mathrm{d}x \qquad\qquad (2)$$

```
\usepackage{amsmath,xcolor}
\begin{flalign*}
    && \color{red}12(x-1)+20(y-3)+14(z-2) &= 0\\
\text{\color{blue}expand and rearrange}
    &&              \boxed{6x+10y+7z-50} &= 0
\end{flalign*}
```

$$12(x-1)+20(y-3)+14(z-2) = 0$$
$$\text{expand and rearrange} \qquad \boxed{6x+10y+7z-50} = 0$$

### 6.3.4 aligned environment

The aligned environment corresponds to array, supporting multi-line formulae that are assigned a single equation number, but it actually results in much better horizontal alignment of the parts of the formula. However, the aligned environment has to be used within another math environment.

$$2x + 3 = 7 \qquad 2x + 3 - 3 = 7 - 3$$
$$2x = 4 \qquad \frac{2x}{2} = \frac{4}{2} \qquad (1)$$
$$x = 2$$

```
\usepackage{amsmath}

\begin{align} \begin{aligned}
2x+3 &= 7 &      2x+3-3 &=7-3     \\
2x   &= 4 & \frac{2x}2 &=\frac42\\
x    &= 2
\end{aligned} \end{align}
```

06-03-12

### 6.3.5 gather environment

Use the gather environment when you want equations to be horizontally centred *line-by-line*.

$$\boxed{i_{11} = 0.25} \qquad (1)$$
$$\boxed{i_{21} = \frac{1}{3} i_{11}}$$
$$\boxed{i_{31} = 0.33 i_{22}} \qquad (2)$$

```
\usepackage{amsmath}

\begin{gather}
\boxed{i_{11}=0.25}\\
\boxed{i_{21}=\frac{1}{3}i_{11}}\nonumber\\
\boxed{i_{31}=0.33i_{22}}
\end{gather}
```

06-03-13

### 6.3.6 multline environment

The multline environment, another of the multi-line environments, offers advantages especially for very long equations. Its internal structure is left – centred – ... – centred – right (cf. example 06-03-14). Only the last line is assigned an equation number, and in the starred version even this is suppressed.

06-03-14

```
\usepackage{amsmath,xcolor}
\color{blue}\begin{multline}
  A = \lim_{n\rightarrow\infty}\Delta x\left(a^{2}+\left(a^{2}+2a \Delta x
    +\left(\Delta x\right)^{2}\right)\right.\\
    +\left(a^{2}+2\cdot2a\Delta x+2^{2}\left(\Delta x\right)^{2}\right)\\
    + \ldots\\
  \left.+\left(a^{2}+2\cdot(n-1)a\Delta x
    +(n-1)^{2}\left(\Delta x\right)^{2}\right)\right)\\
  = \color{red}\frac{1}{3}\left( b^{3}-a^{3}\right)
\end{multline}
```

06-03-15

$$A = \lim_{n \to \infty} \Delta x \left(a^2 + \left(a^2 + 2a\Delta x + (\Delta x)^2\right)\right.$$
$$+ \left(a^2 + 2 \cdot 2a\Delta x + 2^2 (\Delta x)^2\right)$$
$$+ \dots$$
$$\left. + \left(a^2 + 2 \cdot (n-1)a\Delta x + (n-1)^2 (\Delta x)^2\right)\right)$$
$$= \frac{1}{3} \left(b^3 - a^3\right) \quad (1)$$

You can change the default alignment of the individual lines as "lc…cr" through the \shoveleft and \shoveright commands, which let you shift several lines to the left or the right.

06-03-16

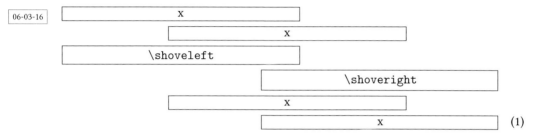

### 6.3.7 split environment

The split environment is similar to multline and is used for equations that are too long for a single line. Again it *must* be part of another math environment. If split is used without column separators, all lines are right-aligned; if a single column separator is given, they are centred, but without space at the centre unless a mathematical comparison operator occurs.

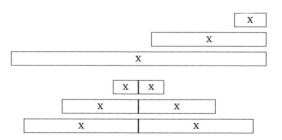

### 6.3.8 cases environment

cases offers better support for case distinctions than standard LaTeX, but *must* be part of another math environment.

\begin{cases} …&…\\…& …\\…\end{cases}

\usepackage{amsmath}

```
\begin{align}
x &= \begin{cases}
    0 & \text{falls }A=\ldots\\    1 & \text{falls }B=\ldots\\
    x & \parbox{7cm}{\raggedright This text can be as long as you want
    because of the \texttt{\textbackslash parbox}; this means that there are no problems wit
    line breaks.}
\end{cases}
\end{align}
```

$$
x = \begin{cases}
0 & \text{falls } A = \dots\\
1 & \text{falls } B = \dots\\
x & \text{This text can be as long as you want because of}\\
  & \text{the \textbackslash parbox; this means that there are no}\\
  & \text{problems with line breaks.}
\end{cases} \tag{1}
$$

### 6.3.9 Matrix environment

**Table 6.3:** Summary of the different matrix environments

|           |                                                               |           |                                                    |             |                                              |
|-----------|---------------------------------------------------------------|-----------|----------------------------------------------------|-------------|----------------------------------------------|
| Vmatrix   | $\begin{Vmatrix} a & b \\ c & d \end{Vmatrix}$                | Bmatrix   | $\begin{Bmatrix} a & b \\ c & d \end{Bmatrix}$     | matrix      | $\begin{matrix} a & b \\ c & d \end{matrix}$ |
| vmatrix   | $\begin{vmatrix} a & b \\ c & d \end{vmatrix}$                | bmatrix   | $\begin{bmatrix} a & b \\ c & d \end{bmatrix}$     | pmatrix     | $\begin{pmatrix} a & b \\ c & d \end{pmatrix}$ |
|           |                                                               |           |                                                    | smallmatrix | $\begin{smallmatrix} a & b \\ c & d \end{smallmatrix}$ |

All matrix environments must be part of another math environment or command. They can be nested arbitrarily. The maximum number of columns for matrices without explicit column definition is limited to 10 by default, but you can change this limit through the internal MaxMatrixCols counter, for example \setcounter{*MaxMatrixCols*}{*20*}.

```
\usepackage{amsmath}
\newcommand\mat{\begin{align*}\begin{bmatrix} a & b\\
    \begin{Vmatrix}A&B\\C&D\end{Vmatrix} c & d\end{bmatrix}\end{align*}}
\begin{minipage}{0.45\linewidth}\mat\end{minipage}
\delimiterfactor=1100
\begin{minipage}{0.45\linewidth}\mat\end{minipage}
```

$$
\begin{bmatrix} & a & & b \\ \begin{Vmatrix} A & B \\ C & D \end{Vmatrix} & c & & d \end{bmatrix} \qquad \begin{bmatrix} & a & & b \\ \begin{Vmatrix} A & B \\ C & D \end{Vmatrix} & c & & d \end{bmatrix}
$$

The alignment of the individual elements for all matrix environments is centred by default; this can be changed by redefining the matrix environment.

06-03-20

$$\begin{pmatrix} 1 & -2 & 1 & 2 \\ 2 & 3 & -2 & 3 \\ 4 & -1 & 3 & -1 \\ 3 & 2 & -4 & 5 \end{pmatrix} \quad (1)$$

```
\usepackage{amsmath}

\begin{align}
\begin{pmatrix} % -> preamble
  1 &-2 & 1 & 2\\ 2 & 3 &-2 & 3\\
  4 &-1 & 3 &-1\\ 3 & 2 &-4 & 5
\end{pmatrix}
\end{align}
\begin{align}
\left(\begin{smallmatrix}% -> preamble
  1 &-2 & 1 & 2\\ +2 & 3 &-2 & 3\\
  4 &-1 & 3 &-1\\ +3 & 2 &-4 & 5
\end{smallmatrix}\right)
\end{align}
```

$$\begin{pmatrix} 1 & -2 & 1 & 2 \\ +2 & 3 & -2 & 3 \\ 4 & -1 & 3 & -1 \\ +3 & 2 & -4 & 5 \end{pmatrix} \quad (2)$$

## 6.3.10 subequations environment

The subequations environment allows for extended numbering by introducing an additional level.

06-03-21

$$y = d \qquad (1a)$$
$$y = cx + d \qquad (1b)$$
$$y = bx^2 + cx + d \qquad (1c)$$
$$y = ax^3 + bx^2 + cx + d \qquad (1d)$$

```
\usepackage{amsmath}

\begin{subequations}
\begin{align}
y &= d\\ y &= cx+d\\ y &= bx^{2}+cx+d\\
y &= ax^{3}+bx^{2}+cx+d
\end{align}
\end{subequations}
```

Modifications of the equation number must be done *after* the start of the subequations if the \theparentequation command is used, as this is only defined inside the environment.

## 6.3.11 Additional commands

| name | description |
|------|-------------|
| \allowdisplaybreaks [*value*] | Allows page breaks between equation lines of the current and lower level groups. The optional argument *value* may take integer values between 0 and 4 and specifies the urgency of the page break; a value of 0 prevents page breaks. |
| \binom{*top*}{*bottom*} | Typesets a binomial coefficient: $\binom{m}{n}$. |
| \bmod{*expression*} | $a\bmod{n^{2}}=b \rightarrow a \bmod n^2 = b$ |
| \boxed{*expression*} | Typesets the mathematical *expression* inside a frame. *expression* may not contain the end of a paragraph. |
| \cfrac [*pos*] {*dividend*}{*divisor*} | Allows you to typeset continued fractions. *pos* specifies the alignment of numerator and denominator and may take one of the values l, r or c. |

continued ...

| name | description |
|---|---|

**\dbinom**{*top*}{*bottom*}     Typesets a binomial coefficient in \displaystyle: $\binom{m}{n}$.

**\ddddot**{*character*} → $\ddddot{x}$

**\dddot**{*character*} → $\dddot{x}$

**\dfrac**{*dividend*}{*divisor*}     Typesets a fraction in \displaystyle $-\dfrac{x}{y}$.

**\displaybreak** [*value*]     Allows page breaks after the next end of line. The optional argument *value* may take integer values between 0 and 4 and specifies the urgency of the page break; a value of 4 forces a page break.

**\genfrac**{*left*}{*right*}{*line width*}{*math style*}{*dividend*}{*divisor*}     Allows the definition of custom fractions or binomial coefficients. *math style* may be one of \displaystyle, \textstyle, \scriptstyle or \scriptscriptstyle.

**\hdotsfor** [*step size*] {*number of columns*}     Allows you to draw a dotted line across several columns in an array or matrix environment.

**\intertext**{*expression*}     Typesets *expression* within a math expression as a separate line of text; spaces are preserved.

**\leftroot**{*value*}     Moves the current point by *value* in a horizontal direction. The *value* is interpreted internally in mu (math units). This command is useful for improving the alignment of root exponents.

**\mathaccent**{*accent character*}{*base character*}     $\mathaccent\cdot\cup$ → $\cup$

**\mod**{*expression*}     $a\mod{n^{2}}=b$ → $a \mod n^2 = b$

**\operatorname**{*name*}     Declares *name* to be an operator, which means that it will be typeset with upright letters.

**\operatornamewithlimits**{*name*}     Declares *name* to be an operator, which means that it will be typeset with upright letters and the \limits command can be used.

**\overset**{*high*}{*normal*}     $\overset{high}{normal}$ → $\overset{high}{normal}$

**\pmod**{*expression*}     $a\pmod{n^{2}}=b$ → $a \pmod{n^2} = b$

**\pod**{*expression*}     $a\pod{n^{2}}=b$ → $a\ (n^2) = b$

**\sideset**{_*lowerLeft*}^{*upperLeft*}{_{*lowerRight*}}^{*upperRight*}{*operator*}     Inserts super- and subscripts at all four corners of a \sum or \prod operator. It may also be used without an explicit operator.

$$\text{\sideset\{\_\{LL\}^\{UL\}\}\{\_\{LR\}^\{UR\}\}\sum\_\{B\}^\{T\}} \Rightarrow {}^{UL}_{LL}\sum_{B}^{T}{}^{UR}_{LR}$$

**\smash** [*pos*] {*radicand*}     Moves the mathematical centre line. *pos* may take one of the following values:
t: leaves the base and changes the height
b: leaves the height and changes the base
tb: changes the base as well as the height

continued ...

| name | description |
|------|-------------|

**\substack**{...\\...\\...}   Provides a stack notation for multiple limits: \prod_{\substack{x=1\\y=3}}\ldots $\Rightarrow \prod\limits_{\substack{x=1\\y=3}} \ldots$

**\tag** * {*expression*}   Instead of an equation number, *expression* is output. The starred version suppresses the parentheses.

**\tbinom**{*top*}{*bottom*}   Typesets a binomial coefficient in \textstyle $- \binom{m}{n}$.

**\text**{*expression*}   Typesets *expression* within a mathematical expression as pure text with spaces preserved.

**\tfrac**{*dividend*}{*divisor*}   Typesets a fraction in \textstyle $- \frac{x}{y}$.

**\underset**{*low*}{*normal*}   $\underset{low}{normal}$ $\Rightarrow \underset{low}{normal}$

**\uproot**{*value*}   Moves the current point by *value* in a vertical direction. The *value* is interpreted internally in mu (math units). This command is useful for improving the alignment of root exponents: compare $\sqrt[kn]{a}$ to $\sqrt[kn]{a}$, result of \sqrt[\uproot{3}k_n]{a}.

# Chapter 7

# Fonts

This chapter looks at the fonts that are available in every system, or are freely available and of interest to many users. Many more fonts are in fact available in a TeX distribution – the number is very large and the specific fonts vary from distribution to distribution; there are too many to cover them all explicitly here.

## 7.1  Font sizes

The standard book, report and article classes and those classes derived from them define at least the commands and corresponding font sizes listed in Table 7.1 on the following page.

## 7.2  Font commands and their parameters

Remember that all font parameters that are given to the commands only take effect after the \selectfont command has been executed!

```
\selectfont
```

Alternatively, the \usefont command can be used – it is simpler when several or all attributes need to be changed. It implicitly executes \selectfont.

**Table 7.1:** The font sizes of the font commands depending on the base font size (the examples refer to the current base font size of 10pt)

| | base font size | | | |
|---|---|---|---|---|
| command | 10 pt | 11 pt | 12 pt | current |
| \tiny | 5 | 6 | 6 | \tiny |
| \scriptsize | 7 | 8 | 8 | \scriptsize |
| \footnotesize | 8 | 9 | 10 | \footnotesize |
| \small | 9 | 10 | 10.95 | \small |
| \normalsize | 10 | 10.95 | 12 | \normalsize |
| \large | 12 | 12 | 14.4 | \large |
| \Large | 14.4 | 14.4 | 17.28 | \Large |
| \LARGE | 17.28 | 17.28 | 20.74 | \LARGE |
| \huge | 20.74 | 20.74 | 24.88 | \huge |
| \Huge | 24.88 | 24.88 | 24.88 | \Huge |

> \usefont{*encoding*}{*family*}{*series*}{*shape*}

## 7.2.1 \fontencoding

The encoding defines the character table, which is saved in a .fd file according to the pattern *encodingfamily*.fd, for example t1ptm.fd. The possible encodings are listed in Table 7.2 on the next page.

> \fontencoding{*encoding type*}

Usually, the T1 encoding will be used for western documents (Latin) and will be specified as a parameter when loading the package fontenc, for example \usepackage [*T1*] {*fontenc*}.

## 7.2.2 \fontfamily

The family is specified by an abbreviation that can be taken from the documentation of the respective font, for example lmmi for "latin modern math italic". Other examples can be found in the font summary below.

> \fontfamily{*font family*}

## 7.2.3 \fontseries

The font series defines the weight and the width of a font. Table 7.3 on the facing page shows a summary of all possible attributes. Few fonts support all attributes, however.

> \fontseries{*font series*}

| encoding | description |
|---|---|
| T1 | LaTeX text encoding (Latin) ("Cork" encoding) |
| TS1 | LaTeX symbol encoding (Latin) |
| T2A,B,C | LaTeX text encoding (Cyrillic) |
| T3 | phonetic alphabet of the tipa package |
| TS3 | same for symbols |
| T4 | text encoding for African languages |
| T5 | text encoding for Vietnamese |
| T7 | text encoding for Greek |
| OT1 | original TeX encoding by Donald Knuth |
| OT4 | TeX encoding for Polish extensions |
| OML | original TeX encoding for math characters by Donald Knuth |
| OMS | original TeX encoding for math symbols by Donald Knuth |
| OMX | same with extensions |
| U | nondescript encoding |
| L.. | local encoding for customizations |
| LY1 | alternative to T1 |

Table 7.2: Selection of standard font encodings in LaTeX

| name | abbreviation | name | abbreviation |
|---|---|---|---|
| Ultra Light | ul | Ultra Condensed | uc |
| Extra Light | el | Extra Condensed | ec |
| Light | l | Condensed | c |
| Semi Light | sl | Semi Condensed | sc |
| Medium (normal) | m | | |
| Semi Bold | sb | Semi Expanded | sx |
| Bold | b | Expanded | x |
| Extra Bold | eb | Extra Expanded | ex |
| Ultra Bold | ub | Ultra Expanded | ux |

Table 7.3: Abbreviations for font weight and width (series)

## 7.2.4 \fontshape

Not all combinations of shape are supported by the respective font. This is the reason why the font was changed in the example column in Table 7.4 to cmr in order to be able to show all the options.

`\fontshape{font shape}`

| name | | example | name | | example |
|---|---|---|---|---|---|
| upright (normal) | n | upright | italic | it | italic |
| slanted/oblique | sl | slanted | small caps | sc | SMALL CAPS |
| upright italic | ui | italic upright | outline | ol | Outline shape |

Table 7.4: Names and abbreviations for the font shape

### 7.2.5 \fontsize

The nine commands available to change the font size (\tiny...\Huge) are usually sufficient, so changing the font size manually is only necessary in exceptional cases.

| \fontsize{*font size*}{*line feed*} |

Without an explicit unit, pt is assumed; all other TeX-compatible units can be used as well (cf. Section 5.1 on page 71). If the *font size* (\baselineskip) is smaller than the character size (\f@size), it is only taken into account if the difference between *linefeed* and *font size* is not smaller than \lineskiplimit (default 0 pt). Otherwise, the \lineskip value (default 1 pt) is assumed for the line spacing, see example in the following table.

**Table 7.5:** Examples for font sizes

| parameter | example |
|---|---|
| {10}{10} | This is a pointless sentence which only demonstrates font size and line height and does not serve any other purpose. |
| {10}{0} | This is a pointless sentence that only demonstrates font size and line height and does not serve any other purpose. |
| {10}{15} | This is a pointless sentence that only demonstrates font size and line height and does not serve any other purpose. |
| {5}{5.5} | This is a pointless sentence that only demonstrates font size and line height and does not serve any other purpose. This is a pointless sentence that only demonstrates font size and line height and does not serve any other purpose. |
| {10}{11} | This is a pointless sentence that only demonstrates font size and line height and does not serve any other purpose. |
| {8}{8.7} | This is a pointless sentence that only demonstrates font size and line height and does not serve any other purpose. |
| {16}{17} | This is a pointless sentence that only demonstrates font size and line height and does not serve any other purpose. |
| {1cm}{1.1cm} | This is a pointless sentence ... |

## 7.3 Serif fonts

If a font package is loaded, it automatically switches to the respective font.

### 7.3.1 Bera Serif – fve, \usepackage{*beraserif*}

Alternatively, loading the bera package provides all three bera fonts and the textcomp package.

| *encod.* | *family* | *series* | *shape* | *example* |
|---|---|---|---|---|
| T1 | fve | m | n | abcdefghijklmnopqrstuvwxyzäöüß<br>ABCDEFGHIJKLMNOPQRSTUVWXYZÄÖÜ<br>0123456789<>,.!"§§%&()=?+# |
| T1 | fve | m | sl | *abcdefghijklmnopqrstuvwxyzäöüß*<br>*ABCDEFGHIJKLMNOPQRSTUVWXYZÄÖÜ*<br>*0123456789<>,.!"§§%&()=?+#* |
| T1 | fve | b | n | **abcdefghijklmnopqrstuvwxyzäöüß**<br>**ABCDEFGHIJKLMNOPQRSTUVWXYZÄÖÜ**<br>**0123456789<>,.!"§§%&()=?+#** |
| T1 | fve | b | sl | ***abcdefghijklmnopqrstuvwxyzäöüß***<br>***ABCDEFGHIJKLMNOPQRSTUVWXYZÄÖÜ***<br>***0123456789<>,.!"§§%&()=?+#*** |

## 7.3.2 Computer Modern Roman – cmr

The default font in TeX, which is available on every system and contains a math character set as well (cf. Section 7.7.1 on page 116). It also exists as a T1 font.

| *encod.* | *family* | *series* | *shape* | *example* |
|---|---|---|---|---|
| OT1 | cmr | m | n | abcdefghijklmnopqrstuvwxyzäöüß<br>ABCDEFGHIJKLMNOPQRSTUVWXYZÄÖÜ<br>0123456789¡¿,.!"§§%&()=?+# |
| OT1 | cmr | m | it | *abcdefghijklmnopqrstuvwxyzäöüß*<br>*ABCDEFGHIJKLMNOPQRSTUVWXYZÄÖÜ*<br>*0123456789¡¿,.!"§§%&()=?+#* |
| OT1 | cmr | m | sl | *abcdefghijklmnopqrstuvwxyzäöüß*<br>*ABCDEFGHIJKLMNOPQRSTUVWXYZÄÖÜ*<br>*0123456789¡¿,.!"§§%&()=?+#* |
| OT1 | cmr | m | sc | ABCDEFGHIJKLMNOPQRSTUVWXYZÄÖÜSS<br>ABCDEFGHIJKLMNOPQRSTUVWXYZÄÖÜ<br>0123456789<>,.!"§§%&()=?+# |
| OT1 | cmr | b | n | abcdefghijklmnopqrstuvwxyzäöüß<br>**ABCDEFGHIJKLMNOPQRSTUVWXYZÄÖÜ**<br>**0123456789¡¿,.!"§§%&()=?+#** |
| OT1 | cmr | bx | n | abcdefghijklmnopqrstuvwxyzäöüß<br>**ABCDEFGHIJKLMNOPQRSTUVWXYZÄÖÜ**<br>**0123456789¡¿,.!"§§%&()=?+#** |
| OT1 | cmr | bx | it | *abcdefghijklmnopqrstuvwxyzäöüß*<br>***ABCDEFGHIJKLMNOPQRSTUVWXYZÄÖÜ***<br>***0123456789¡¿,.!"§§%&()=?+#*** |
| OT1 | cmr | bx | sl | *abcdefghijklmnopqrstuvwxyzäöüß*<br>***ABCDEFGHIJKLMNOPQRSTUVWXYZÄÖÜ***<br>***0123456789¡¿,.!"§§%&()=?+#*** |

### 7.3.3 Bookman – pbk, \usepackage{*bookman*}

| *encod.* | *family* | *series* | *shape* | *example* |
|---|---|---|---|---|
| T1 | pbk | m | n | abcdefghijklmnopqrstuvwxyzäöüß<br>ABCDEFGHIJKLMNOPQRSTUVWXYZÄÖÜ<br>0123456789<>,.!"§$%&()=?+# |
| T1 | pbk | m | it | *abcdefghijklmnopqrstuvwxyzäöüß*<br>*ABCDEFGHIJKLMNOPQRSTUVWXYZÄÖÜ*<br>*0123456789<>,.!"§$%&()=?+#* |
| T1 | pbk | m | sl | *abcdefghijklmnopqrstuvwxyzäöüß*<br>*ABCDEFGHIJKLMNOPQRSTUVWXYZÄÖÜ*<br>*0123456789<>,.!"§$%&()=?+#* |
| T1 | pbk | m | sc | ABCDEFGHIJKLMNOPQRSTUVWXYZÄÖÜSS<br>ABCDEFGHIJKLMNOPQRSTUVWXYZÄÖÜ<br>0123456789<>,.!"§$%&()=?+# |
| T1 | pbk | b | n | **abcdefghijklmnopqrstuvwxyzäöüß**<br>**ABCDEFGHIJKLMNOPQRSTUVWXYZÄÖÜ**<br>**0123456789<>,.!"§$%&()=?+#** |
| T1 | pbk | b | it | ***abcdefghijklmnopqrstuvwxyzäöüß***<br>***ABCDEFGHIJKLMNOPQRSTUVWXYZÄÖÜ***<br>***0123456789<>,.!"§$%&()=?+#*** |
| T1 | pbk | b | sl | ***abcdefghijklmnopqrstuvwxyzäöüß***<br>***ABCDEFGHIJKLMNOPQRSTUVWXYZÄÖÜ***<br>***0123456789<>,.!"§$%&()=?+#*** |
| T1 | pbk | b | sc | **ABCDEFGHIJKLMNOPQRSTUVWXYZÄÖÜSS**<br>**ABCDEFGHIJKLMNOPQRSTUVWXYZÄÖÜ**<br>**0123456789<>,.!"§$%&()=?+#** |

### 7.3.4 Charter – bch, \usepackage{*charter*}

| *encod.* | *family* | *series* | *shape* | *example* |
|---|---|---|---|---|
| T1 | bch | m | n | abcdefghijklmnopqrstuvwxyzäöüß<br>ABCDEFGHIJKLMNOPQRSTUVWXYZÄÖÜ<br>0123456789<>,.!"§§%&()=?+# |
| T1 | bch | m | it | *abcdefghijklmnopqrstuvwxyzäöüß*<br>*ABCDEFGHIJKLMNOPQRSTUVWXYZÄÖÜ*<br>*0123456789<>,.!"§§%&()=?+#* |
| T1 | bch | m | sl | *abcdefghijklmnopqrstuvwxyzäöüß*<br>*ABCDEFGHIJKLMNOPQRSTUVWXYZÄÖÜ*<br>*0123456789<>,.!"§§%&()=?+#* |
| T1 | bch | m | sc | ABCDEFGHIJKLMNOPQRSTUVWXYZÄÖÜSS<br>ABCDEFGHIJKLMNOPQRSTUVWXYZÄÖÜ<br>0123456789<>,.!"§§%&()=?+# |

| | | | | |
|---|---|---|---|---|
| T1 | bch | b | n | abcdefghijklmnopqrstuvwxyzäöüß<br>ABCDEFGHIJKLMNOPQRSTUVWXYZÄÖÜ<br>0123456789<>,.!"§§%&()=?+# |
| T1 | bch | b | it | abcdefghijklmnopqrstuvwxyzäöüß<br>ABCDEFGHIJKLMNOPQRSTUVWXYZÄÖÜ<br>0123456789<>,.!"§§%&()=?+# |
| T1 | bch | b | sl | abcdefghijklmnopqrstuvwxyzäöüß<br>ABCDEFGHIJKLMNOPQRSTUVWXYZÄÖÜ<br>0123456789<>,.!"§§%&()=?+# |
| T1 | bch | b | sc | ABCDEFGHIJKLMNOPQRSTUVWXYZÄÖÜSS<br>ABCDEFGHIJKLMNOPQRSTUVWXYZÄÖÜ<br>0123456789<>,.!"§§%&()=?+# |

### 7.3.5  Concrete – `ccr`, \usepackage{*beton*}

| encod. | family | series | shape | example |
|---|---|---|---|---|
| T1 | ccr | m | n | abcdefghijklmnopqrstuvwxyzäöüß<br>ABCDEFGHIJKLMNOPQRSTUVWXYZÄÖÜ<br>0123456789<>,.!"§§%&()=?+# |
| T1 | ccr | m | it | abcdefghijklmnopqrstuvwxyzäöüß<br>ABCDEFGHIJKLMNOPQRSTUVWXYZÄÖÜ<br>0123456789<>,.!"§§%&()=?+# |
| T1 | ccr | m | sl | abcdefghijklmnopqrstuvwxyzäöüß<br>ABCDEFGHIJKLMNOPQRSTUVWXYZÄÖÜ<br>0123456789<>,.!"§§%&()=?+# |
| T1 | ccr | m | sc | ABCDEFGHIJKLMNOPQRSTUVWXYZÄÖÜSS<br>ABCDEFGHIJKLMNOPQRSTUVWXYZÄÖÜ<br>0123456789<>,.!"§§%&()=?+# |
| OT1 | ccr | c | sl | abcdefghijklmnopqrstuvwxyzäöüß<br>ABCDEFGHIJKLMNOPQRSTUVWXYZÄÖÜ<br>0123456789¡¿,.!"§§%&()=?+# |

### 7.3.6  Euler Roman – `eur`, \usepackage{*euler*}

| encod. | family | series | shape | example |
|---|---|---|---|---|
| U | eur | m | n | abcdefghijklmnopqrstuvwxyzäöüß<br>ABCDEFGHIJKLMNOPQRSTUVWXYZÄÖÜ<br>0123456789<>ωε§$/ϑ |
| U | eur | b | n | abcdefghijklmnopqrstuvwxyzäöüß<br>ABCDEFGHIJKLMNOPQRSTUVWXYZÄÖÜ<br>0123456789<>ωε§$/ϑ |

### 7.3.7 kpFonts – jkp, \usepackage{*kpfonts*}

The kpfonts project is a complete set of fonts and the package provides a lot of optional arguments.

| *encod.* | *family* | *series* | *shape* | *example* |
|---|---|---|---|---|
| T1 | jkp | m | n | abcdefghijklmnopqrstuvwxyzäöüß<br>ABCDEFGHIJKLMNOPQRSTUVWXYZÄÖÜ<br>0123456789<>,.!"§§%&()=?+# |
| T1 | jkp | m | it | *abcdefghijklmnopqrstuvwxyzäöüß*<br>*ABCDEFGHIJKLMNOPQRSTUVWXYZÄÖÜ*<br>*0123456789<>,.!"§§%&()=?+#* |
| T1 | jkp | m | sc | ABCDEFGHIJKLMNOPQRSTUVWXYZÄÖÜss<br>ABCDEFGHIJKLMNOPQRSTUVWXYZÄÖÜ<br>0123456789<>,.!"§§%&()=?+# |
| T1 | jkp | m | scsl | *ABCDEFGHIJKLMNOPQRSTUVWXYZÄÖÜss*<br>*ABCDEFGHIJKLMNOPQRSTUVWXYZÄÖÜ*<br>*0123456789<>,.!"§§%&()=?+#* |
| T1 | jkp | m | sl | *abcdefghijklmnopqrstuvwxyzäöüß*<br>*ABCDEFGHIJKLMNOPQRSTUVWXYZÄÖÜ*<br>*0123456789<>,.!"§§%&()=?+#* |
| T1 | jkp | b | n | **abcdefghijklmnopqrstuvwxyzäöüß**<br>**ABCDEFGHIJKLMNOPQRSTUVWXYZÄÖÜ**<br>**0123456789<>,.!"§§%&()=?+#** |
| T1 | jkp | b | it | ***abcdefghijklmnopqrstuvwxyzäöüß***<br>***ABCDEFGHIJKLMNOPQRSTUVWXYZÄÖÜ***<br>***0123456789<>,.!"§§%&()=?+#*** |
| T1 | jkp | b | sl | ***abcdefghijklmnopqrstuvwxyzäöüß***<br>***ABCDEFGHIJKLMNOPQRSTUVWXYZÄÖÜ***<br>***0123456789<>,.!"§§%&()=?+#*** |
| T1 | jkp | b | sc | **ABCDEFGHIJKLMNOPQRSTUVWXYZÄÖÜss**<br>**ABCDEFGHIJKLMNOPQRSTUVWXYZÄÖÜ**<br>**0123456789<>,.!"§§%&()=?+#** |
| T1 | jkp | b | scsl | ***ABCDEFGHIJKLMNOPQRSTUVWXYZÄÖÜss***<br>***ABCDEFGHIJKLMNOPQRSTUVWXYZÄÖÜ***<br>***0123456789<>,.!"§§%&()=?+#*** |
| T1 | jkp | bx | n | **abcdefghijklmnopqrstuvwxyzäöüß**<br>**ABCDEFGHIJKLMNOPQRSTUVWXYZÄÖÜ**<br>**0123456789<>,.!"§§%&()=?+#** |
| T1 | jkp | bx | it | ***abcdefghijklmnopqrstuvwxyzäöüß***<br>***ABCDEFGHIJKLMNOPQRSTUVWXYZÄÖÜ***<br>***0123456789<>,.!"§§%&()=?+#*** |
| T1 | jkp | bx | sl | ***abcdefghijklmnopqrstuvwxyzäöüß***<br>***ABCDEFGHIJKLMNOPQRSTUVWXYZÄÖÜ***<br>***0123456789<>,.!"§§%&()=?+#*** |

| | | | |
|---|---|---|---|
| T1 | jkp | bx | sc | ABCDEFGHIJKLMNOPQRSTUVWXYZÄÖÜSS<br>ABCDEFGHIJKLMNOPQRSTUVWXYZÄÖÜ<br>0123456789<>,.!"§§$%&()=?+# |
| T1 | jkp | bx | scsl | *ABCDEFGHIJKLMNOPQRSTUVWXYZÄÖÜSS*<br>*ABCDEFGHIJKLMNOPQRSTUVWXYZÄÖÜ*<br>*0123456789<>,.!"§§$%&()=?+#* |

## 7.3.8  kpFonts light – jkpl, \usepackage[*light*]{*kpfonts*}

| encod. | family | series | shape | example |
|---|---|---|---|---|
| T1 | jkpl | m | n | abcdefghijklmnopqrstuvwxyzäöüß<br>ABCDEFGHIJKLMNOPQRSTUVWXYZÄÖÜ<br>0123456789<>,.!"§§$%&()=?+# |
| T1 | jkpl | m | it | *abcdefghijklmnopqrstuvwxyzäöüß*<br>*ABCDEFGHIJKLMNOPQRSTUVWXYZÄÖÜ*<br>*0123456789<>,.!"§§$%&()=?+#* |
| T1 | jkpl | m | sc | ABCDEFGHIJKLMNOPQRSTUVWXYZÄÖÜSS<br>ABCDEFGHIJKLMNOPQRSTUVWXYZÄÖÜ<br>0123456789<>,.!"§§$%&()=?+# |
| T1 | jkpl | m | scsl | *ABCDEFGHIJKLMNOPQRSTUVWXYZÄÖÜSS*<br>*ABCDEFGHIJKLMNOPQRSTUVWXYZÄÖÜ*<br>*0123456789<>,.!"§§$%&()=?+#* |
| T1 | jkpl | m | sl | *abcdefghijklmnopqrstuvwxyzäöüß*<br>*ABCDEFGHIJKLMNOPQRSTUVWXYZÄÖÜ*<br>*0123456789<>,.!"§§$%&()=?+#* |
| T1 | jkpl | b | n | abcdefghijklmnopqrstuvwxyzäöüß<br>ABCDEFGHIJKLMNOPQRSTUVWXYZÄÖÜ<br>0123456789<>,.!"§§$%&()=?+# |
| T1 | jkpl | b | it | *abcdefghijklmnopqrstuvwxyzäöüß*<br>*ABCDEFGHIJKLMNOPQRSTUVWXYZÄÖÜ*<br>*0123456789<>,.!"§§$%&()=?+#* |
| T1 | jkpl | b | sl | *abcdefghijklmnopqrstuvwxyzäöüß*<br>*ABCDEFGHIJKLMNOPQRSTUVWXYZÄÖÜ*<br>*0123456789<>,.!"§§$%&()=?+#* |
| T1 | jkpl | b | sc | ABCDEFGHIJKLMNOPQRSTUVWXYZÄÖÜSS<br>ABCDEFGHIJKLMNOPQRSTUVWXYZÄÖÜ<br>0123456789<>,.!"§§$%&()=?+# |
| T1 | jkpl | b | scsl | *ABCDEFGHIJKLMNOPQRSTUVWXYZÄÖÜSS*<br>*ABCDEFGHIJKLMNOPQRSTUVWXYZÄÖÜ*<br>*0123456789<>,.!"§§$%&()=?+#* |
| T1 | jkpl | bx | n | abcdefghijklmnopqrstuvwxyzäöüß<br>ABCDEFGHIJKLMNOPQRSTUVWXYZÄÖÜ<br>0123456789<>,.!"§§$%&()=?+# |

| | | | | |
|---|---|---|---|---|
| T1 | jkpl | bx | it | *abcdefghijklmnopqrstuvwxyzäöüß* <br> *ABCDEFGHIJKLMNOPQRSTUVWXYZÄÖÜ* <br> *0123456789<>,.!"§§%&()=?+#* |
| T1 | jkpl | bx | sl | *abcdefghijklmnopqrstuvwxyzäöüß* <br> *ABCDEFGHIJKLMNOPQRSTUVWXYZÄÖÜ* <br> *0123456789<>,.!"§§%&()=?+#* |
| T1 | jkpl | bx | sc | ABCDEFGHIJKLMNOPQRSTUVWXYZÄÖÜss <br> ABCDEFGHIJKLMNOPQRSTUVWXYZÄÖÜ <br> 0123456789<>,.!"§§%&()=?+# |
| T1 | jkpl | bx | scsl | *ABCDEFGHIJKLMNOPQRSTUVWXYZÄÖÜss* <br> *ABCDEFGHIJKLMNOPQRSTUVWXYZÄÖÜ* <br> *0123456789<>,.!"§§%&()=?+#* |

## 7.3.9 Libertine – flx, \usepackage{*libertine*}

| encod. | family | series | shape | example |
|---|---|---|---|---|
| T1 | fxl | m | n | abcdefghijklmnopqrstuvwxyzäöüß <br> ABCDEFGHIJKLMNOPQRSTUVWXYZÄÖÜ <br> 0123456789<>,.!"§§%&()=?+# |
| T1 | fxl | m | it | *abcdefghijklmnopqrstuvwxyzäöüß* <br> *ABCDEFGHIJKLMNOPQRSTUVWXYZÄÖÜ* <br> *0123456789<>,.!"§§%&()=?+#* |
| T1 | fxl | b | n | **abcdefghijklmnopqrstuvwxyzäöüß** <br> **ABCDEFGHIJKLMNOPQRSTUVWXYZÄÖÜ** <br> **0123456789<>,.!"§§%&()=?+#** |
| T1 | fxl | b | it | ***abcdefghijklmnopqrstuvwxyzäöüß*** <br> ***ABCDEFGHIJKLMNOPQRSTUVWXYZÄÖÜ*** <br> ***0123456789<>,.!"§§%&()=?+#*** |
| T1 | fxl | m | sc | ABCDEFGHIJKLMNOPQRSTUVWXYZÄÖÜß <br> ABCDEFGHIJKLMNOPQRSTUVWXYZÄÖÜ <br> 0123456789<>,.!"§§%&()=?+# |
| T1 | fxl | b | sc | **ABCDEFGHIJKLMNOPQRSTUVWXYZÄÖÜß** <br> **ABCDEFGHIJKLMNOPQRSTUVWXYZÄÖÜ** <br> **0123456789<>,.!"§§%&()=?+#** |
| T1 | fxl | m | ic | *ABCDEFGHIJKLMNOPQRSTUVWXYZÄÖÜß* <br> *ABCDEFGHIJKLMNOPQRSTUVWXYZÄÖÜ* <br> *0123456789<>,.!"§§%&()=?+#* |
| T1 | fxl | b | ic | *ABCDEFGHIJKLMNOPQRSTUVWXYZÄÖÜß* <br> ***ABCDEFGHIJKLMNOPQRSTUVWXYZÄÖÜ*** <br> ***0123456789<>,.!"§§%&()=?+#*** |

## 7.3.10  New Century Schoolbook – pnc, \usepackage{*newcent*}

| *encod.* | *family* | *series* | *shape* | *example* |
|---|---|---|---|---|
| T1 | pnc | m | n | abcdefghijklmnopqrstuvwxyzäöüß ABCDEFGHIJKLMNOPQRSTUVWXYZÄÖÜ 0123456789<>,.!"§§%&()=?+# |
| T1 | pnc | m | it | *abcdefghijklmnopqrstuvwxyzäöüß ABCDEFGHIJKLMNOPQRSTUVWXYZÄÖÜ 0123456789<>,.!"§§%&()=?+#* |
| T1 | pnc | m | sl | *abcdefghijklmnopqrstuvwxyzäöüß ABCDEFGHIJKLMNOPQRSTUVWXYZÄÖÜ 0123456789<>,.!"§§%&()=?+#* |
| T1 | pnc | m | sc | ABCDEFGHIJKLMNOPQRSTUVWXYZÄÖÜSS ABCDEFGHIJKLMNOPQRSTUVWXYZÄÖÜ 0123456789<>,.!"§$%&()=?+# |
| T1 | pnc | b | n | **abcdefghijklmnopqrstuvwxyzäöüß ABCDEFGHIJKLMNOPQRSTUVWXYZÄÖÜ 0123456789<>,.!"§§%&()=?+#** |
| T1 | pnc | b | it | ***abcdefghijklmnopqrstuvwxyzäöüß ABCDEFGHIJKLMNOPQRSTUVWXYZÄÖÜ 0123456789<>,.!"§§%&()=?+#*** |
| T1 | pnc | b | sl | ***abcdefghijklmnopqrstuvwxyzäöüß ABCDEFGHIJKLMNOPQRSTUVWXYZÄÖÜ 0123456789<>,.!"§§%&()=?+#*** |
| T1 | pnc | b | sc | **ABCDEFGHIJKLMNOPQRSTUVWXYZÄÖÜSS ABCDEFGHIJKLMNOPQRSTUVWXYZÄÖÜ 0123456789<>,.!"§$%&()=?+#** |

## 7.3.11  Palatino – ppl, \usepackage{*mathpazo*}

| *encod.* | *family* | *series* | *shape* | *example* |
|---|---|---|---|---|
| T1 | ppl | m | n | abcdefghijklmnopqrstuvwxyzäöüß ABCDEFGHIJKLMNOPQRSTUVWXYZÄÖÜ 0123456789<>,.!"§§%&()=?+# |
| T1 | ppl | m | it | *abcdefghijklmnopqrstuvwxyzäöüß ABCDEFGHIJKLMNOPQRSTUVWXYZÄÖÜ 0123456789<>,.!"§§%&()=?+#* |
| T1 | ppl | m | sl | *abcdefghijklmnopqrstuvwxyzäöüß ABCDEFGHIJKLMNOPQRSTUVWXYZÄÖÜ 0123456789<>,.!"§§%&()=?+#* |
| T1 | ppl | m | sc | ABCDEFGHIJKLMNOPQRSTUVWXYZÄÖÜSS ABCDEFGHIJKLMNOPQRSTUVWXYZÄÖÜ 0123456789<>,.!"§$%&()=?+# |

| | | | | |
|---|---|---|---|---|
| T1 | ppl | b | n | abcdefghijklmnopqrstuvwxyzäöüß ABCDEFGHIJKLMNOPQRSTUVWXYZÄÖÜ 0123456789<>,.!"§$%&()=?+# |
| T1 | ppl | b | it | abcdefghijklmnopqrstuvwxyzäöüß ABCDEFGHIJKLMNOPQRSTUVWXYZÄÖÜ 0123456789<>,.!"§$%&()=?+# |
| T1 | ppl | b | sl | abcdefghijklmnopqrstuvwxyzäöüß ABCDEFGHIJKLMNOPQRSTUVWXYZÄÖÜ 0123456789<>,.!"§$%&()=?+# |
| T1 | ppl | b | sc | ABCDEFGHIJKLMNOPQRSTUVWXYZÄÖÜSS ABCDEFGHIJKLMNOPQRSTUVWXYZÄÖÜ 0123456789<>,.!"§$%&()=?+# |

## 7.3.12 Times Roman – ptm, \usepackage{*mathptmx*}

| *encod.* | *family* | *series* | *shape* | *example* |
|---|---|---|---|---|
| T1 | ptm | m | n | abcdefghijklmnopqrstuvwxyzäöüß ABCDEFGHIJKLMNOPQRSTUVWXYZÄÖÜ 0123456789<>,.!"§$%&()=?+# |
| T1 | ptm | m | it | abcdefghijklmnopqrstuvwxyzäöüß ABCDEFGHIJKLMNOPQRSTUVWXYZÄÖÜ 0123456789<>,.!"§$%&()=?+# |
| T1 | ptm | m | sl | abcdefghijklmnopqrstuvwxyzäöüß ABCDEFGHIJKLMNOPQRSTUVWXYZÄÖÜ 0123456789<>,.!"§$%&()=?+# |
| T1 | ptm | m | sc | ABCDEFGHIJKLMNOPQRSTUVWXYZÄÖÜSS ABCDEFGHIJKLMNOPQRSTUVWXYZÄÖÜ 0123456789<>,.!"§$%&()=?+# |
| T1 | ptm | b | n | abcdefghijklmnopqrstuvwxyzäöüß ABCDEFGHIJKLMNOPQRSTUVWXYZÄÖÜ 0123456789<>,.!"§$%&()=?+# |
| T1 | ptm | b | it | abcdefghijklmnopqrstuvwxyzäöüß ABCDEFGHIJKLMNOPQRSTUVWXYZÄÖÜ 0123456789<>,.!"§$%&()=?+# |
| T1 | ptm | b | sl | abcdefghijklmnopqrstuvwxyzäöüß ABCDEFGHIJKLMNOPQRSTUVWXYZÄÖÜ 0123456789<>,.!"§$%&()=?+# |
| T1 | ptm | b | sc | ABCDEFGHIJKLMNOPQRSTUVWXYZÄÖÜSS ABCDEFGHIJKLMNOPQRSTUVWXYZÄÖÜ 0123456789<>,.!"§$%&()=?+# |

## 7.3.13  Utopia – put, \usepackage{*utopia*}

| *encod.* | *family* | *series* | *shape* | *example* |
|---|---|---|---|---|
| T1 | put | m | n | abcdefghijklmnopqrstuvwxyzäöüß<br>ABCDEFGHIJKLMNOPQRSTUVWXYZÄÖÜ<br>0123456789<>,.!"§§%&()=?+# |
| T1 | put | m | it | *abcdefghijklmnopqrstuvwxyzäöüß*<br>*ABCDEFGHIJKLMNOPQRSTUVWXYZÄÖÜ*<br>*0123456789<>,.!"§§%&()=?+#* |
| T1 | put | m | sl | abcdefghijklmnopqrstuvwxyzäöüß<br>ABCDEFGHIJKLMNOPQRSTUVWXYZÄÖÜ<br>0123456789<>,.!"§§%&()=?+# |
| T1 | put | m | sc | ABCDEFGHIJKLMNOPQRSTUVWXYZÄÖÜSS<br>ABCDEFGHIJKLMNOPQRSTUVWXYZÄÖÜ<br>0123456789<>,.!"§§%&()=?+# |
| T1 | put | b | n | **abcdefghijklmnopqrstuvwxyzäöüß**<br>**ABCDEFGHIJKLMNOPQRSTUVWXYZÄÖÜ**<br>**0123456789<>,.!"§§%&()=?+#** |
| T1 | put | b | it | ***abcdefghijklmnopqrstuvwxyzäöüß***<br>***ABCDEFGHIJKLMNOPQRSTUVWXYZÄÖÜ***<br>***0123456789<>,.!"§§%&()=?+#*** |
| T1 | put | b | sl | ***abcdefghijklmnopqrstuvwxyzäöüß***<br>***ABCDEFGHIJKLMNOPQRSTUVWXYZÄÖÜ***<br>***0123456789<>,.!"§§%&()=?+#*** |
| T1 | put | b | sc | **ABCDEFGHIJKLMNOPQRSTUVWXYZÄÖÜSS**<br>**ABCDEFGHIJKLMNOPQRSTUVWXYZÄÖÜ**<br>**0123456789<>,.!"§§%&()=?+#** |

## 7.3.14  URW Antiqua Condensed – uaq

| *encod.* | *family* | *series* | *shape* | *example* |
|---|---|---|---|---|
| T1 | uaq | mc | n | abcdefghijklmnopqrstuvwxyzäöüß<br>ABCDEFGHIJKLMNOPQRSTUVWXYZÄÖÜ<br>0123456789<>,.!"§§%&()=?+# |
| T1 | uaq | mc | sl | abcdefghijklmnopqrstuvwxyzäöüß<br>ABCDEFGHIJKLMNOPQRSTUVWXYZÄÖÜ<br>0123456789<>,.!"§§%&()=?+# |
| T1 | uaq | mc | sc | ABCDEFGHIJKLMNOPQRSTUVWXYZÄÖÜSS<br>ABCDEFGHIJKLMNOPQRSTUVWXYZÄÖÜ<br>0123456789<>,.!"§§%&()=?+# |

## 7.4 Sans-serif fonts

### 7.4.1 Avant Garde – **pag**, \usepackage{*avant*}

| encod. | family | series | shape | example |
|---|---|---|---|---|
| T1 | pag | m | n | abcdefghijklmnopqrstuvwxyzäöüß ABCDEFGHIJKLMNOPQRSTUVWXYZÄÖÜ 0123456789<>,.!"§§%&()=?+# |
| T1 | pag | m | it | abcdefghijklmnopqrstuvwxyzäöüß ABCDEFGHIJKLMNOPQRSTUVWXYZÄÖÜ 0123456789<>,.!"§§%&()=?+# |
| T1 | pag | m | sl | abcdefghijklmnopqrstuvwxyzäöüß ABCDEFGHIJKLMNOPQRSTUVWXYZÄÖÜ 0123456789<>,.!"§§%&()=?+# |
| T1 | pag | m | sc | ABCDEFGHIJKLMNOPQRSTUVWXYZÄÖÜSS ABCDEFGHIJKLMNOPQRSTUVWXYZÄÖÜ 0123456789<>,.!"§§%&()=?+# |
| T1 | pag | b | n | abcdefghijklmnopqrstuvwxyzäöüß ABCDEFGHIJKLMNOPQRSTUVWXYZÄÖÜ 0123456789<>,.!"§§%&()=?+# |
| T1 | pag | b | sl | abcdefghijklmnopqrstuvwxyzäöüß ABCDEFGHIJKLMNOPQRSTUVWXYZÄÖÜ 0123456789<>,.!"§§%&()=?+# |
| T1 | pag | b | sc | ABCDEFGHIJKLMNOPQRSTUVWXYZÄÖÜSS ABCDEFGHIJKLMNOPQRSTUVWXYZÄÖÜ 0123456789<>,.!"§§%&()=?+# |
| T1 | pag | db | n | abcdefghijklmnopqrstuvwxyzäöüß ABCDEFGHIJKLMNOPQRSTUVWXYZÄÖÜ 0123456789<>,.!"§§%&()=?+# |
| T1 | pag | db | sl | abcdefghijklmnopqrstuvwxyzäöüß ABCDEFGHIJKLMNOPQRSTUVWXYZÄÖÜ 0123456789<>,.!"§§%&()=?+# |
| T1 | pag | db | sc | ABCDEFGHIJKLMNOPQRSTUVWXYZÄÖÜSS ABCDEFGHIJKLMNOPQRSTUVWXYZÄÖÜ 0123456789<>,.!"§§%&()=?+# |

### 7.4.2 Bera Sans – **fvs**, \usepackage{*berasans*}

| encod. | family | series | shape | example |
|---|---|---|---|---|
| T1 | fvs | m | n | abcdefghijklmnopqrstuvwxyzäöüß ABCDEFGHIJKLMNOPQRSTUVWXYZÄÖÜ 0123456789<>,.!"§§%&()=?+# |
| T1 | fvs | m | it | abcdefghijklmnopqrstuvwxyzäöüß ABCDEFGHIJKLMNOPQRSTUVWXYZÄÖÜ 0123456789<>,.!"§§%&()=?+# |

| | | | | |
|---|---|---|---|---|
| T1 | fvs | b | n | **abcdefghijklmnopqrstuvwxyzäöüß**<br>**ABCDEFGHIJKLMNOPQRSTUVWXYZÄÖÜ**<br>**0123456789<>,.!"§§%&()=?+#** |
| T1 | fvs | b | it | ***abcdefghijklmnopqrstuvwxyzäöüß***<br>***ABCDEFGHIJKLMNOPQRSTUVWXYZÄÖÜ***<br>***0123456789<>,.!"§§%&()=?+#*** |

## 7.4.3 Biolinum – fxb, \usepackage{*libertine*}

To typeset the entire document in Biolinum, you must also change the default font \renewcommand\familydefault{\\*sfdefault*}.

| *encod.* | *family* | *series* | *shape* | *example* |
|---|---|---|---|---|
| T1 | fxb | m | n | abcdefghijklmnopqrstuvwxyzäöüß<br>ABCDEFGHIJKLMNOPQRSTUVWXYZÄÖÜ<br>0123456789<>,.!"§§%&()=?+# |
| T1 | phv | b | n | **abcdefghijklmnopqrstuvwxyzäöüß**<br>**ABCDEFGHIJKLMNOPQRSTUVWXYZÄÖÜ**<br>**0123456789<>,.!"§§%&()=?+#** |
| T1 | phv | m | sc | ABCDEFGHIJKLMNOPQRSTUVWXYZÄÖÜSS<br>ABCDEFGHIJKLMNOPQRSTUVWXYZÄÖÜ<br>0123456789<>,.!"§§%&()=?+# |
| T1 | phv | b | sc | **ABCDEFGHIJKLMNOPQRSTUVWXYZÄÖÜSS**<br>**ABCDEFGHIJKLMNOPQRSTUVWXYZÄÖÜ**<br>**0123456789<>,.!"§§%&()=?+#** |

## 7.4.4 Computer Modern Bright – cmbr, \usepackage{*cmbright*}

| *encod.* | *family* | *series* | *shape* | *example* |
|---|---|---|---|---|
| T1 | cmbr | m | n | abcdefghijklmnopqrstuvwxyzäöüß<br>ABCDEFGHIJKLMNOPQRSTUVWXYZÄÖÜ<br>0123456789<>,.!"§§%&()=?+# |
| T1 | cmbr | m | sl | *abcdefghijklmnopqrstuvwxyzäöüß*<br>*ABCDEFGHIJKLMNOPQRSTUVWXYZÄÖÜ*<br>*0123456789<>,.!"§§%&()=?+#* |
| T1 | cmbr | sb | n | abcdefghijklmnopqrstuvwxyzäöüß<br>ABCDEFGHIJKLMNOPQRSTUVWXYZÄÖÜ<br>0123456789<>,.!"§§%&()=?+# |
| T1 | cmbr | sb | sl | *abcdefghijklmnopqrstuvwxyzäöüß*<br>*ABCDEFGHIJKLMNOPQRSTUVWXYZÄÖÜ*<br>*0123456789<>,.!"§§%&()=?+#* |
| T1 | cmbr | bx | n | abcdefghijklmnopqrstuvwxyzäöüß<br>ABCDEFGHIJKLMNOPQRSTUVWXYZÄÖÜ<br>0123456789<>,.!"§§%&()=?+# |

### 7.4.5 Computer Modern Sans Serif – cmss

cmss is the default font of every TeX system for sans-serif fonts. It also exists as a T1 font as
cm-super.

| encod. | family | series | shape | example |
|--------|--------|--------|-------|---------|
| OT1 | cmss | m | n | abcdefghijklmnopqrstuvwxyzäöüß<br>ABCDEFGHIJKLMNOPQRSTUVWXYZÄÖÜ<br>0123456789¡¿,.!"§$%&()=?+# |
| OT1 | cmss | m | sl | abcdefghijklmnopqrstuvwxyzäöüß<br>ABCDEFGHIJKLMNOPQRSTUVWXYZÄÖÜ<br>0123456789¡¿,.!"§$%&()=?+# |
| OT1 | cmss | bx | n | abcdefghijklmnopqrstuvwxyzäöüß<br>ABCDEFGHIJKLMNOPQRSTUVWXYZÄÖÜ<br>0123456789¡¿,.!"§$%&()=?+# |
| OT1 | cmss | sbc | n | abcdefghijklmnopqrstuvwxyzäöüß<br>ABCDEFGHIJKLMNOPQRSTUVWXYZÄÖÜ<br>0123456789¡¿,.!"§$%&()=?+# |

### 7.4.6 Helvetica – phv, \usepackage[scaled]{helvet}

To typeset the entire document in Helvetica, you must also change the default font:
\renewcommand\familydefault{\sfdefault}.

| encod. | family | series | shape | example |
|--------|--------|--------|-------|---------|
| T1 | phv | m | n | abcdefghijklmnopqrstuvwxyzäöüß<br>ABCDEFGHIJKLMNOPQRSTUVWXYZÄÖÜ<br>0123456789<>,.!"§$%&()=?+# |
| T1 | phv | m | sl | abcdefghijklmnopqrstuvwxyzäöüß<br>ABCDEFGHIJKLMNOPQRSTUVWXYZÄÖÜ<br>0123456789<>,.!"§$%&()=?+# |
| T1 | phv | m | sc | ABCDEFGHIJKLMNOPQRSTUVWXYZÄÖÜSS<br>ABCDEFGHIJKLMNOPQRSTUVWXYZÄÖÜ<br>0123456789<>,.!"§$%&()=?+# |
| T1 | phv | b | n | abcdefghijklmnopqrstuvwxyzäöüß<br>ABCDEFGHIJKLMNOPQRSTUVWXYZÄÖÜ<br>0123456789<>,.!"§$%&()=?+# |
| T1 | phv | b | sl | abcdefghijklmnopqrstuvwxyzäöüß<br>ABCDEFGHIJKLMNOPQRSTUVWXYZÄÖÜ<br>0123456789<>,.!"§$%&()=?+# |
| T1 | phv | b | sc | ABCDEFGHIJKLMNOPQRSTUVWXYZÄÖÜSS<br>ABCDEFGHIJKLMNOPQRSTUVWXYZÄÖÜ<br>0123456789<>,.!"§$%&()=?+# |
| T1 | phv | bc | n | abcdefghijklmnopqrstuvwxyzäöüß<br>ABCDEFGHIJKLMNOPQRSTUVWXYZÄÖÜ<br>0123456789<>,.!"§$%&()=?+# |

T1   phv   bc   sl   *abcdefghijklmnopqrstuvwxyzäöüß*
*ABCDEFGHIJKLMNOPQRSTUVWXYZÄÖÜ*
*0123456789<>,.!"§$%&()=?+#*

T1   phv   bc   sc   ABCDEFGHIJKLMNOPQRSTUVWXYZÄÖÜSS
**ABCDEFGHIJKLMNOPQRSTUVWXYZÄÖÜ**
**0123456789<>,.!"§$%&()=?+#**

## 7.4.7   kpFonts – jkpss, \usepackage{*kpfonts*}

| encod. | family | series | shape | example |
|--------|--------|--------|-------|---------|
| T1 | jkpss | m | n | abcdefghijklmnopqrstuvwxyzäöüß<br>ABCDEFGHIJKLMNOPQRSTUVWXYZÄÖÜ<br>0123456789<>,.!"§$%&()=?+# |
| T1 | jkpss | m | sc | ABCDEFGHIJKLMNOPQRSTUVWXYZÄÖÜSS<br>ABCDEFGHIJKLMNOPQRSTUVWXYZÄÖÜ<br>0123456789<>,.!"§$%&()=?+# |
| T1 | jkpss | m | scsl | *ABCDEFGHIJKLMNOPQRSTUVWXYZÄÖÜSS*<br>*ABCDEFGHIJKLMNOPQRSTUVWXYZÄÖÜ*<br>*0123456789<>,.!"§$%&()=?+#* |
| T1 | jkpss | m | sl | *abcdefghijklmnopqrstuvwxyzäöüß*<br>*ABCDEFGHIJKLMNOPQRSTUVWXYZÄÖÜ*<br>*0123456789<>,.!"§$%&()=?+#* |
| T1 | jkpss | b | n | **abcdefghijklmnopqrstuvwxyzäöüß**<br>**ABCDEFGHIJKLMNOPQRSTUVWXYZÄÖÜ**<br>**0123456789<>,.!"§$%&()=?+#** |
| T1 | jkpss | b | sl | ***abcdefghijklmnopqrstuvwxyzäöüß***<br>***ABCDEFGHIJKLMNOPQRSTUVWXYZÄÖÜ***<br>***0123456789<>,.!"§$%&()=?+#*** |
| T1 | jkpss | b | sc | **ABCDEFGHIJKLMNOPQRSTUVWXYZÄÖÜSS**<br>**ABCDEFGHIJKLMNOPQRSTUVWXYZÄÖÜ**<br>**0123456789<>,.!"§$%&()=?+#** |
| T1 | jkpss | b | scsl | ***ABCDEFGHIJKLMNOPQRSTUVWXYZÄÖÜSS***<br>***ABCDEFGHIJKLMNOPQRSTUVWXYZÄÖÜ***<br>***0123456789<>,.!"§$%&()=?+#*** |
| T1 | jkpss | bx | n | **abcdefghijklmnopqrstuvwxyzäöüß**<br>**ABCDEFGHIJKLMNOPQRSTUVWXYZÄÖÜ**<br>**0123456789<>,.!"§$%&()=?+#** |
| T1 | jkpss | bx | sl | ***abcdefghijklmnopqrstuvwxyzäöüß***<br>***ABCDEFGHIJKLMNOPQRSTUVWXYZÄÖÜ***<br>***0123456789<>,.!"§$%&()=?+#*** |
| T1 | jkpss | bx | sc | **ABCDEFGHIJKLMNOPQRSTUVWXYZÄÖÜSS**<br>**ABCDEFGHIJKLMNOPQRSTUVWXYZÄÖÜ**<br>**0123456789<>,.!"§$%&()=?+#** |

```
T1 jkpss bx scsl ABCDEFGHIJKLMNOPQRSTUVWXYZÄÖÜSS
                  ABCDEFGHIJKLMNOPQRSTUVWXYZÄÖÜ
                  0123456789<>,.!"§$%&()=?+#
```

## 7.4.8 URW Grotesk Bold Condensed – ugq

| encod. | family | series | shape | example |
|--------|--------|--------|-------|---------|
| T1 | ugq | b | n | **abcdefghijklmnopqrstuvwxyzäöüß**<br>**ABCDEFGHIJKLMNOPQRSTUVWXYZÄÖÜ**<br>**0123456789<>,.!"§$%&()=?+#** |
| T1 | ugq | b | sl | *abcdefghijklmnopqrstuvwxyzäöüß*<br>*ABCDEFGHIJKLMNOPQRSTUVWXYZÄÖÜ*<br>*0123456789<>,.!"§$%&()=?+#* |

# 7.5 Typewriter fonts

There are only a few free typewriter fonts that also have a bold version. The often-used
`Courier` does not have a particularly nice design. It is advisable to used a scalable font like
`Latin Modern`, `Beramono` or `Luximono`.

## 7.5.1 Bera Mono – fvm, \usepackage{*beramono*}

| encod. | family | series | shape | example |
|--------|--------|--------|-------|---------|
| T1 | fvm | m | n | abcdefghijklmnopqrstuvwxyzäöüß<br>ABCDEFGHIJKLMNOPQRSTUVWXYZÄÖÜ<br>0123456789<>,.!"§$%&()=?+# |
| T1 | fvm | m | sl | *abcdefghijklmnopqrstuvwxyzäöüß*<br>*ABCDEFGHIJKLMNOPQRSTUVWXYZÄÖÜ*<br>*0123456789<>,.!"§$%&()=?+#* |
| T1 | fvm | b | n | **abcdefghijklmnopqrstuvwxyzäöüß**<br>**ABCDEFGHIJKLMNOPQRSTUVWXYZÄÖÜ**<br>**0123456789<>,.!"§$%&()=?+#** |
| T1 | fvm | b | sl | ***abcdefghijklmnopqrstuvwxyzäöüß***<br>***ABCDEFGHIJKLMNOPQRSTUVWXYZÄÖÜ***<br>***0123456789<>,.!"§$%&()=?+#*** |

## 7.5.2 Computer Modern Typewriter – cmtt

| encod. | family | series | shape | example |
|--------|--------|--------|-------|---------|
| OT1 | cmtt | m | n | abcdefghijklmnopqrstuvwxyzäöüß<br>ABCDEFGHIJKLMNOPQRSTUVWXYZÄÖÜ<br>0123456789<>,.!"§$%&()=?+# |

```
OT1   cmtt   m   it   abcdefghijklmnopqrstuvwxyzäöüß
                       ABCDEFGHIJKLMNOPQRSTUVWXYZÄÖÜ
                       0123456789<>,.!"§$%&()=?+#
OT1   cmtt   m   sl   abcdefghijklmnopqrstuvwxyzäöüß
                       ABCDEFGHIJKLMNOPQRSTUVWXYZÄÖÜ
                       0123456789<>,.!"§$%&()=?+#
OT1   cmtt   m   sc   ABCDEFGHIJKLMNOPQRSTUVWXYZÄÖÜSS
                       ABCDEFGHIJKLMNOPQRSTUVWXYZÄÖÜ
                       0123456789<>,.!"§$%&()=?+#
```

### 7.5.3 Computer Modern Typewriter light – cmtl

| encod. | family | series | shape | example |
|--------|--------|--------|-------|---------|
| OT1 | cmtl | m | n | abcdefghijklmnopqrstuvwxyzäöüß<br>ABCDEFGHIJKLMNOPQRSTUVWXYZÄÖÜ<br>0123456789<>,.!"§$%&()=?+# |
| OT1 | cmtl | m | sl | abcdefghijklmnopqrstuvwxyzäöüß<br>ABCDEFGHIJKLMNOPQRSTUVWXYZÄÖÜ<br>0123456789<>,.!"§$%&()=?+# |

### 7.5.4 Computer Modern Typewriter (variable) – cmvtt

| encod. | family | series | shape | example |
|--------|--------|--------|-------|---------|
| OT1 | cmvtt | m | n | abcdefghijklmnopqrstuvwxyzäöüß<br>ABCDEFGHIJKLMNOPQRSTUVWXYZÄÖÜ<br>0123456789¡¿,.!"§$%&()=?+# |
| OT1 | cmvtt | m | it | abcdefghijklmnopqrstuvwxyzäöüß<br>ABCDEFGHIJKLMNOPQRSTUVWXYZÄÖÜ<br>0123456789¡¿,.!"§$%&()=?+# |

### 7.5.5 Courier – pcr, \usepackage{courier}

| encod. | family | series | shape | example |
|--------|--------|--------|-------|---------|
| T1 | pcr | m | n | abcdefghijklmnopqrstuvwxyzäöüß<br>ABCDEFGHIJKLMNOPQRSTUVWXYZÄÖÜ<br>0123456789<>,.!"§$%&()=?+# |
| T1 | pcr | m | sl | abcdefghijklmnopqrstuvwxyzäöüß<br>ABCDEFGHIJKLMNOPQRSTUVWXYZÄÖÜ<br>0123456789<>,.!"§$$%&()=?+# |
| T1 | pcr | m | sc | ABCDEFGHIJKLMNOPQRSTUVWXYZÄÖÜSS<br>ABCDEFGHIJKLMNOPQRSTUVWXYZÄÖÜ<br>0123456789<>,.!"§$%&()=?+# |

| | | | |
|---|---|---|---|
| T1 | pcr | b | n | abcdefghijklmnopqrstuvwxyzäöüß<br>ABCDEFGHIJKLMNOPQRSTUVWXYZÄÖÜ<br>0123456789<>,.!"§$%&()=?+# |
| T1 | pcr | b | sl | *abcdefghijklmnopqrstuvwxyzäöüß*<br>*ABCDEFGHIJKLMNOPQRSTUVWXYZÄÖÜ*<br>*0123456789<>,.!"§$%&()=?+#* |
| T1 | pcr | b | sc | ABCDEFGHIJKLMNOPQRSTUVWXYZÄÖÜS S<br>ABCDEFGHIJKLMNOPQRSTUVWXYZÄÖÜ<br>0123456789<>,.!"§$%&()=?+# |

## 7.5.6 Inconsolata – fi4, \usepackage{*inconsolata*}

| encod. | family | series | shape | example |
|---|---|---|---|---|
| T1 | fi4 | m | n | ˋ´ˆ˜¨˝°˘¸˙ ‚‹›""„«» 1J<br>␣!"#$%&'()*+,-./0123456789:;<=>?<br>@ABCDEFGHIJKLMNOPQRSTUVWXYZ[\]^_<br>`abcdefghijklmnopqrstuvwxyz{|}~ |

## 7.5.7 kpFonts – jkptt, \usepackage{*kpfonts*}

| encod. | family | series | shape | example |
|---|---|---|---|---|
| T1 | jkptt | m | n | ˋ´ˆ˜¨˝°˘˙ ‚‹›""„«»---ol Jfffiflfffiffl<br>␣!"#$%&'()*+,-./0123456789:;<=>?<br>@ABCDEFGHIJKLMNOPQRSTUVWXYZ[\]^_<br>`abcdefghijklmnopqrstuvwxyz{|}~- |
| T1 | jkptt | m | sl | *ˋ´ˆ˜¨˝°˘˙ ‚‹›""„«»---ol Jfffiflfffiffl*<br>*␣!"#$%&'()*+,-./0123456789:;<=>?*<br>*@ABCDEFGHIJKLMNOPQRSTUVWXYZ[\]^_*<br>*`abcdefghijklmnopqrstuvwxyz{|}~-* |
| T1 | jkptt | b | n | ˋ´ˆ˜¨˝°˘˙ ‚‹›""„«»---ol Jfffiflfffiffl<br>␣!"#$%&'()*+,-./0123456789:;<=>?<br>@ABCDEFGHIJKLMNOPQRSTUVWXYZ[\]^_<br>`abcdefghijklmnopqrstuvwxyz{|}~- |
| T1 | jkptt | b | sl | *ˋ´ˆ˜¨˝°˘˙ ‚‹›""„«»---ol Jfffiflfffiffl*<br>*␣!"#$%&'()*+,-./0123456789:;<=>?*<br>*@ABCDEFGHIJKLMNOPQRSTUVWXYZ[\]^_*<br>*`abcdefghijklmnopqrstuvwxyz{|}~-* |

## 7.5.8 Latin Modern Typewriter – `lmtt`, `\usepackage`{*lmodern*}

| encod. | family | series | shape | example |
|--------|--------|--------|-------|---------|
| T1 | lmtt | m | n | `˙ ` ´ ^ ˜ ¨ ˝ ° ˇ ˘ ¯ ˙ ¸ ˛ ‹ › " " „ « » – – ₒ 1 J`<br>`␣ ! " # $ % & ' ( ) * + , - . / 0123456789 : ; < = > ?`<br>`@ABCDEFGHIJKLMNOPQRSTUVWXYZ [ \ ] ^ _`<br>`‘abcdefghijklmnopqrstuvwxyz { | } ˜ ¨` |
| T1 | lmtt | m | it | `˙ ` ´ ^ ˜ ¨ ˝ ° ˇ ˘ ¯ ˙ ¸ ˛ ‹ › " " „ « » – – ₒ ı J`<br>`␣ ! " # $ % & ' ( ) * + , - . / 0123456789 : ; < = > ?`<br>`@ABCDEFGHIJKLMNOPQRSTUVWXYZ [ \ ] ^ _`<br>`‘abcdefghijklmnopqrstuvwxyz { | } ˜ ¨` |
| T1 | lmtt | m | sc | `˙ ` ´ ^ ˜ ¨ ˝ ° ˇ ˘ ¯ ˙ ¸ ˛ ‹ › " " „ « » – – ₒ I J`<br>`␣ ! " # $ % & ' ( ) * + , - . / 0123456789 : ; < = > ?`<br>`@ABCDEFGHIJKLMNOPQRSTUVWXYZ [ \ ] ^ _`<br>`‘ABCDEFGHIJKLMNOPQRSTUVWXYZ { | } ˜ ¨` |
| T1 | lmtt | m | scsl | `˙ ` ´ ^ ˜ ¨ ˝ ° ˇ ˘ ¯ ˙ ¸ ˛ ‹ › " " „ « » – – ₒ I J`<br>`␣ ! " # $ % & ' ( ) * + , - . / 0123456789 : ; < = > ?`<br>`@ABCDEFGHIJKLMNOPQRSTUVWXYZ [ \ ] ^ _`<br>`‘ABCDEFGHIJKLMNOPQRSTUVWXYZ { | } ˜ ¨` |
| T1 | lmtt | l | n | `˙ ` ´ ^ ˜ ¨ ˝ ° ˇ ˘ ¯ ˙ ¸ ˛ ‹ › " " „ « » – – ₒ 1 J`<br>`␣ ! " # $ % & ' ( ) * + , - . / 0123456789 : ; < = > ?`<br>`@ABCDEFGHIJKLMNOPQRSTUVWXYZ [ \ ] ^ _`<br>`‘abcdefghijklmnopqrstuvwxyz { | } ˜ ¨` |
| T1 | lmtt | l | it | `˙ ` ´ ^ ˜ ¨ ˝ ° ˇ ˘ ¯ ˙ ¸ ˛ ‹ › " " „ « » – – ₒ 1 J`<br>`␣ ! " # $ % & ' ( ) * + , - . / 0123456789 : ; < = > ?`<br>`@ABCDEFGHIJKLMNOPQRSTUVWXYZ [ \ ] ^ _`<br>`‘abcdefghijklmnopqrstuvwxyz { | } ˜ ¨` |
| T1 | lmtt | lc | n | `˙ ` ´ ^ ˜ ¨ ˝ ° ˇ ˘ ¯ ˙ ¸ ˛ ‹ › " " „ « » – – ₒ 1 J`<br>`␣ ! " # $ % & ' ( ) * + , - . / 0123456789 : ; < = > ?`<br>`@ABCDEFGHIJKLMNOPQRSTUVWXYZ [ \ ] ^ _`<br>`‘abcdefghijklmnopqrstuvwxyz { | } ˜ ¨` |
| T1 | lmtt | lc | it | `˙ ` ´ ^ ˜ ¨ ˝ ° ˇ ˘ ¯ ˙ ¸ ˛ ‹ › " " „ « » – – ₒ 1 J`<br>`␣ ! " # $ % & ' ( ) * + , - . / 0123456789 : ; < = > ?`<br>`@ABCDEFGHIJKLMNOPQRSTUVWXYZ [ \ ] ^ _`<br>`‘abcdefghijklmnopqrstuvwxyz { | } ˜ ¨` |
| T1 | lmtt | b | n | `˙ ` ´ ^ ˜ ¨ ˝ ° ˇ ˘ ¯ ˙ ¸ ˛ ‹ › " " „ « » – – ₒ 1 J`<br>`␣ ! " # $ % & ' ( ) * + , - . / 0123456789 : ; < = > ?`<br>`@ABCDEFGHIJKLMNOPQRSTUVWXYZ [ \ ] ^ _`<br>`‘abcdefghijklmnopqrstuvwxyz { | } ˜ ¨` |
| T1 | lmtt | b | it | `˙ ` ´ ^ ˜ ¨ ˝ ° ˇ ˘ ¯ ˙ ¸ ˛ ‹ › " " „ « » – – ₒ 1 J`<br>`␣ ! " # $ % & ' ( ) * + , - . / 0123456789 : ; < = > ?`<br>`@ABCDEFGHIJKLMNOPQRSTUVWXYZ [ \ ] ^ _`<br>`‘abcdefghijklmnopqrstuvwxyz { | } ˜ ¨` |

### 7.5.9 Latin Modern Typewriter (variable) – `lmvtt`

| *encod.* | *family* | *series* | *shape* | *example* |
|---|---|---|---|---|
| T1 | lmvtt | m | n | ˋ ˊ ˆ ˜ ˝ ° ˇ ˘ ¯ ˙ ¸ ˛ ‹ › "" „ « » —— oı ȷ ff fi fl ffi ffl |
| | | | | ␣ ! " # $ % & ' ( ) * + , - . / 0123456789 : ; < = > ? |
| | | | | @ABCDEFGHIJKLMNOPQRSTUVWXYZ[\]^_ |
| | | | | `abcdefghijklmnopqrstuvwxyz{|}~- |
| T1 | lmvtt | m | it | ˋ ˊ ˆ ˜ ˝ ° ˇ ˘ ¯ ˙ ¸ ˛ ‹ › "" „ « » —— oı ȷ ff fi fl ffi ffl |
| | | | | ␣ ! " # $ % & ' ( ) * + , - . / 0123456789 : ; < = > ? |
| | | | | @ABCDEFGHIJKLMNOPQRSTUVWXYZ[\]^_ |
| | | | | `abcdefghijklmnopqrstuvwxyz{|}~- |
| T1 | lmvtt | l | n | ˋ ˊ ˆ ˜ ˝ ° ˇ ˘ ¯ ˙ ¸ ˛ ‹ › "" „ « » —— oı ȷ ff fi fl ffi ffl |
| | | | | ␣ ! " # $ % & ' ( ) * + , - . / 0123456789 : ; < = > ? |
| | | | | @ABCDEFGHIJKLMNOPQRSTUVWXYZ[\]^_ |
| | | | | `abcdefghijklmnopqrstuvwxyz{|}~- |
| T1 | lmvtt | l | it | ˋ ˊ ˆ ˜ ˝ ° ˇ ˘ ¯ ˙ ¸ ˛ ‹ › "" „ « » —— oı ȷ ff fi fl ffi ffl |
| | | | | ␣ ! " # $ % & ' ( ) * + , - . / 0123456789 : ; < = > ? |
| | | | | @ABCDEFGHIJKLMNOPQRSTUVWXYZ[\]^_ |
| | | | | `abcdefghijklmnopqrstuvwxyz{|}~- |
| T1 | lmvtt | b | n | ˋ ˊ ˆ ˜ ˝ ° ˇ ˘ ¯ ˙ ¸ ˛ ‹ › "" „ « » —— oı ȷ ff fi fl ffi ffl |
| | | | | ␣ ! " # $ % & ' ( ) * + , - . / 0123456789 : ; < = > ? |
| | | | | @ABCDEFGHIJKLMNOPQRSTUVWXYZ[\]^_ |
| | | | | `abcdefghijklmnopqrstuvwxyz{|}~- |
| T1 | lmvtt | b | it | ˋ ˊ ˆ ˜ ˝ ° ˇ ˘ ¯ ˙ ¸ ˛ ‹ › "" „ « » —— oı ȷ ff fi fl ffi ffl |
| | | | | ␣ ! " # $ % & ' ( ) * + , - . / 0123456789 : ; < = > ? |
| | | | | @ABCDEFGHIJKLMNOPQRSTUVWXYZ[\]^_ |
| | | | | `abcdefghijklmnopqrstuvwxyz{|}~- |

### 7.5.10 Luxi Mono – `ul9`, \usepackage[*scaled*]{*luximono*}

As typewriter fonts usually appear larger, you can assign the optional `scaled` parameter a decimal percent value to make the font smaller; the default is `scaled=0.87`.

| *encod.* | *family* | *series* | *shape* | *example* |
|---|---|---|---|---|
| T1 | ul9 | m | n | abcdefghijklmnopqrstuvwxyzäöüß |
| | | | | ABCDEFGHIJKLMNOPQRSTUVWXYZÄÖÜ |
| | | | | 0123456789<>,.!"§§%&()=?+# |
| T1 | ul9 | m | sl | abcdefghijklmnopqrstuvwxyzäöüß |
| | | | | ABCDEFGHIJKLMNOPQRSTUVWXYZÄÖÜ |
| | | | | 0123456789<>,.!"§§%&()=?+# |
| T1 | ul9 | b | n | abcdefghijklmnopqrstuvwxyzäöüß |
| | | | | ABCDEFGHIJKLMNOPQRSTUVWXYZÄÖÜ |
| | | | | 0123456789<>,.!"§§%&()=?+# |

T1   ul9   b   sl   *abcdefghijklmnopqrstuvwxyzäöüß*
                    ***ABCDEFGHIJKLMNOPQRSTUVWXYZÄÖÜ***
                    ***0123456789<>,.!"§$%&()=?+#***

## 7.6  Special fonts

### 7.6.1  Euler Script and Gothic – eus – euf, \usepackage{*euler*}

| encod. | family | series | shape | example |
|--------|--------|--------|-------|---------|
| U | eus | m | n | {}\|\§¨¨¨¨ß <br> $\mathcal{ABCDEFGHIJKLMNOPQRSTUVWXYZÄÖÜ}$ <br> $\mathcal{R§$J}$ |
| U | euf | m | n | abcdefghijklmnopqrstuvwrŋзäöüß <br> ABCDEFGHIJKLMNOPQRSTUVWXYZЗÄÖÜ <br> 0123456789,.!§$&()=?+ |

### 7.6.2  Euro Symbol – eurosym, \usepackage{*eurosym*}

The character string e ABC and \symbol{*0*} were used for the example. Usually, the Euro symbol is accessed within the document through \euro. You can use the lines defined by ABC for custom definitions of the Euro symbol. The symbol € can be achieved through \symbol{0}.

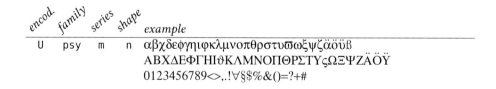

| encod. | family | series | shape | example | encod. | family | series | shape | example |
|--------|--------|--------|-------|---------|--------|--------|--------|-------|---------|
| U | eurosym | m | n | € === € | U | eurosym | m | sl | € === € |
| U | eurosym | m | ol | € === € | U | eurosym | bx | n | € === € |
| U | eurosym | bx | sl | € === € | U | eurosym | bx | ol | € === € |

### 7.6.3  Symbol Font – psy, \usepackage{*pifont*}

| encod. | family | series | shape | example |
|--------|--------|--------|-------|---------|
| U | psy | m | n | αβχδεφγηιφκλμνοπθρστυϖωξψζäöüß <br> ΑΒΧΔΕΦΓΗΙϑΚΛΜΝΟΠΘΡΣΤΥςΩΞΨΖÄÖŸ <br> 0123456789<>,.!∀§$%&()=?+# |

### 7.6.4 Zapf Chancery – `pzc`, `\usepackage`{*chancery*}

| encod. | family | series | shape | example |
|--------|--------|--------|-------|---------|
| T1 | pzc | mb | it | *abcdefghijklmnopqrstuvwxyzäöüß* |
|  |  |  |  | *ABCDEFGHIJKLMNOPQRSTUVWXYZÄÖÜ* |
|  |  |  |  | *0123456789<>,.!'§$%&()=?+#* |

### 7.6.5 Zapf Dingbats – `pzd`, `\usepackage`{*pifont*}

| encod. | family | series | shape | example |
|--------|--------|--------|-------|---------|
| U | pzd | m | n | ❁❂✳❃❉❊✱❋✽✼✾●○■□❑❒▲▼◆❖▶◀◗☐◆ß |
|  |  |  |  | ✥✛✜✚✦✢★✩☆✪✫✬✭✮✯✰✴✵✶✷✸✹✺✻✼✽✾ |
|  |  |  |  | ✏✐✍✓✔✗✘✖☙❀✠✜❦☜✁✂✄§$☎☛✈↘☞✝✞✟✡✌ |

## 7.7 Math fonts

In principle, there is only one freely-available complete font that has text as well as math characters. This is the default TEX font Computer Modern Roman, or `lmodern` as the corresponding T1 font. All other complete fonts are either not freely available or draw the math symbols partly from other fonts. [25]

### 7.7.1 Computer Modern – `cm`, `ms`

The default font for math, available on every TEX system.

| encod. | family | series | shape | example |
|--------|--------|--------|-------|---------|
| OT1 | cmr | m | n | ΓΔΘΛΞΠΣΥΦΨΩ fffiflffiffl ıȷ ` ´ ˇ ˘ ¯ ˚ ¸ ß æœø ÆŒØ |
|  |  |  |  | -!"#$%&'()*+,-./0123456789:;¡=¿? |
|  |  |  |  | @ABCDEFGHIJKLMNOPQRSTUVWXYZ["]^˙ |
|  |  |  |  | 'abcdefghijklmnopqrstuvwxyz——"˜¨ |
| OT1 | cmr | m | it | *ΓΔΘΛΞΠΣΥΦΨΩ fffiflffiffl ıȷ ` ´ ˇ ˘ ¯ ˚ ¸ ß æœø ÆŒØ* |
|  |  |  |  | *-!"#£%&'()*+,-./0123456789:;¡=¿?* |
|  |  |  |  | *@ABCDEFGHIJKLMNOPQRSTUVWXYZ["]^˙* |
|  |  |  |  | *'abcdefghijklmnopqrstuvwxyz——"˜¨* |
| OT1 | cmr | bx | n | **ΓΔΘΛΞΠΣΥΦΨΩ fffiflffiffl ıȷ ` ´ ˇ ˘ ¯ ˚ ¸ ß æœø ÆŒØ** |
|  |  |  |  | **-!"#$%&'()*+,-./0123456789:;¡=¿?** |
|  |  |  |  | **@ABCDEFGHIJKLMNOPQRSTUVWXYZ["]^˙** |
|  |  |  |  | **'abcdefghijklmnopqrstuvwxyz——"˜¨** |
| OML | cmm | m | it | *ΓΔΘΛΞΠΣΥΦΨΩ αβγδεζηθικλμνξπρστυφχ* |
|  |  |  |  | *ψωεϑϖϱςφ ⌣ ← — → ⇁ ◃▹ ⊲ 0123456789.,</>⋆* |
|  |  |  |  | *∂ABCDEFGHIJKLMNOPQRSTUVWXYZ♭♮ ⌣ ⌢* |
|  |  |  |  | *ℓabcdefghijklmnopqrstuvwxyzıȷ℘ ⃗ ⌢* |

| OMS | cmsy | m | n |  |
| OT1 | cmss | m | n | |
| OT1 | cmtt | m | n | |
| OMX | cmex | m | n | |
| U | msa | m | n | |
| U | msb | m | n | |

## 7.7.2  Computer Modern Bright– cmbr, \usepackage{*cmbright*}

| *encod.* | *family* | *series* | *shape* | *example* |
|---|---|---|---|---|
| OML | cmbrm | m | it | $\Gamma\Delta\Theta\Lambda\Xi\Pi\Sigma\Upsilon\Phi\Psi\Omega\alpha\beta\gamma\delta\epsilon\zeta\eta\theta\iota\kappa\lambda\mu\nu\xi\pi\rho\sigma\tau\upsilon\phi\chi$ $\psi\omega\varepsilon\varpi\varrho\varsigma\varphi\leftharpoonup\leftharpoondown\rightharpoonup\rightharpoondown$ ͡ ▷◁0123456789.,</>⋆ $\partial ABCDEFGHIJKLMNOPQRSTUVWXYZ\flat\natural\sharp$ ⌣ ⌢ $\ell abcdefghijklmnopqrstuvwxyz\imath\jmath\wp$ ⃗ ⃑ |
| OML | cmbrm | b | it | $\Gamma\Delta\Theta\Lambda\Xi\Pi\Sigma\Upsilon\Phi\Psi\Omega\alpha\beta\gamma\delta\epsilon\zeta\eta\theta\iota\kappa\lambda\mu\nu\xi\pi\rho\sigma\tau\upsilon\phi\chi$ $\psi\omega\varepsilon\varpi\varrho\varsigma\varphi\leftharpoonup\leftharpoondown\rightharpoonup\rightharpoondown$ ͡ ▷◁0123456789.,</>⋆ $\partial ABCDEFGHIJKLMNOPQRSTUVWXYZ\flat\natural\sharp$ ⌣ ⌢ |

$\ell abcdefghijklmnopqrstuvwxyzıȷ\wp$

| OMS | cmbrs | m | n |  |

### 7.7.3 Concrete Math – cc, \usepackage{concmath}

| encod. | family | series | shape | example |
|--------|--------|--------|-------|---------|
| OML | ccm | m | it | $\Gamma\Delta\Theta\Lambda\Xi\Pi\Sigma\Upsilon\Phi\Psi\Omega\alpha\beta\gamma\delta\epsilon\zeta\eta\theta\iota\kappa\lambda\mu\nu\xi\pi\rho\sigma\tau\upsilon\phi\chi$ $\psi\omega\varepsilon\vartheta\varpi\varrho\varsigma\varphi \leftharpoonup\leftharpoondown\rightharpoonup\rightharpoondown \triangleright\triangleleft 0123456789.,</>\star$ $\partial ABCDEFGHIJKLMNOPQRSTUVWXYZ\flat\natural\sharp\smile\frown$ $\ell abcdef ghijklmnopqrstuvwxyzıȷ\wp$ |
| OMS | ccsy | m | n | 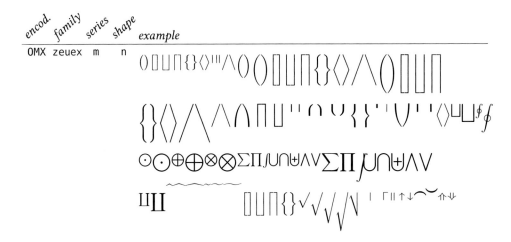 |

### 7.7.4 Euler Math – eu, \usepackage{eulervm}

| encod. | family | series | shape | example |
|--------|--------|--------|-------|---------|
| OMX | zeuex | m | n |  |

### 7.7.5 Fourier-Gutenberg fonts – fut, \usepackage{fourier}

| encod. | family | series | shape | example |
|--------|--------|--------|-------|---------|
| OML | futm | m | it | $\Gamma\Delta\Theta\Lambda\Xi\Pi\Sigma\Upsilon\Phi\Psi\Omega\alpha\beta\gamma\delta\epsilon\zeta\eta\theta\iota\kappa\lambda\mu\nu\xi\pi\rho\sigma\tau\upsilon\phi\chi$ $\psi\omega\varepsilon\vartheta\varpi\varrho\varsigma\varphi\leftharpoonup\rightharpoonup\triangleright\triangleleft 0123456789.,</>\star$ $\partial ABCDEFGHIJKLMNOPQRSTUVWXYZ\flat\natural\sharp\smile\frown$ |

| OML | futmi | m | it | $\ell abcdefghijklmnopqrstuvwxyz\imath\jmath\wp\vec{}\frown$ <br> $\Gamma\Delta\Theta\Lambda\Xi\Pi\Sigma\Upsilon\Phi\Psi\Omega\alpha\beta\gamma\delta\epsilon\zeta\eta\theta\iota\kappa\lambda\mu\nu\xi\pi\rho\sigma\tau\upsilon\phi\chi$ <br> $\psi\omega\vartheta\varpi\varrho\varsigma\varphi\leftharpoonup\leftharpoondown\rightharpoonup\rightharpoondown\triangleright\triangleleft 0123456789.,</>\star$ <br> $\partial ABCDEFGHIJKLMNOPQRSTUVWXYZ\flat\natural\sharp\smile\frown$ |
|-----|-------|---|----|----|
| OMS | futm | m | n | $\ell abcdefghijklmnopqrstuvwxyz\imath\jmath\wp\vec{}\frown$ <br> $-\cdot\times*\div\diamond\pm\mp\oplus\ominus\otimes\oslash\odot\bigcirc\circ\bullet\asymp\equiv\subseteq\supseteq\leq\geq\preceq\succeq\sim\approx\subset\supset\ll\gg\prec\succ$ <br> $\leftarrow\rightarrow\uparrow\downarrow\leftrightarrow\nearrow\searrow\simeq\Leftarrow\Rightarrow\Uparrow\Downarrow\Leftrightarrow\nwarrow\swarrow\propto\infty\in\ni\triangle\bigtriangledown\not\exists\neg\emptyset\Re\Im\top\bot$ <br> $\aleph ABCDEFGHIJKLMNOPQRSTUVWXYZ\cup\cap\uplus\wedge\vee$ <br> $\vdash\dashv\lfloor\rfloor\lceil\rceil\{\}\langle\rangle\|\updownarrow\Updownarrow\backslash\wr\surd\coprod\nabla\int\sqcup\sqcap\sqsubseteq\sqsupseteq\S\dagger\ddagger\P\clubsuit\diamondsuit\heartsuit\spadesuit$ |

## 7.7.6  kp-Fonts – jkp, \usepackage{*kpfonts*}

| encod. | family | series | shape | example |
|--------|--------|--------|-------|---------|
| OT1 | jkp | m | n | $\Gamma\Delta\Theta\Lambda\Xi\Pi\Sigma\Upsilon\Phi\Psi\Omega$ffffiflffiffl\i\j ```` ´´ ˜˜ ¯ ° ¸ ßæœøÆŒØ <br> ¡!"#\$%&'()*+,-./0123456789:;¡=¿? <br> @ABCDEFGHIJKLMNOPQRSTUVWXYZ["]^` <br> 'abcdefghijklmnopqrstuvwxyz——˝˜¨ |
| OML | jkp | m | it | $\Gamma\Delta\Theta\Lambda\Xi\Pi\Sigma\Upsilon\Phi\Psi\Omega\alpha\beta\gamma\delta\epsilon\zeta\eta\theta\iota\kappa\lambda\mu\nu\xi\pi\rho\sigma\tau\upsilon\phi\chi$ <br> $\psi\omega\vartheta\varpi\varrho\varsigma\varphi\leftharpoonup\leftharpoondown\rightharpoonup\rightharpoondown\triangleright\triangleleft 0123456789.,</>\star$ <br> $\partial ABCDEFGHIJKLMNOPQRSTUVWXYZ\flat\natural\sharp\smile\frown$ <br> $\ell abcdefghijklmnopqrstuvwxyz\imath\jmath\wp\vec{}\frown$ |
| OMS | jkp | m | n | $-\cdot\times*\div\diamond\mp\oplus\ominus\otimes\oslash\odot\bigcirc\circ\bullet\asymp\equiv\subseteq\supseteq\leq\geq\preceq\succeq\sim\approx\subset\supset\ll\gg\prec\succ$ <br> $\leftarrow\rightarrow\uparrow\downarrow\leftrightarrow\nearrow\searrow\simeq\Leftarrow\Rightarrow\Uparrow\Downarrow\Leftrightarrow\nwarrow\swarrow\propto\infty\in\ni\triangle\bigtriangledown\not\exists\neg\emptyset\Re\Im\top\bot$ <br> $\aleph ABCDEFGHIJKLMNOPQRSTUVWXYZ\cup\cap\uplus\wedge\vee$ <br> $\vdash\dashv\lfloor\rfloor\lceil\rceil\{\}\langle\rangle\|\updownarrow\Updownarrow\backslash\wr\surd\coprod\nabla\int\sqcup\sqcap\sqsubseteq\sqsupseteq\S\dagger\ddagger\P\clubsuit\diamondsuit\heartsuit\spadesuit$ |
| OMX | jkp | m | n | |
| U | jkpexa | m | n | |

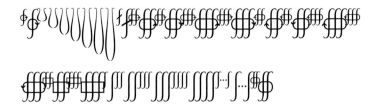

### 7.7.7 Latin Modern – `lm`, `\usepackage{`*lmodern*`}`

| encod. | family | series | shape | example |
|---|---|---|---|---|
| OML | lmm | m | it | $\Gamma\Delta\Theta\Lambda\Xi\Pi\Sigma\Upsilon\Phi\Psi\Omega\alpha\beta\gamma\delta\epsilon\zeta\eta\theta\iota\kappa\lambda\mu\nu\xi\pi\rho\sigma\tau\upsilon\phi\chi$ $\psi\omega\vartheta\varrho\varsigma\varphi{\leftharpoonup}{\leftharpoondown}{\rightharpoonup}{\rightharpoondown}\triangleright\triangleleft 0123456789.,</>\star$ $\partial ABCDEFGHIJKLMNOPQRSTUVWXYZ\flat\natural\sharp\smile\frown$ $\ell abcdefghijklmnopqrstuvwxyz\imath\jmath\wp\vec{}$ |
| OT1 | lmr | m | n | $\Gamma\Delta\Theta\Lambda\Xi\Pi\Sigma\Upsilon\Phi\Psi\Omega$ff fi fl ffi ffl ı ȷ ` ´ ˇ ˘ ˉ ˚ ¸ ß æ œ ø Æ Œ Ø -!"#\$%&'()*+,-./0123456789:;¡=¿? @ABCDEFGHIJKLMNOPQRSTUVWXYZ["]^˙ 'abcdefghijklmnopqrstuvwxyz——"˜¨ |
| OMS | lmsy | m | n | $-\cdot\times*\div\diamond\pm\mp\oplus\ominus\otimes\oslash\odot\bigcirc\circ\bullet\asymp\equiv\subseteq\supseteq\leq\geq\preceq\succeq\sim\approx\subset\supset\ll\gg\prec\succ$ $\leftarrow\rightarrow\uparrow\downarrow\leftrightarrow\nearrow\searrow\simeq\Leftarrow\Rightarrow\Uparrow\Downarrow\Leftrightarrow\nwarrow\swarrow\propto\prime\infty\in\ni\triangle\bigtriangledown\not\mapsto\forall\exists\neg\emptyset\Re\Im\top\bot$ $\aleph\mathcal{ABCDEFGHIJKLMNOPQRSTUVWXYZ}\cup\cap\uplus\wedge\vee$ $\vdash\dashv\lfloor\rfloor\lceil\rceil\{\}\langle\rangle\|\updownarrow\Updownarrow\backslash\wr\surd\amalg\nabla\int\sqcup\sqcap\sqsubseteq\sqsupseteq\S\dagger\ddagger\P\clubsuit\diamondsuit\heartsuit\spadesuit$ |
| OT1 | lmr | bx | n | **$\Gamma\Delta\Theta\Lambda\Xi\Pi\Sigma\Upsilon\Phi\Psi\Omega$ff fi fl ffi ffl ı ȷ ` ´ ˇ ˘ ˉ ˚ ¸ ß æ œ ø Æ Œ Ø -!"#\$%&'()*+,-./0123456789:;¡=¿? @ABCDEFGHIJKLMNOPQRSTUVWXYZ["]^˙ 'abcdefghijklmnopqrstuvwxyz——"˜¨** |
| OT1 | lmss | m | n | $\Gamma\Delta\Theta\Lambda\Xi\Pi\Sigma\Upsilon\Phi\Psi\Omega$ff fi fl ffi ffl ı ȷ ` ´ ˇ ˘ ˉ ˚ ¸ ß æ œ ø Æ Œ Ø -!"#\$%&'()*+,-./0123456789:;¡=¿? @ABCDEFGHIJKLMNOPQRSTUVWXYZ["]^˙ 'abcdefghijklmnopqrstuvwxyz——"˜¨ |
| OT1 | lmr | m | it | *$\Gamma\Delta\Theta\Lambda\Xi\Pi\Sigma\Upsilon\Phi\Psi\Omega$ff fi fl ffi ffl ı ȷ ` ´ ˇ ˘ ˉ ˚ ¸ ß æ œ ø Æ Œ Ø -!"#\$%&'()*+,-./0123456789:;¡=¿? @ABCDEFGHIJKLMNOPQRSTUVWXYZ["]^˙ 'abcdefghijklmnopqrstuvwxyz——"˜¨* |
| OT1 | lmtt | m | n | `ΓΔΘΛΞΠΣΤΦΨΩ↑↓'¡¿ıȷ` ` ´ ˇ ˘ ˉ ˚ ¸ ß æ œ ø Æ Œ Ø ␣!"#\$%&'()*+,-./0123456789:;<=>? @ABCDEFGHIJKLMNOPQRSTUVWXYZ[\]^_ 'abcdefghijklmnopqrstuvwxyz{|}~¨` |
| OMX | lmex | m | n | $($ $)$ $\lfloor$ $\rfloor$ $\lceil$ $\rceil$ $\{$ $\}$ $\langle$ $\rangle$ $\|$ $\|$ $/$ $\backslash$ $($ $)$ $($ $)$ $\lfloor$ $\rfloor$ $\lceil$ $\rceil$ $\{$ $\}$ $\langle$ $\rangle$ $/$ $\backslash$ $($ $)$ $\lfloor$ $\rfloor$ $\lceil$ $\rceil$ |

## 7.7.8 Mathdesign – md, \usepackage[*bitstream-charter*]{*mathdesign*}

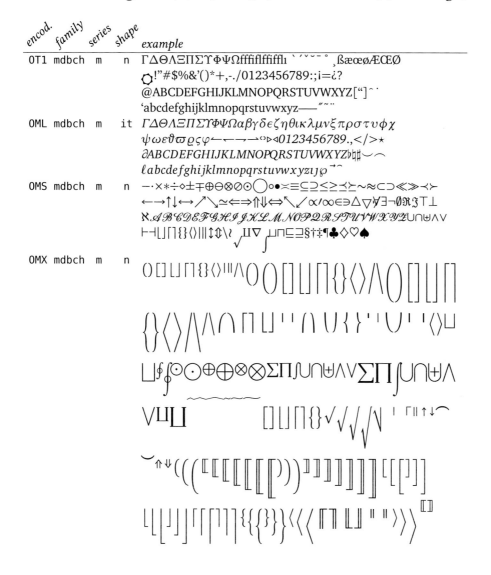

⁄⁄|\\\\√√√‛'

OT1 mdbch b   n   ΓΔΘΛΞΠΣΥΦΨΩfffiflffiffl ı `´ˇ˘¯˚ ¸ßæœøÆŒØ
◯!"#$%&'()*+,-./0123456789:;¡=¿?
@ABCDEFGHIJKLMNOPQRSTUVWXYZ["]ˆ`
'abcdefghijklmnopqrstuvwxyz—''˝~¨

OML mdbch b   it  ΓΔΘΛΞΠΣΥΦΨΩαβγδεζηθικλμνξπρστυφχ
ψωεϑϖςϕ↼↽⇀⇁'▸◂0123456789.,</>⋆
∂ABCDEFGHIJKLMNOPQRSTUVWXYZ♭♮⌣⌢
ℓabcdefghijklmnopqrstuvwxyzıȷ℘⃗⃔

OMS mdbch b   n   −·×∗÷⋄±∓⊕⊖⊗⊘⊙◯∘•≍≡⊆⊇≤≥⪯⪰∼≈⊂⊃≪≫◁▷
←→↑↓↔↗↘≃⇐⇒⇑⇓⇔↖↙α∝∞∈∋△▽⋢⌐∅♣ℑℜ⊤⊥
ℵ.𝒜ℬ𝒞𝒟ℰℱ𝒢ℋℐ𝒥𝒦ℒℳ𝒩𝒪𝒫𝒬ℛ𝒮𝒯𝒰𝒱𝒲𝒳𝒴𝒵∪∩⊎⋀⋁
⊢⊣⌊⌋⌈⌉{}⟨⟩∥|↕\⋁√⊔∇∫⌢⌣⊏⊐§†‡¶♣◇♡♠

OMX mdbch b   n

‛'⇑⇓((⎛⟦⟦⟦⟦⟦⎡⎢⎢⎢⎢⎢⟧⟧⟧⟧⟧⟧⟧⎤⎢⎢⎢⎢⟧⟧
⌊⌊⌋⌋⌉⌈⌈⌉⌉{{⦃}}⟪⟪⟨⎴⎴⎵⎵"""⟩⟩⟩⟦⟧

⁄⁄|\\\\√√√‛'

`\usepackage[urw-garamond]{mathdesign}`

| encod. | family | series | shape | example |
|--------|--------|--------|-------|---------|
| OT1 | mdugm | m | n | ΓΔΘΛΞΠΣΥΦΨΩ fffifl ffl ffi ffl ı ` ´ ˇ ˘ ¯ ˚ ¸ ßæœø ÆŒØ ⬡!"#$%&'()*+,-./0123456789:;¡=¿? @ABCDEFGHIJKLMNOPQRSTUVWXYZ["]ˆ˙ 'abcdefghijklmnopqrstuvwxyz-–—"˜¨ |
| OML | mdugm | m | it | ΓΔΘΛΞΠΣΥΦΨΩ αβγδεζηθιϰλμνξπρστυφχ ψωεϑϖϱςϕ←⇐→⇀▷◁0123456789.,</>⋆ ∂ABCDEFGHIJKLMNOPQRSTUVWXYZ♭♮♯⌣⌢ ℓabcdefghijklmnopqrstuvwxyzı℘⃗⌢ |
| OMS | mdugm | m | n | −·×∗÷⋄±∓⊕⊖⊗⊘⊙◯∘•≍≡⊆⊇≤≥≺≻∼≈⊂⊃≪≫≺≻ ←→↑↓↖↗∖∧≃⇐⇒⇑⇕⇔↘∕∝∞∋△▽⅄¬⊘ℜℑ⊤⊥ ℵ𝒜ℬ𝒞𝒟ℰℱ𝒢ℋℐ𝒥𝒦ℒℳ𝒩𝒪𝒫𝒬ℛ𝒮𝒯𝒰𝒱𝒲𝒳𝒴𝒵⊔⊓∀∨ ⊢⊣⊔⊓{}⟨⟩‖‖↕↨∖∫√⨿∇∫⊔⊓⊑⊒§†‡¶♣♢♡♠ |
| OMX | mdugm | m | n | |
| OT1 | mdugm | b | n | ΓΔΘΛΞΠΣΥΦΨΩ fffifl ffl ffi ffl ı ` ´ ˇ ˘ ¯ ˚ ¸ ßæœø ÆŒØ ⬡!"#$%&'()*+,-./0123456789:;¡=¿? @ABCDEFGHIJKLMNOPQRSTUVWXYZ["]ˆ˙ 'abcdefghijklmnopqrstuvwxyz-–—"˜¨ |

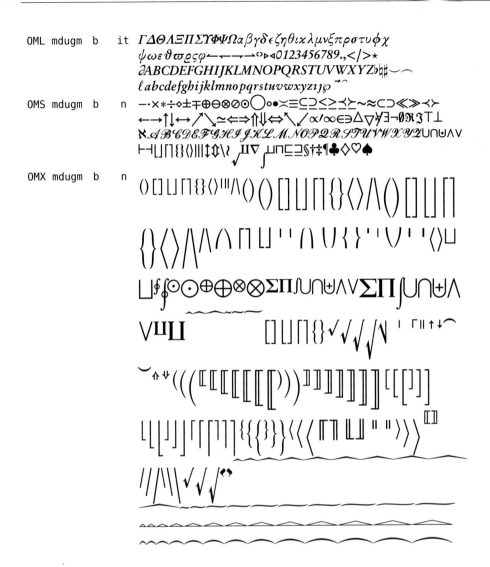

| encod. | family | series | shape | example |
|---|---|---|---|---|
| OML | mdugm | b | it | $\Gamma\Delta\Theta\Lambda\Xi\Pi\Sigma\Upsilon\Phi\Psi\Omega\alpha\beta\gamma\delta\epsilon\zeta\eta\theta\iota\kappa\lambda\mu\nu\xi\pi\rho\sigma\tau\upsilon\phi\chi$ $\psi\omega\varepsilon\vartheta\varpi\varrho\varsigma\varphi\longleftarrow\leftarrow\longrightarrow\rightarrow$↺▷◁0123456789.,</>⋆ $\partial ABCDEFGHIJKLMNOPQRSTUVWXYZ$♭♮⌣⌢ $\ell abcdefghijklmnopqrstuvwxyz\imath\jmath\wp$⃗⌢ |
| OMS | mdugm | b | n | $-\cdot\times*\div\pm\mp\oplus\ominus\otimes\oslash\odot\bigcirc\circ\bullet\asymp\equiv\subseteq\supseteq\leq\geq\preceq\succeq\sim\approx\subset\supset\ll\gg\prec\succ$ $\leftarrow\rightarrow\uparrow\downarrow\leftrightarrow\nearrow\searrow\simeq\Leftarrow\Rightarrow\Uparrow\Downarrow\Leftrightarrow\nwarrow\swarrow\propto\prime\infty\in\ni\triangle\nabla\forall\exists\neg\Re\Im\top\bot$ ℵ$\mathcal{ABCDEFGHIJKLMNOPQRSTUVWXYZ}\cup\cap\uplus\wedge\vee$ $\vdash\dashv\lfloor\rfloor\lceil\rceil\{\}\langle\rangle\|\updownarrow\Updownarrow\backslash$℧∇$\smallint\sqcup\sqcap$⊏⊐$\S\dagger\ddagger\P\clubsuit\diamondsuit\heartsuit\spadesuit$ |
| OMX | mdugm | b | n |  |

\usepackage[adobe-utopia]{mathdesign}

| encod. | family | series | shape | example |
|---|---|---|---|---|
| OT1 | mdput | m | n | $\Gamma\Delta\Theta\Lambda\Xi\Pi\Sigma\Upsilon\Phi\Psi\Omega$ffffiflffiffl ` ´ ˇ ˘ ¯ ˚ ¸ ß æ œ ø Æ Œ Ø ❀!"#$%&'()*+,-./0123456789:;¡=¿? @ABCDEFGHIJKLMNOPQRSTUVWXYZ["]ˆ˙ 'abcdefghijklmnopqrstuvwxyz—–"˜¨ |
| OML | mdput | m | it | $\Gamma\Delta\Theta\Lambda\Xi\Pi\Sigma\Upsilon\Phi\Psi\Omega\alpha\beta\gamma\delta\epsilon\zeta\eta\theta\iota\kappa\lambda\mu\nu\xi\pi\rho\sigma\tau\upsilon\phi\chi$ $\psi\omega\varepsilon\vartheta\varpi\varrho\varsigma\varphi\longleftarrow\leftarrow\longrightarrow\rightarrow$↺▷◁0123456789.,</>⋆ |

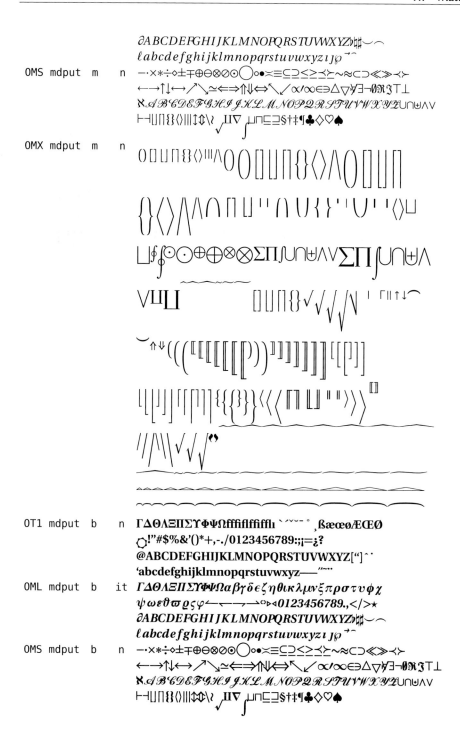

| OMS mdput | m | n |
| OMX mdput | m | n |
| OT1 mdput | b | n |
| OML mdput | b | it |
| OMS mdput | b | n |

OMX mdput b n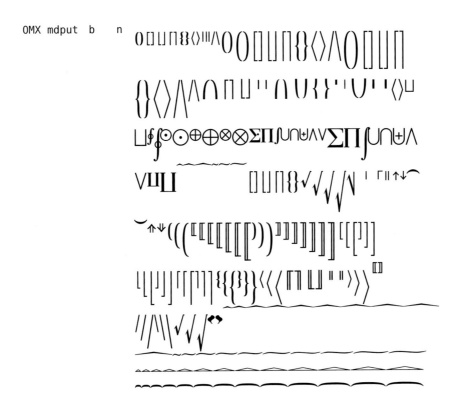

## 7.7.9 PX fonts – px, \usepackage{*pxfonts*}

| encod. | family | series | shape | example |
|---|---|---|---|---|
| OML | pxmi | m | it | $\Gamma\Delta\Theta\Lambda\Xi\Pi\Sigma\Upsilon\Phi\Psi\Omega\alpha\beta\gamma\delta\epsilon\zeta\eta\theta\iota\kappa\lambda\mu\nu\xi\pi\rho\sigma\tau\upsilon\phi\chi$ $\psi\omega\varepsilon\vartheta\varpi\varrho\varsigma\varphi\leftharpoonup\leftharpoondown\rightharpoonup\rightharpoondown$ʿʾ◁▷◀0123456789.,</>★ $\partial ABCDEFGHIJKLMNOPQRSTUVWXYZ\flat\natural\sharp \smallsmile\smallfrown$ $\ell abcdefghijklmnopqrstuvwxyz\imath\jmath\wp \vec{}\,\frown$ |
| OML | pxmi | bx | it | $\Gamma\Delta\Theta\Lambda\Xi\Pi\Sigma\Upsilon\Phi\Psi\Omega\alpha\beta\gamma\delta\epsilon\zeta\eta\theta\iota\kappa\lambda\mu\nu\xi\pi\rho\sigma\tau\upsilon\phi\chi$ $\psi\omega\varepsilon\vartheta\varpi\varrho\varsigma\varphi\leftharpoonup\leftharpoondown\rightharpoonup\rightharpoondown$ʿʾ◁▷◀0123456789.,</>★ $\partial ABCDEFGHIJKLMNOPQRSTUVWXYZ\flat\natural\sharp \smallsmile\smallfrown$ $\ell abcdefghijklmnopqrstuvwxyz\imath\jmath\wp \vec{}\,\frown$ |
| OMS | pxsy | m | n | $-\cdot\times *\div\circ\pm\mp\oplus\ominus\otimes\oslash\odot\bigcirc\circ\bullet\asymp\equiv\subseteq\supseteq\leq\geq\sim\approx\subset\supset\ll\gg\prec\succ$ $\leftarrow\rightarrow\uparrow\downarrow\leftrightarrow\nearrow\searrow\simeq\Leftarrow\Rightarrow\Uparrow\Downarrow\nwarrow\swarrow\propto\infty\in\ni\triangle\nabla\not\vdash\not\dashv\exists\neg\emptyset\Re\Im\top\bot$ $\aleph ABCDEFGHIJKLMNOPQRSTUVWXYZ\cup\cap\uplus\wedge$ $\vdash\dashv\sqcup\sqcap\int\oint\smallint\sqsubset\sqsupset\S\dagger\ddagger\P\clubsuit\diamondsuit\heartsuit\spadesuit$ |
| OMS | pxsy | bx | n | $-\cdot\times *\div\circ\pm\mp\oplus\ominus\otimes\oslash\odot\bigcirc\circ\bullet\asymp\equiv\subseteq\supseteq\leq\geq\sim\approx\subset\supset\ll\gg\prec\succ$ $\leftarrow\rightarrow\uparrow\downarrow\leftrightarrow\nearrow\searrow\simeq\Leftarrow\Rightarrow\Uparrow\Downarrow\nwarrow\swarrow\propto\infty\in\ni\triangle\nabla\not\vdash\not\dashv\exists\neg\emptyset\Re\Im\top\bot$ $\aleph ABCDEFGHIJKLMNOPQRSTUVWXYZ\cup\cap\uplus\wedge$ |

| U | pxsya | m | n | ... |
| U | pxsya | bx | n | ... |
| U | pxsyb | m | n | ... |
| U | pxsyb | bx | n | ... |

## 7.7.10   TX fonts – tx, \usepackage{txfonts}

| encod. | family | series | shape | example |
|---|---|---|---|---|
| OML | txmi | m | it | *ΓΔΘΛΞΠΣΥΦΨΩαβγδεζηθικλμνξπρστυφχ ψωεθϖϱςφ←↩→↪⌣⌢◁▷0123456789.,</>★ ∂ABCDEFGHIJKLMNOPQRSTUVWXYZ♭♮♯⌣⌢ ℓabcde fghi jklmnopqrstuvwxyzıȷ℘↗⌢* |
| OML | txmi | bx | it | ***ΓΔΘΛΞΠΣΥΦΨΩαβγδεζηθικλμνξπρστυφχ ψωεθϖϱςφ←↩→↪⌣⌢◁▷0123456789.,</>★ ∂ABCDEFGHIJKLMNOPQRSTUVWXYZ♭♮♯⌣⌢ ℓabcde fghi jklmnopqrstuvwxyzıȷ℘↗⌢*** |
| OMS | txms | m | n | ... |
| U | txsya | m | n | ... |
| U | txsya | bx | n | ... |
| U | txsyb | m | n | ... |

U  txsyb  bx    n

ℲABCDEFGHIJKLMNOPQRSTUVWXYZ

ꟻↃ℧ð≈⊐⅂⌐◁▷ᛚᛉ⫴∖~≈≊≨≩⌢⌣Ƒϰƙℏℏǝ

ℲABCDEFGHIJKLMNOPQRSTUVWXYZ

ꟻↃ℧ð≈⊐⅂◁▷ᛚᛉ⫴∖~≈≊≨≩⌢⌣Ƒϰƙℏℏǝ

Chapter $8$

# Packages

This chapter briefly covers a few select packages that are widely used and can be loaded by any document. The selection is fairly arbitrary, as there is no clear distinction from less widely used packages.

## 8.1 fontenc

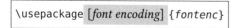

```
\usepackage [font encoding] {fontenc}
```

By default, the T1 encoding will be used, which also provides characters for correctly hyphenating words with non-ASCII characters. This encoding has nothing to do with the Type1 fonts of PostScript. The font encodings that are valid in general are listed in Table 7.2 on page 95. The fontenc package should be loaded by default with the correct font encoding, usually with the option T1, as almost all used fonts are vector fonts.

## 8.2 inputenc

This package lets you specify the input encoding; this only refers to non-ASCII characters.

```
\usepackage [name of encoding] {inputenc}
\inputencoding{name of encoding}
```

The `\inputencoding` command allows you to change the encoding for individual parts of the text; for example for short CJK sequences (Chinese–Japanese–Korean).
The most important encodings for the input encoding are:
- `ascii` ASCII for character range 32–127.
- `latin1` ISO Latin-1 encoding.
- `latin9` ISO Latin-9 encoding (with Euro symbol).
- `utf8` 8-bit Unicode Transformation Format.
- `applemac` Macintosh Encoding.
- `ansinew` Windows ANSI Encoding, extension of Latin-1 (synonym for `cp1252`)

Additional encodings can be taken from the documentation of the package → texdoc *inputenc*. When multiple authors are working on the same document, problems can arise if different input encodings are used. The recode program (or similar) lets you re-encode easily into the general LaTeX format that only uses commands.

```
recode --diacritics --touch --verbose latin1..LaTeX <file name>
```

In this example, `latin1` encoding would be converted to LaTeX, that is for example ä→\"a. Alternatively, the switch could have been made with `\inputencoding`.

## 8.3 graphicx

### 8.3.1 \includegraphics

The `\includegraphics *` command requires the `graphicx` package, which automatically loads the `graphics` package. After loading it, the following command, among others, is available.

```
\usepackage [settings] {graphicx}
...
\includegraphics * [settings] {file name}
```

- The optional specification of the driver can usually be omitted, as the configuration file can determine the used mode itself, for example `dvips` or `pdftex`.
- The file name should be given without extension to allow the driver to choose the right one, for example `.eps` in LaTeX mode.
- If the file name contains characters that don't correspond to normal alphanumeric characters for TeX, you need to use the `grffile` package by Heiko Oberdiek. In particular this allows for several dots or spaces in file names.
- Without a path, TeX first looks in the directory of the document, in the local TeX tree and then in the normal TeX tree.
- Additional search paths can be specified through `\graphicspath` or the environment variable `TEXINPUTS`.
- The starred version clips the graphic to the bounding box.

The following examples all use the same graphic:

```
\usepackage{graphicx}
  X\_\fbox{\includegraphics[width=2cm]{B}}\_X
  X\_\fbox{\includegraphics[height=2cm]{B}}\_X
  X\_\fbox{\includegraphics[width=2cm,height=2cm,keepaspectratio=false]{B}}\_X
  X\_\fbox{\includegraphics[width=2cm,height=2cm,keepaspectratio]{B}}\_X
```

08-03-1

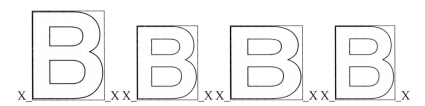

```
\usepackage{graphicx}
  X\_\fbox{\includegraphics[scale=0.5]{B}}\_X
  X\_\fbox{\includegraphics[trim=9 18 30 15]{B}}\_X\qquad
  X\_\fbox{\includegraphics[trim=9 18 30 15, clip]{B}}\_X\qquad
  X\_\fbox{\includegraphics[viewport=20 10 80 80]{B}}\_X
```

08-03-2

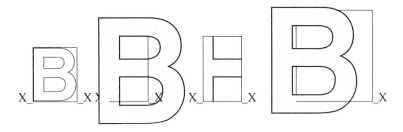

```
\usepackage{graphicx}
  X\_\fbox{\includegraphics[viewport=20 10 80 80,clip]{B}}\_X
  X\_\fbox{\includegraphics[trim=10 10 5 5, clip]{B}}\_X
  X\_\fbox{\includegraphics[angle=45, width=2cm]{B}}\_X
  X\_\fbox{\includegraphics[width=2cm, angle=45]{B}}\_X
```

08-03-3

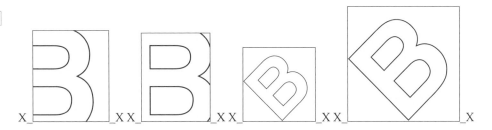

```
\usepackage{graphicx}
  X\_\fbox{\includegraphics[origin=rt,angle=45,width=2cm]{B}}\_X
  X\_\fbox{\includegraphics[origin=lC,angle=45,width=2cm]{B}}\_X
  X\_\fbox{\includegraphics[origin=rb,angle=45,width=2cm]{B}}\_X
  X\_\fbox{\includegraphics[draft,width=2cm]{B}}\_X
```

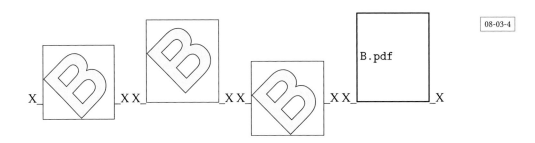

## 8.4 `caption`

It's a good idea always to load the `caption` package by Axel Sommerfeld as it significantly improves the functionality for adding figure and table captions, which otherwise is very restricted in standard LaTeX. You can change the settings for the labels through either the optional argument of `\usepackage` or the `\captionsetup` command. If you change the settings within a floating environment, they remain local to that environment; otherwise they are valid for all successive occurrences of `\caption` until they are changed again. The `caption` package has no effect on the placement of the label; if it is to appear above a table, it must be set *before* the table. However, automatic placement is possible through the `floatrow` package. The options that may only appear in the preamble of a document are shown in Table 8.1. They may be set as part of the optional argument of `\usepackage` or as parameters of `\captionsetup`.

**Table 8.1:** Summary of the package options for `caption` that may only appear in the preamble.

| *name* | *default* | *meaning* |
|---|---|---|
| compatibility | true | Stay compatible with other packages. |
| figurename | \figurename | Specify label name, which is usually specified by the document class. |
| figureposition | – | Placement parameter for objects in a `figure` environment. The default depends on which document class and other packages are loaded. |
| figurewithin | – | Activates superior counters for the `figure` environment. |
| tablename | \tablename | Specify label name, which is usually specified by the document class. |
| tableposition | – | Placement parameter for objects in a `table` environment. The default depends on which document class and other packages are loaded. |
| tablewithin | – | Activates superior counters for the `table` environment. |

```
\captionsetup [type] {settings}
\caption [TOC entry] {label}
\caption*{label}
\captionof{type} [TOC entry] {label}
\captionof*{type}{label}
```

- The starred versions prevent the entry being added to the respective table of contents. Alternatively you can achieve the same result through an empty optional argument, e. g. \caption[]{A table.}.
- \captionof enables you to set the type independent of the containing floating environment.

Note that the \caption command may only appear within a floating environment (or an error message is given "! *LaTeX Error: \caption outside float.*"), whereas \captionof is allowed within as well as outside a floating environment, so you can use it to label non-floating objects. Table 8.2 on page 137 shows a summary of the possible options; they may be changed globally in the preamble or locally in the text through \captionsetup.

*\caption*
*versus*
*\captionof*

## 8.4.1 Global formatting of labels

A label in general consists of three parts – the identifier, the separator and the text. You can change label formatting globally through the format option. Valid settings are:

**plain** Default LaTeX behaviour; the label is typeset as a separate paragraph without additional formatting. The indention option changes the indentation from the second line; both positive and negative indentation are possible, e. g. indention=-2em. The values refer to the start of the label text.

**hang** The label text is typeset as a separate paragraph next to the identifier and separator. Again the indention option changes the indentation from the second line.

**...** Reserved for custom formats, which can be defined through \DeclareCaptionFormat:

\DeclareCaptionFormat{*name*}{*code with #1, #2 and #3*}

Definitions of custom formats must appear in the preamble and *may* use the three parameters #1 for the identifier, #2 for the separator and #3 for the text. You can choose any *name* that is not already taken.

## 8.4.2 Label

The label, composed of the identifier and a consecutive number, is typeset according to the specifications of the used document class – usually just the identifier followed by a space and the number. The labelformat option changes this behaviour. Possible values are:

**default** The identifier is typeset according to the specifications of the used document class.  *labelformat*

**empty** The identifier is not output; only the number appears.

**simple** The label is composed of the identifier and the number without any additional formatting.

**brace** The identifier is terminated by a single (closing) parenthesis.

**parens** The number of the label is enclosed in parentheses.

**...** Reserved for custom values defined through \DeclareCaptionLabelFormat:

\DeclareCaptionLabelFormat{*name*}{*code with #1 and #2*}

You can change the space between identifier and parenthesis through the labelsep option. Possible values are:

**none** No separator is assumed.    *labelsep*

**colon** The separator consists of a colon followed by a space.

**period** The separator consists of a dot followed by a space.

**space** The separator consists of just a space. If there is no identifier, it is omitted.

**quad** The separator consists of the \quad command.

**newline** The separator consists of a linebreak character; note that this doesn't work with the hang format.

**endash** A dash – is used as the separator.

**...** Reserved for custom values defined through \DeclareCaptionLabelSeparator:

```
\DeclareCaptionLabelSeparator{name}{code}
```

### 8.4.3 Label text

*textformat* The textformat option doesn't control the actual formatting of the label text, but the formatting of what is appended to the end of the text. You can use this for example to make sure that all labels are terminated with a period. Possible values are:

**simple** No change.

**period** The text is terminated with a period.

**...** Reserved for custom values defined through \DeclareCaptionTextFormat:

```
\DeclareCaptionTextFormat{name}{code with #1}
```

The #1 parameter will be replaced by the label text.

*justification* You can control the justification of the label text, for example the formatting of the paragraph, through the justification option. Possible values are:

**justified** Default justified paragraph.

**centering** Centring without hyphenation.

**centerlast** The last line of the text is centred.

**centerfirst** The first line of the text is centred.

**raggedright** The text is left-aligned without hyphenation.

**RaggedRight** The text is left-aligned with hyphenation. This automatically loads the ragged2e package. Whether the package is required or not is determined by caption at runtime; an additional subsequent LaTeX run may be necessary.

**raggedleft** The text is right-aligned without hyphenation.

**...** Reserved for custom values defined through \DeclareCaptionJustification.

*singlelinecheck* In standard LaTeX single-line labels are centred automatically, while multi-line labels are always justified. The caption package lets you suppress this check such that the justification parameter is always evaluated. To achieve this, set the singlelinecheck option to false or alternatively *no, off* or *0*.

*font* The character formatting is done through three optional arguments. font is the top-level
*labelfont* option and applies to the entire label – identifier, number and label text. labelfont only
*textfont* applies to identifier and separator and textfont only to the label text. Both overwrite the
*font+* specifications from the font option. The alternative options added through the "+" character
*labelfont+* amend existing definitions. All three, or rather six, versions may take the values listed below.
*textfont+* Multiple values must be separated by commas and may need to be enclosed in {...}.

**default:** The default can be set with normal as a combination of normalcolor, normalfont, normalsize and singlespacing.

**font size:** scriptsize, footnotesize, small, normalsize, large and Large.

| font: | **normalfont** | normal font | **up** | upright font |
|---|---|---|---|---|
| | **it** | *italic font* | **sl** | *slanted font* |
| | **sc** | SMALL CAPS FONT | **md** | medium font series |
| | **bf** | **bold font series** | **rm** | Roman font family |
| | **sf** | sans serif font family | **tt** | `typewriter font family` |

**line spacing:** `singlespacing`, `onehalfspacing`, `doublespacing` and `stretch`; the last one must be assigned a value. If the `setspace` package has been loaded, *single-line* mode is set automatically for labels.

**colour:** `normalcolor` or `color=<colour>`. Requires either the `color` or `xcolor` package.

**...** Reserved for custom values defined through `\DeclareCaptionFont`.

You can combine any of these values arbitrarily as long as the current font supports the combination.

You can change the margins either by explicit specification through `margin` or by implicit specification through `width` (text width of the label). The values must be absolute lengths; relative lengths like the width of the table or figure aren't possible. These can be specified however through the `floatrow` or `threeparttable` packages. If only one value is specified for `margin`, it refers to both left and right margins. Two separate values for left and right must be separated by a comma and enclosed in {...}, for example `margin={0pt,10pt}`. Different inner and outer margins in two-sided documents are adapted automatically to even and odd pages. you can switch this behaviour off through the `oneside` option and back on through `twoside`. If the width of the figure or table is known, the same width can be used for the label. *margin* *width* *oneside* *oneside* *twoside*

## 8.4.4 Horizontal spacing

The `margin*` option sets the margins unless a text width that defines margins accordingly has been specified before through `width`. If the margins are set globally, problems may occur if multi-column mode is used within the document. In these cases, you can use `minmargin` and `maxmargin` to specify minimum and maximum margins, for example `maxmargin=0.1\linewidth`. *margin\** *minmargin* *maxmargin*

The `caption` package also lets you use several paragraphs as label text, which is not possible with standard LaTeX. An alternative text without paragraphs must be specified through the optional argument of `\caption` for the respective table of contents however. You can set the paragraph spacing through the `parskip` option and the hanging indentation after the first line through `hangindent`. *parskip* *hangindent*

## 8.4.5 Vertical spacing

You can alter the default value for either the `\belowcaptionskip` or `\abovecaptionskip` space through the `skip` option. The position of this space is specified through `position`. Possible values are `top` or `above` (object on top, caption below), `bottom` or `below` (object below, caption above) and `auto`. The specification of the position only refers to `skip`, but not to the placement of the caption – it appears where it appears in the source code. An automatic placement is only possible with packages like `floatrow` or `threeparttable`. The value `auto` only *tries* to evaluate the value for `skip` correctly. You can assign a value to a specific type of floating environment through the optional argument of `\captionsetup`: *skip* *position*

`\captionsetup[table]{position=below}`.

The same thing can also be achieved through the optional argument of \usepackage with the
figureposition and tableposition options:

`\usepackage[tableposition=below]{caption}`

The specification of the spacing through the caption package depends on the behaviour of
the respective document class and other packages that affect floating environments and the
two lengths \belowcaptionskip and \abovecaptionskip. Problems with assigning spaces
are therefore not uncommon.

### 8.4.6 Styles

*style* Multiple options can be combined into a style to make it easier to set the options. Two styles
are predefined in the caption package:

**base:** format=plain, labelformat=default, margin=0pt, labelsep=colon, font={},
justification=justified, labelfont={}, textfont={}, indention=0pt, parindent=0pt,
hangindent=0pt, singlelinecheck=true.

**default:** format=default, labelformat=default, margin=0pt, font=default, labelsep=default,
textfont=default, indention=0pt, labelfont=default, parindent=0pt, hangindent=0pt,
justification=default, singlelinecheck=true.

If the caption fits on a single line, justification=centering and indention=0pt are used
regardless of the chosen style. You can change this through the *additional options* argument
of the \DeclareCaptionStyle command:

`\DeclareCaptionStyle{`*name*`}` *[additional options]* `{`*options*`}`

All newly-defined styles are based on the base style; only values that differ from it have to be
specified. The values defined in *additional options* only affect single-line captions if the check
for it has not been disabled through singlelinecheck=false.

### 8.4.7 Table of contents

It has already been mentioned that an empty optional argument for \caption prevents an
*list* entry into the table of contents of the respective floating environment. If you want this to
*listformat* apply globally for a document or starting from a specific point, assign the list option the
*package* value false, no or off. The normal behaviour is achieved through list=true. However, the
*subfig* subfig package doesn't support this option. Instead, you must set the lofdepth or lotdepth
counters to zero. The formatting of the table of contents is determined by the listformat
option. The following values are possible:

**empty** The number of the floating environment is not given.

**simple** The number is given with counter prefix.

**parens** The number is given with prefix in parentheses.

**subsimple** As simple but without prefix (default).

**subparens** As parens but without prefix.

**...** Reserved for custom list formats defined through \DeclareCaptionListFormat:

`\DeclareCaptionListFormat{`*name*`}{`*code with #1 and #2*`}`

Within the document, #1 is replaced with the identifier prefix (e. g. \p@figure – figure) and #2 with the reference number (e. g. \thefigure).

If no subfigures are created with the subcaption or subfig packages, no prefix is assumed in the normal case. Then simple and subsimple give the same result, as do parens and subparens. In contrast to the captions themselves, no type (like "figure") is specified in the table of contents, as this is obvious from the caption of the respective table of contents.

**Table 8.2:** Summary of the optional arguments for the caption package that can be changed locally through the \captionsetup command. For *Boolean* variables, the values true, yes, on or 1 and false, no, off or 0 are possible.

| *name* | *default* | *meaning* |
|---|---|---|
| aboveskip | \abovecaptionskip | Space above the caption. |
| belowskip | \belowcaptionskip | Space below the caption. |
| font | – | Global font for the caption. Possible values are scriptsize, footnotesize, normalsize, large, Large, normalfont, up, it, sl, sc, md, bf, rm, sf, tt, singlespacing, onehalfspacing, doublespacing, stretch=<value>, normalcolor, color=<colour> and normal. |
| font+ | – | Additional option for the current specification. Possible values cf. font. |
| format | plain | Formatting of the caption. Possible values are plain and hang. |
| FPlist | caption | Specification of the reference for a FPfigure or FPtable environment. Possible values are caption and figure. |
| FPref | figure | The same for a reference. |
| hangindent | 0pt | Sets the value for the hanging indentation after the first line. |
| hypcap | true | Sets the anchor for hyperref to the start of the floating environment. |
| hypcapspace | 0pt | Vertical space between link and object. |
| indention | 0pt | Sets the value for the hanging indentation. |
| justification | justified | Horizontal formatting of the caption. Possible values are justified, centering, centerlast, centerfirst, raggedright, RaggedRight and raggedleft. |
| labelfont | – | Formatting of the label. Possible values cf. font. |
| labelfont+ | – | Formatting of the label. Possible values cf. font+. |
| labelformat | default | Formatting of the label. Possible values are default, empty, simple, brace and parens. |
| labelsep | colon | Character between label and label text. Possible values are none, colon, period, space, quad, endash and newline. |
| labelseparator | colon | The same as labelsep. |
| list | on | Add captions to table of contents. |
| listfigurename | – | Caption of the list of figures; the default depends on the used document class. |
| listformat | subsimple | Formatting of the number in the list of figures and tables. Possible values are empty, simple, parens, subsimple, subparens. |
| listtablename | – | Similar to listfigurename. |
| margin | 0pt | Specification of the left and right margin for the labels. If only one value is specified, it is assumed for both margins. Two specifications for {left,right} must be separated by a comma and enclosed in curly braces. |
| margin* | 0pt | Margins are only set if width is not defined. |

continued ...

| name | default | meaning |
|------|---------|---------|
| maxmargin | – | Maximum margin. |
| minmargin | – | Minimum margin. |
| name | – | Similar to figurename and tablename, but applies only to the current floating environment. |
| oneside | – | Sets the document option to one-sided. |
| parindent | \parindent | Sets the paragraph indentation. |
| parskip | \parskip | Sets the dynamic paragraph spacing. |
| position | auto | Position of the caption. Possible values are d, default, t, top, above, b, bottom, below, a and auto. |
| singlelinecheck | true | Special treatment of single-line captions. |
| skip | 10pt | Space between caption and object. |
| strut | on | Use the \struts command. |
| style | – | Assign a user-defined style. |
| subtype | – | Sets the type of a sub floating environment. |
| textfont | – | Sets the font for the label text (cf. font). |
| textfont+ | – | Additional font attributes (cf. font+). |
| textformat | plain | Formatting of the caption. Possible values are plain and hang. |
| twoside | – | Sets the document option to two-sided. |
| type | – | Sets the type of the current floating environment and a hyperlink. |
| type* | – | Same as above but without hyperlink. |
| width | \linewidth | Sets the width of a caption. |

## 8.5 floatrow

The floatrow package by Olga Lapko is an extension of the float and rotfloat packages. It does much more however, in particular supporting horizontal and vertical arrangements of several figures, tables or other arbitrary objects within a floating environment. floatrow is
*subtables and* especially suitable for creating subfigures and subtables and you should use it in preference to
*subfigures* the subfig or subcaption packages.

The floatrow package uses the core of the caption package (described in Section 8.4 on page 132) and therefore works especially well with it. The package supports:

 - defining new floating environments
 - specifying a width of the floating environment, for example to make captions of the same width as the object
 - captions on the side
 - arranging several subfigures or subtables next to each other
 - footnotes within a float box
 - creating legends as footnotes
 - defining custom styles for any kind of floating environment.

### 8.5.1 Optional arguments

Specify all options that should apply globally either when loading the package or afterwards through the \floatsetup command, which allows for global or local specifications. To enable floatrow to pass options to caption, you must load it *after* caption.

```
\usepackage [settings] {caption}
\usepackage [settings] {floatrow}
\floatsetup [type] {options}
\thisfloatsetup{definitions}
\clearfloatsetup{type}
```

## 8.5.2 Summary of parameters

The package provides many parameters for customizations of the floating environments, which are listed below. The default values for the parameters after loading the package are:

| | |
|---|---|
| font=normalsize | Same as the caption package. |
| footfont=footnotesize | Font size for footnotes and legends. |
| capposition=bottom | Vertical positioning of the caption. |
| capbesideposition=left | Horizontal positioning of the caption. |
| capbesideframe=no | Frame caption on the side. |
| footposition=default | Vertical positioning of footnotes and legends. |
| heightadjust=none | Vertical arrangement of the elements in a float box. |
| facing=no | Observe different alignment of the margins for two-sided documents. |
| margins=centering | Specify horizontal alignment of object and caption. |
| objectset=centering | Similar to the setting of the caption package with justification=centering. |
| floatrowsep=columnsep | Horizontal spacing between two float boxes. |
| capbesidesep=columnsep | Spacing between object and caption for horizontal alignment. |
| precode=none | Code to be executed before the start of a float box. |
| rowprecode=none | Code to be executed before the start of a float line. |
| postcode=none | Code to be executed at the end of a float box. |
| rowpostcode=none | Code to be executed at the end of a float line. |
| framearound=none | Frame around object and caption. |
| rowfill=no | Specification if a frame or the lines above and below a float box should span the whole width of the line. |
| midcode=captionskip | Code to be executed between an object and the caption; only possible for captions that appear above or below. |
| captionskip=10p | Space between object and label. |

## 8.5.3 Styles for floating environments

The floatrow package provides a large number of predefined styles, some of which rely on additional packages. The following table shows a summary.

**Table 8.3:** Listing of the floating environment styles defined by floatrow.

| name | parameters | meaning |
|---|---|---|
| plain | – | Corresponds to the layout of standard LATEX for floating environments. |

08-05-1

Figure 1: A not so long caption for a floating environment.

Table 1: A not so long caption for a floating environment.

| plaintop | capposition=top | Corresponds to the plain style except that the labels are placed above the object. |
|---|---|---|

08-05-2

Figure 1: A not so long caption for a floating environment.

Table 1: A not so long caption for a floating environment.

| Plaintop | capposition=Top | Corresponds to the plain style except that the labels are placed above the object and both caption and object are aligned with the upper edge. Assumes that you are using the floatrow environment. |
|---|---|---|

08-05-3

Figure 1: A not so long caption for a figure.

Table 1: A not so long table caption.

continued . . .

| name | parameters | meaning |
|------|-----------|---------|
| ruled | capposition=top, precode=thickrule, midcode=rule, postcode=lowrule, heightadjust=all | Creates a grey line above and below the "float box" and a thin black line between object and caption. 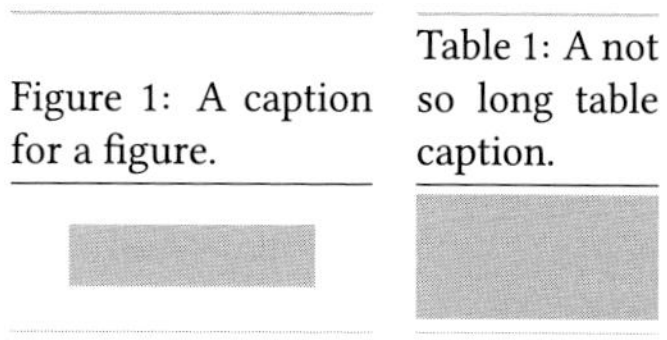 |
| Ruled | style=ruled, capposition=Top | Like the ruled style with Plaintop. 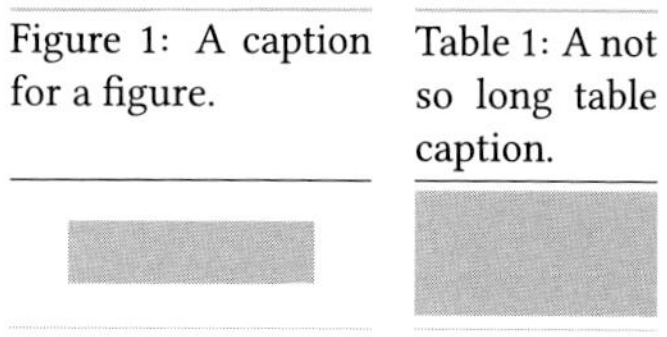 |
| boxed | captionskip=2pt, framestyle=fbox, heightadjust=object, framearound=object | The \fbox is typeset with the default values for \fboxsep and 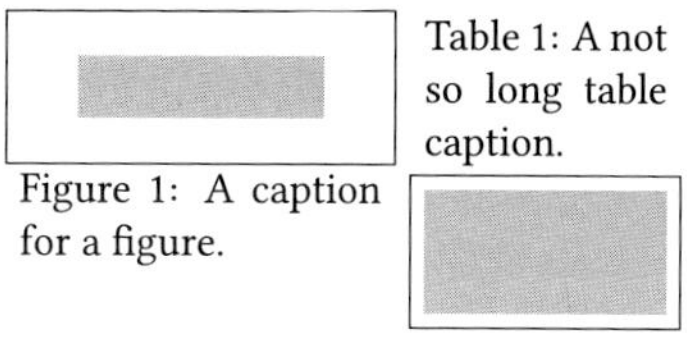 \fboxrule. |
| Boxed | style=boxed, framefit=yes | The frames are typeset according to the optional length parameter of the \ffigbox and \ttabbox commands. 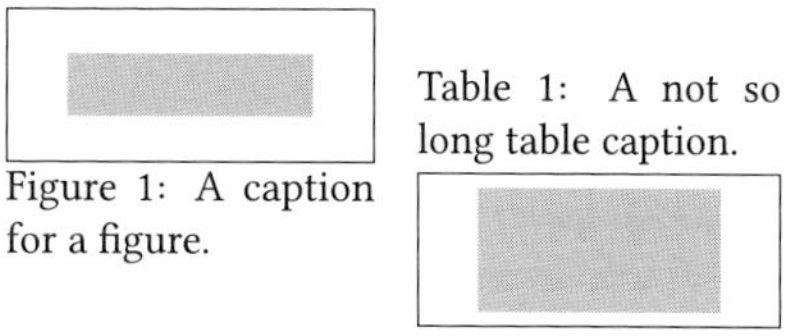 |
| BOXED | framestyle=fbox, framefit=yes, heightadjust=all, framearound=all | Both object and label are in the box. 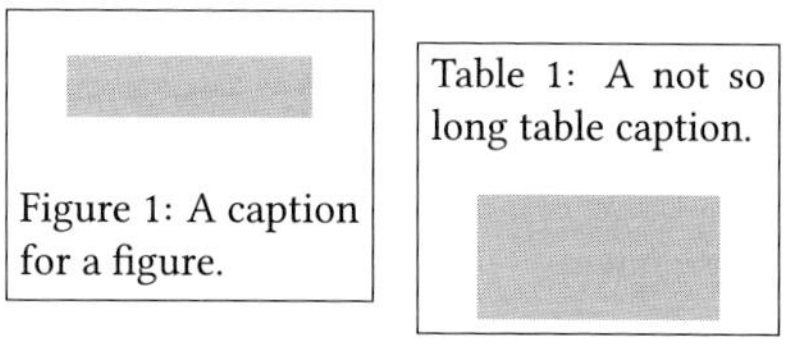 |

08-05-4

Figure 1: A caption for a figure.

Table 1: A not so long table caption.

08-05-5

Figure 1: A caption for a figure.

Table 1: A not so long table caption.

08-05-6

Table 1: A not so long table caption.

Figure 1: A caption for a figure.

08-05-7

Table 1: A not so long table caption.

Figure 1: A caption for a figure.

08-05-8

Table 1: A not so long table caption.

Figure 1: A caption for a figure.

### 8.5.4 Further parameters

Examples for all possible parameters are beyond the scope of this book. The following summary provides an overview and description of a few more useful parameters that haven't been mentioned yet.

Table 8.4: Summary of additional parameters for the `floatrow` package.

| name | meaning |
| --- | --- |
| `capbesidesep` | Corresponds to the `labelsep` parameter from the `caption` package and determines the space between object and label on the side. The space has to be defined symbolically as one of the following values: <br> **`columnsep`** Corresponds to `\columnsep=10.0pt`. <br> **`quad`** Corresponds to 1em. <br> **`qquad`** Corresponds to 2em. <br> **`hfil`** Corresponds to the dynamic space `\hfil`. <br> **`hfill`** Corresponds to the dynamic space `\hfill`. <br> **...** Additional spaces defined through `\DeclareFloatSeparators`. |
| `capbesidewidth` | Specifies the width of a label on the side. Expects either an explicit length, `none` or `sidefil` (default). |
| `captionskip` | Defines the space between object and caption; defaults to 10 pt. Used as the default for the `midcode` parameter. |
| `colorframeset` | Specifies the fill colour for boxes set as `framestyle=colorbox`. There is no default value for this parameter – values have to be defined through the `\DeclareColorBox` command, for example `\DeclareColorBox{cbox}{\fcolorbox{red}{blue}}`. As usual you can make such an assignment through `\floatsetup{colorframeset=mycolorbox}`. |
| `floatrowsep` | The space between two floating objects within the `floatrow` environment. |
| `floatwidth` | The width of the "float box", which is usually defined by the figure or table. This can be used to make captions the same width as a *figure*. The parameter expects the same values as `capbesidewidth`. |
| `font` | Similar to the `caption` package, the style of the label can be specified. Multiple attributes must be enclosed in curly braces and separated by commas. You can assign colours through the `\color` command, for example `font={small,color={blue}}`. |
| `footnoterule` | Defines the appearance of the separating line before footnotes. Possible values are: <br> **`normal`** The line corresponds to the standard LaTeX one. <br> **`limited`** The same, but the maximum length is the length specified through `\frulemax`, which can be overwritten through for example `\renewcommand\frulemax{3cm}`. <br> **`fullsize`** Line across the whole width of the text. <br> **`none`** No line. <br> **...** Additional lines defined through `\DeclareFloatFootnoterule`. |
| `footskip` | Space before a legend or footnote, default 4 pt. |
| `framearound` | Specification of what should be framed. Possible values are: <br> **`none`** No frame. <br> **`object`** Frame around the object. <br> **`all`** Frame around the object, the caption and footnotes/legend. <br> **`row`** Frame around an entire "float" line created with the `floatrow` environment. |
| `framefit` | A Boolean parameter specifying whether the frame should be adapted to the width of the caption. Possible values are `no` and `yes`. |

continued ...

| *name* | *meaning* |
|---|---|

**frameset**    Can be used to define thickness and spacing of the frame, for example `frameset={\fboxrule=1pt\fboxsep=12pt}`

**framestyle**    Defines a frame style, by default only the `fbox` and `colorbox` types make sense. If colours aren't supported, `framestyle=fbox` is set automatically. Additional frames are available if the `fr-fancy` package is loaded.

**margins**    Defines horizontal as well as vertical spaces. Possible values are:

     **centering**   The object is centred.

     **raggedright**   The object is left-aligned.

     **raggedleft**   The object is right-aligned.

     **hangleft**   For the starred versions ("wide floats"); specifies that the floating environment protrudes into the left margin, which is extended by `\marginparwidth` and `\marginparsep`. The values of `\leftskip` and `\rightskip` are added as well.

     **hangright**   The same, but on the other side.

     **hanginside**   The same, but refers to the inner margin for a two-sided document.

     **hangoutside**   The same, but refers to the outer margin for a two-sided document.

     **...**   Additional formats defined through `\DeclareMarginSet`.

**midcode**    The same between an object and the caption. Only possible for captions that appear above or below an object.

**precode**    Code that is executed before the start of a "float box", usually defining a space. May take the following values:

     **none**   The same as an empty specification `precode=`.

     **thickrule**   A line of width 0.8 pt with 2 pt space to the object.

     **rule**   The same but 0.4 pt thick, used asa centre line.

     **lowrule**   The same but 0.4 pt thick, used as the bottom line.

     **captionskip**   Vertical space given by the `captionskip` parameter. Used if nothing was specified for `midcode` (see below).

     **...**   Additional spaces/lines/... defined through `\DeclareFloatVCode`.

**postcode**    The same at the end of a "float box".

**rawfloats**    Resets all standard floating environments and all new ones to the standard LaTeX behaviour. You may only specify this as a package option in conjunction with `\usepackage`.

**rowpostcode**    The same at the end of a "float" line.

**rowprecode**    The same before the start of a "float" line.

**rowfill**    A Boolean parameter specifying whether a frame spans the whole width of the line.

## 8.6 **hyperref**

The comprehensive `hyperref` package by Sebastian Rahtz and Heiko Oberdiek takes care of hyperlinks. It tries to hook into all possible references, links, footnotes and other references and control all pointers. Thus, for example, it creates hyperlinks from a footnote number to the corresponding footnote text. In general you should load the `hyperref` package after all other packages. There are some exceptions to this rule, detailed below – in these cases *load* the loading order should be considered carefully in order to ensure correct operation. Also *hyperref* note that the `IEEEtran` document class requires a version of `hyperref` $>= 1.6b$ because of `\@makecaption`.

**Table 8.5:** Order of packages when using `hyperref`.

| packet(s) | remarks |
|---|---|
| `algorithm` | `\usepackage{float}`<br>`\usepackage{hyperref}`<br>`\usepackage[chapter]{algorithm}% as example` |
| `amsmath` | `\usepackage{amsmath}`<br>`\let\equation\gather`<br>`\let\endequation\endgather` |
| `amsrefs` | `\usepackage{hyperref}`<br>`\usepackage{amsrefs}` |
| `arydshln`<br>`longtable` | `\usepackage{longtable}`<br>`\usepackage{hyperref}`<br>`\usepackage{arydshln}` |
| `bibentry` | `\makeatletter\let\saved@bibitem\@bibitem\makeatother`<br>`\usepackage{bibentry} \usepackage{hyperref}`<br>`\begin{document}`<br>`\begingroup`<br>`\makeatletter\let\@bibitem\saved@bibitem`<br>`  \nobibliography{database}`<br>`\endgroup` |
| `chappg` | `\usepackage{hyperref}`<br>`\usepackage{chappg}` |
| `cite` | `\usepackage{cite}`<br>`\makeatletter`<br>`\def\NAT@parse{\typeout{This is a fake Natbib command to fool Hyperref.}}`<br>`\makeatother`<br>`\usepackage[hypertex]{hyperref}`<br>`\cite` works as usual, but no hyperlinks are created. |
| `dblaccnt` | `% pd1enc.def or puenc.def must be loaded before`<br>`\usepackage{hyperref}`<br>`\usepackage{dblaccnt}` |
| `easyeqn` | Can't be used with `hyperref` currently! |
| `ellipsis` | This package redefines `\textellipses` and must be loaded *after* `hyperref`.<br>`\usepackage{hyperref}`<br>`\usepackage{ellipsis}` |
| `float` | Doesn't support several `\caption` commands within a single floating environment. If the style is controlled by the `float` package, the anchor of `hyperref` is at the upper edge of the object.<br>`\usepackage{float}`<br>`\usepackage{hyperref}` |
| `endnotes` | Package is not supported. |
| `footnote` | Package is not supported and `hyperref` must be loaded with the option `hyperref=false`. |

continued ...

| packet(s) | remarks |
|---|---|
| geometry | There are only problems when using the dvipdfm driver and the program of the same name to convert the DVI file, so use the dvipdfmx program instead. |
| index | A version >= 1995/09/28 v4.1 should be used because of the redefinition of \addcontentsline. |
| linguex | \usepackage{hyperref} \usepackage{linguex} |
| ltabptch | \usepackage{longtable} \usepackage{ltabptch}<br>\usepackage{hyperref} |
| nomencl | Examples for links of the page number:<br>\renewcommand*{\pagedeclaration}[1]{\unskip, \hyperpage{#1}}<br>For equation numbers:<br>\renewcommand*\eqdeclaration[1]{\hyperlink{equation.#1}{(Equation~#1)}} |
| prettyref | \usepackage{prettyref} \usepackage[pdftex]{hyperref}<br>%\newrefformat{FIG}{Figure~\ref{#1}}% without hyperref<br>\newrefformat{FIG}{\hyperref[{#1}]{Figure~\ref*{#1}}}<br>\begin{document}<br>A reference to~\prettyref{FIG:ONE}. \newpage<br>\begin{figure}<br>\caption{This is my figure.}\label{FIG:ONE}<br>\end{figure}<br>\end{document} |
| ntheorem | Problems may occur depending on the commands used.<br>\usepackage{hyperref}<br>\usepackage[hyperref]{ntheorem} |
| sidecap | There should be no problems with the current version. |
| titleref | \usepackage{nameref}<br>\usepackage{titleref}% without usetoc<br>\usepackage{hyperref} |
| titlesec | nameref supports titlesec but not hyperref. |
| ucs | \usepackage{ucs}<br>\usepackage[utf8x]{inputenc}<br>\usepackage{hyperref}% or with option unicode<br>\PrerenderUnicode{ö}%  or \PrerenderUnicodePage{1}<br>\hypersetup{pdftitle={umlaut example: ö}} |
| varioref | The package is basically not supported by hyperref because of many problems. The following may work though:<br>\usepackage{nameref}<br>\usepackage{varioref}<br>\usepackage{hyperref} |
| verse | Versions from 2005/08/22 v2.22 are supported by hyperref. |

The behaviour of hyperref is almost exclusively controlled through options that you can set as package options or through \hypersetup. However, not all options can be changed through \hypersetup after the package has been loaded. hyperref outputs a warning if an option was changed too late and the change will have no effect.

```
\usepackage [settings] {hyperref}
\hypersetup{key-value list}
```

An alphabetical listing of all known options is shown in Table 8.6. Not all of them can be described here for space reasons.

**Table 8.6:** Summary of the possible options for the hyperref package. If nothing is specified in *default*, the argument is empty.

| name | default | remarks |
|------|---------|---------|
| **a4paper** | | |
| **a5paper** | | |
| **anchorcolor** | black | Anchor colour. |
| **b5paper** | | |
| **backref** | false | Bibliographic back references. |
| **baseurl** | | Base URL for the document. |
| **bookmarks** | true | Create bookmarks. |
| **bookmarksdepth** | | The depth of the bookmarks. Possible values are {} (the \tocdepth counter determines the depth), *<number>*, and *<name>* (*name* must be one of the valid chapter or section names like part, chapter, section...). |
| **bookmarksnumbered** | false | Bookmarks with section number. |
| **bookmarksopen** | false | Show bookmarks in the PDF viewer (controlled through bookmarksopenlevel). |
| **bookmarksopenlevel** | \maxdimen | Depth up to which bookmarks are shown in the viewer. |
| **bookmarkstype** | toc | Type of the bookmarks. |
| **breaklinks** | true | *Internal* specification if the used driver is able to break links. |
| **CJKbookmarks** | false | CJK bookmarks. |
| **citebordercolor** | 0 1 0 | Colour frame for \cite commands. |
| **citecolor** | green | Link colour for \cite commands. |
| **colorlinks** | false | Coloured links instead of a frame; the default is truefor tex4ht and dviwindo drivers. |
| **debug** | false | Output more information into the log file (similar to the verbose option). |
| **draft** | false | Don't create hyperlinks. |
| **dvipdfm** | | dvipdfm driver. |
| **dvipdfmx** | | dvipdfmx driver. |
| **dvips** | | dvips driver. |
| **dvipsone** | | dvipsone driver. |
| **dviwindo** | | dviwindo driver. |
| **encap** | | "Encap" character for the hyperindex. |
| **executivepaper** | | |

continued ...

| name | default | remarks |
| --- | --- | --- |
| **extension** | dvi | Extension for linked files; may be dvi, pdf, htm or html. |
| **filebordercolor** | 0 .5 .5 | Frame colour for file links. |
| **filecolor** | cyan | Link colour for file links. |
| **final** | true | Opposite of the draft option. |
| **frenchlinks** | false | Use \textsc instead of a link colour. |
| **hyperfigures** | false | Link figures. |
| **hyperfootnotes** | true | Link footnotes. |
| **hyperindex** | true | Link indices. |
| **hypertex** | | HyperTeX driver. |
| **hypertexnames** | true | Use names for links. |
| **implicit** | true | Redefine LATEX internals. |
| **latex2html** | | LATEX2HTML driver. |
| **legalpaper** | | |
| **letterpaper** | | |
| **linkbordercolor** | 1 0 0 | Frame colour of links. |
| **linkcolor** | red | Link colour. |
| **linktoc** | section | What to link in the table of contents. Possible values are none (no links), section (corresponds to linktocpage=false), page (corresponds to linktocpage=true) and all (link text as well as page number). |
| **linktocpage** | false | Link the page number instead of the text for all tables of content. |
| **menubordercolor** | 1 0 0 | Frame colour for menu links. |
| **menucolor** | red | Link colour for menu links. |
| **nativepdf** | false | Alias of dvips. |
| **naturalnames** | false | Use LATEX-created names for links. |
| **nesting** | false | Allow nested links. |
| **ocgcolorlinks** | false | Allow colour links in the PDF viewer (OCG=Optional Content Groups) that are printed in black. Such links can't be broken and are only available for pdftex and dvipdfm output drivers and PDF version >= 1.5. |
| **pageanchor** | true | Add an anchor for every page. |
| **pagebackref** | false | Back reference with page number. |
| **pdfa** | false | Try to keep the code output compliant with PDF/A. Some things are not supported, for example XMP metadata, fonts, colours, driver-specific low-level code... |
| **pdfauthor** | | Text for PDF author field. |
| **pdfborder** | 0 0 1 | Width of a link frame, the default for the colorlinks option is 0 0 0. |

continued ...

| name | default | remarks |
|------|---------|---------|
| **pdfcenterwindow** | false | Centre the PDF viewer window on the screen. |
| **pdfcreator** | LaTeX | (with hyperref package) Text for the PDF creator field. |
| **pdfdirection** | | Direction. |
| **pdfdisplaydoctitle** | false | Show document title instead of file name in the menu bar. |
| **pdfduplex** | | Duplex printing. |
| **pdfencoding** | pdfdoc | Internal encoding for bookmarks and entries in the information dictionary. Possible values are auto, pdfdoc and unicode (corresponds to UTF-16BE). |
| **pdfescapeform** | false | Escaping for form fields is disabled by default. For true, the PDF driver escapes for example curly braces such that JavaScript can be input in the usual manner. |
| **pdffitwindow** | false | Fit the window size to the document size. |
| **pdfhighlight** | /I | Highlight PDF links. |
| **pdfkeywords** | | Text for the PDF keywords field. |
| **pdflang** | | PDF language identifier (RFC 3066) |
| **pdfmark** | false | Alias of dvips. |
| **pdfmenubar** | true | Activate menu bar in the PDF viewer. |
| **pdfnewwindow** | | Open links to other PDF files in a new window. Possible values are false and true and the empty argument {}, which is interpreted as (absent). |
| **pdfnonfullscreenpagemode** | | Page display mode when leaving fullscreen mode. |
| **pdfnumcopies** | | Number of copies for printing. |
| **pdfpagelayout** | | Specify /PageLayout. Possible values are SinglePage, OneColumn, TwoColumnLeft and TwoColumnRight. |
| **pdfpagemode** | | Set standard mode for PDF display. |
| **pdfpagelabels** | true | Create PDF page labels. |
| **pdfpagescrop** | | Set crop page size of the PDF document. |
| **pdfpagetransition** | | Set page transition style. |
| **pdfpicktrackbypdfsize** | | Set options for print dialogue. |
| **pdfprintarea** | | Set /PrintArea in the viewer preferences. |
| **pdfprintclip** | | Set /PrintClip in the viewer preferences. |
| **pdfprintpagerange** | | Set /PrintPageRange in the viewer preferences. |
| **pdfprintscaling** | | Set /PrintScaling in the viewer preferences. |
| **pdfproducer** | | Text for the PDF producer field. |
| **pdfstartpage** | 1 | Start page when opening the PDF document. |

continued ...

| name | default | remarks |
|---|---|---|
| **pdfstartview** | Fit | Start mode of the PDF document. Possible values are Fit, FitB, FitH top, FitBH top, FitR x1 y1 x2 y2, FitV left, FitBV left and XYZ left right zoom. |
| **pdfsubject** | | Text for the PDF subject field. |
| **pdftex** | | pdfTEX driver. |
| **pdftitle** | | Text for the PDF title field. |
| **pdftoolbar** | true | Make PDF toolbar visible. |
| **pdfusetitle** | false | The default specifications of \title and \author are used to create pdftitle and pdfauthor. If the document class supports optional specifications, they are taken into account by \hyperref. |
| **pdfversion** | 1.2 | At the moment only used for the code for PDF forms if hyperref can't determine otherwise. Possible values are 1.2, 1.3, ..., 1.7. |
| **pdfview** | XYZ | PDF view when following a link. |
| **pdfviewarea** | | Set /ViewArea in the viewer preferences. |
| **pdfviewclip** | | Set /ViewClip in the viewer preferences. |
| **pdfwindowui** | true | Make the elements of a user-defined interface visible. |
| **plainpages** | false | Typeset page anchor as Arabic numerals. |
| **ps2pdf** | | ps2pdf driver. |
| **raiselinks** | false | Raise links (for HyperTEX driver). |
| **runbordercolor** | 0 .7 .7 | Frame colour of programme links. |
| **runcolor** | filecolor | Colour of programme links. |
| **setpagesize** | true | Set page size through the corresponding driver commands. |
| **tex4ht** | | TEX4ht driver. |
| **textures** | | Textures driver. |
| **unicode** | false | PDF strings in unicode, also see pdfencoding. |
| **urlbordercolor** | 0 1 1 | Frame colour of URL links. |
| **urlcolor** | magenta | Colour of URL links. |
| **verbose** | false | More output in the log file. |
| **vtex** | | VTeX driver. |
| **xetex** | | XeTEX driver. |

Some important commands provided by hyperref are shown below.

| name | description |
|---|---|
| \href{*link*}{*text*} | *Text* internally points to *link*. |
| \hypersetup{*argument*} | *Argument* contains value assignments for the hyperref options. |

*continued ...*

| name | description |
|---|---|
| \nolinkurl{*URL*} | *URL* is treated like an argument of \url, but not linked. |
| \pdfbookmark [*level*] {*bookmark text*}{*anchor name*} | *Bookmark text* is linked to *anchor name*. *Level* 0 corresponds to chapter for the book class. |
| \currentpdfbookmark{*text*}{*name*} | Bookmark for the current level. |
| \subpdfbookmark{*text*}{*name*} | Bookmark one level below the current. |
| \belowpdfbookmark{*text*}{*name*} | The same without changing the current level. |
| \texorpdfstring{*TₑX*}{*PDF*} | Bookmarks must not contain special characters. To enable bookmarks for text containing special characters, for example in captions, you can provide an alternative version of the text for the link. *TₑX* is used for the normal display and *PDF* for the bookmark. |

## 8.7 array

The array package provides better ways for partitioning a table. It's a good idea to use booktabs with it as well. The new possibilities are introduced below, using the same table for comparison. The "normal" column definitions are shown first for completeness. The horizontal and vertical lines don't improve the readability of the table; we use them here only to illustrate the options, but in general it's best to draw tables with only a few horizontal lines and no vertical ones.

| left | right | centred | box |
|---|---|---|---|
| l | r | c | p{2cm} |

```
\begin{tabular}{|l|r|c|p{2cm}|}\hline
left & right & centred & box\\\hline
l & r & c & p\{2cm\}}\\\hline
\end{tabular}
```

08-07-1

\extrarowheight increases the **height** of the row without affecting the depth; this length should not be too large. It is usually used to avoid capital letters touching an upper line.

| left | right | centred | box |
|---|---|---|---|
| l | r | c | p{1.75cm} |

```
\usepackage{array}
\usepackage[table]{xcolor}

\setlength\extrarowheight{8pt}
\begin{tabular}{|l|r|c|p{1.75cm}|}\hline
left & right & centred & box\\\hline
\rowcolor{cyan!40}
l & r & c & p\{1.75cm\}}\\\hline
\end{tabular}
```

08-07-2

\arraybackslash redefines the standard line break command, the double backslash \\. If you use one of the formatting commands \raggedright, \raggedleft or \centering without \arraybackslash in a p-column, the command would not have its original meaning. For a new *row within a column*, you can use \newline but for a new *table row* use \\ or the \tabularnewline command.

08-07-3

| L | | R | C | box |
|---|---|---|---|---|
| l | | r | c | p{2.5cm} |
| | | | | new row with |
| | | | | \newline |
| l | | r | c | new table row |
| | | | | with \\ |
| what now | | | | |

```
\usepackage{array,ragged2e}
\usepackage[table]{xcolor}

\begin{tabular}{|>{\columncolor{yellow}}l|r|c|
   >{\RaggedRight\arraybackslash}p{2.5cm}|}
\hline
L & R & C & box\\\hline
l & r & c & p\{2.5cm\}\newline
   new row with \verb+\newline+\\
l & r & c & new table row with \verb+\\+\\
   what now &&& \\\hline
\end{tabular}
```

08-07-4

| L | | R | C | box |
|---|---|---|---|---|
| l | | r | c | p{2cm} |
| | | | | new row with |
| | | | | \newline |
| l | | r | c | new ta- |
| | | | | ble row with |
| | | | | \tabularnewline |
| what now | | | | |

```
\usepackage{array,ragged2e}
\usepackage[table]{xcolor}

\begin{tabular}
   {|l|r|c|>{\RaggedRight}p{2.5cm}|}\hline
L & R & C & box\tabularnewline\hline
l & r & c & \cellcolor{magenta!40}p\{2cm\}
   \newline new row with \verb+\newline+\\
l & r & c & new table row with
           \Lcs{tabularnewline}\\
what now &&&\tabularnewline\hline
\end{tabular}
```

>{...}, where "..." stands for arbitrary code that is executed *before the start* of the respective column in each row. In this example, bold font is chosen.

08-07-5

| left | right | centred | box |
|---|---|---|---|
| l | r | c | p{1.5cm} |

```
\usepackage{array}
\usepackage[table]{xcolor}

\begin{tabular}{|>{\bfseries}l|r|c|p{1.5cm}|}
\rowcolor{red!30}left & right & centred & box\\
\rowcolor{red!60}l & r & c & p\{1.5cm\}
\end{tabular}
```

<{...}, where "..." stands for arbitrary code that is executed *after* the respective column in each row. In this example, math mode is switched on and off using >{$} to activate display mode and <{$} to deactivate it.

08-07-6

| left | *right* | centred | box |
|---|---|---|---|
| l | *r* | c | p{1.5cm} |

```
\usepackage{array}
\usepackage[table,dvipsnames]{xcolor}

\begin{tabular}{l>{\columncolor{Tan}$}r<{$}
   c|p{1.5cm}|}
left & right & centred & box\\\hline
l & r & c & p\{1.5cm\}
\end{tabular}
```

!{...},, where "..." stands for arbitrary code that is inserted *instead* of a separating line in each row, where the space to the columns left and right is preserved. In this example, a colon or an arrow are inserted instead of the separator.

```
\usepackage[table]{xcolor}
```

08-07-7

```
\begin{tabular}{l!{\color{red}\vline}r
    !{:}c!{\color{blue}$\rightarrow$}p{1.5cm}}
left & right & centred & box\\\hline
\rowcolor[cmyk]{0,.5,.7,0}l&r&c&p\{1.5cm\}
\end{tabular}
```

@{...},, where "…" stands for arbitrary code that is inserted *instead* of a separating line in each row, *without* preserving any space to the columns left and right. In this example, again colons and arrows are inserted instead of the separating line. The difference to the example above is obvious.

```
\usepackage{xcolor}
```

08-07-8

```
\begin{tabular}{@{}l|r@{:}c@{\protect%
    \colorbox{cyan}{$\rightarrow$}}p{1.5cm}@{}}
left & right & centred & box\\\cline{2-4}
l & r & c & p\{1.5cm\}\\\cline{1-1}
\end{tabular}
```

*{number}{column type}, where *number* stands for the number of repetitions and *column type* for arbitrary code.

| l | l | l | r | r | r | r |
|---|---|---|---|---|---|---|
| L | L | L | R | R | R | R |

```
\usepackage[table]{xcolor}
\usepackage{array}
```

08-07-9

```
\begin{tabular}
    {|*{3}{>{\columncolor{blue!40}}l}|*{4}{r|}}\cline{1-3}
l&l&l&r&r&r&r\\    L&L&L&R&R&R&R\\\cline{1-3}
\end{tabular}
```

The \newcolumntype command lets you define arbitrary new column types. You can then use these in abbreviated form in table headers as column definitions.

\newcolumntype{*character*} [*n*] {*column definition*}

*character* can only be a letter and should be different from the ones already reserved. *n* specifies the number of parameters and is discarded if the definition doesn't use parameters. The *column definition* must refer to a column type that already exists. The following examples show how you can use the command:

```
\usepackage{array}
\usepackage[table,svgnames]{xcolor}
\newcolumntype{L}{>{$}l<{$}}  \newcolumntype{T}{>{\ttfamily\small}l}
\rowcolors{1}{Pink}{Orchid!50}% from xcolor
\begin{tabular}{lLT@{\qquad}lLT}
sine & \sin(\alpha) &<value> sin &cosine & \cos(\alpha) & <value> cos \\
tangent&\tan(\alpha) &<value> tan &arc tangent&\arctan(x)&<value1> <value2> atan
\end{tabular}
```

| sine | $\sin(\alpha)$ | <value> sin | cosine | $\cos(\alpha)$ | <value> cos |
|------|------|------|------|------|------|
| tangent | $\tan(\alpha)$ | <value> tan | arc tangent | $\arctan(x)$ | <value1> <value2> atan |

08-07-10

In the following example, the header is rotated to allow the columns to be narrower. This improves the readability of the table. If you need a header of a column to consist of several lines, use the varwidth package by Donald Arseneau. It doesn't need you to set the required width explicitly, unlike the minipage environment.

```
\usepackage{array,rotating}
\usepackage[table,svgnames]{xcolor}   \rowcolors{2}{Peru}{Peru!50}
\newcolumntype{B}{>{\bfseries}c}       \newcolumntype{T}{>{\ttfamily}l}
\newcolumntype{R}[1]{>{\color{Crimson}\begin{turn}{#1}}l<{\end{turn}}}
\begin{tabular}[b]{BTl}
\multicolumn{1}{R{45}}{abbreviation} & \multicolumn{1}{R{45}}{reference column} &
\multicolumn{1}{R{45}}{parameter}\\\hline B & c & - \\ T & l & - \\ R & l & 1\\\hline
\end{tabular} \qquad       \rowcolors{2}{Thistle}{Wheat}
\begin{tabular}[b]{@{}BTl@{}}
\multicolumn{1}{R{90}}{abbreviation} & \multicolumn{1}{R{90}}{reference column} &
\multicolumn{1}{R{90}}{parameter}\\ B & c & - \\ T & l & - \\ R & l & 1
\end{tabular}
```

08-07-11

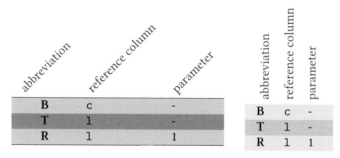

By definition, TEX doesn't hyphenate the first word of a paragraph. However, this is sometimes desirable in narrow columns. To achieve this, define a column type that first writes \hspace0pt into the column. TEX recognizes this as a word of width zero and hyphenates the next regular word. In the following example, the last column of the first table is faulty, but OK in the second table.

08-07-12

| left | right | centred | box |
|------|-------|---------|-----|
| l    | r     | c       | californication |

| left | right | centred | box |
|------|-------|---------|-----|
| l    | r     | c       | californi-cation |

```
\usepackage{array}\usepackage[table]{xcolor}
\newcolumntype{P}[1]{%
   >{\columncolor{green!40}%
   \hspace{0pt}}p{#1}}

\begin{tabular}{|l|r|c>
   {\columncolor{blue!40}}p{1.5cm}}
left & right & centred & box\\\hline
l & r & c & californication
\end{tabular}\\[8mm]
\begin{tabular}{|l|r|cP{1.5cm}}
left & right & centred & box\\\hline
l & r & c & californication
\end{tabular}
```

\raggedleft, \centering and \raggedright alter the horizontal alignment, as mentioned earlier. The modified commands \RaggedLeft, \Centering and \RaggedRight from the ragged2e package by Martin Schröder also allow for word hyphenation.

```
\usepackage{array,ragged2e}  \usepackage[table]{xcolor}
\newcolumntype{L}[1]{>{\color{red}\hspace{0pt}\RaggedRight\arraybackslash}p{#1}}
\newcolumntype{C}[1]{>{\color{green}\hspace{0pt}\Centering\arraybackslash}p{#1}}
\newcolumntype{R}[1]{>{\color{blue}\hspace{0pt}\RaggedLeft\arraybackslash}p{#1}}
\begin{tabular}{@{} L{3cm} C{3cm} R{3cm} @{}}\hline
a flush left, ragged right column & a centred, ragged right column
                              & a flush right, ragged left column\\
L & C & R\\\hline
\end{tabular}
```

| a flush left, ragged right column | a centred, ragged right column | a flush right, ragged left column |
|---|---|---|
| L | C | R |

08-07-13

## 8.8 xcolor

There is a major difference between the xcolor package by Uwe Kern and the color package by David Carlisle with regards to the dvips option. color always activates the dvipsnames option if one of the dvips, oztex or xdvi drivers is being used. This can cause problems if the document is translated with pdftex, which will complain about undefined colours. This is why xcolor expects the named option expected by dvipsnames to be specified explicitly if the predefined colours (cf. Table 8.11 on page 160) should be used.

\usepackage [*settings*] {*xcolor*}

**Table 8.8:** Summary of the most important package options of xcolor.

| option | meaning |
|---|---|
| natural | (default) Use all colours within their model. Exceptions are RGB (converted to rgb), HSB (converted to hsb) and Gray (converted to gray). |
| rgb | Convert all colours into the rgb model. |
| cmy | Convert all colours into the cmy model. |
| cmyk | Convert all colours into the cmyk model. |
| hsb | Convert all colours into the hsb model. |
| gray | Convert all colours into the gray model. |
| RGB | Convert all colours into the RGB model (and then into the rgb model). |
| HTML | Convert all colours into the HTML model (and then into the rgb model). |
| HSB | Convert all colours into the HSB model (and then into the hsb model). |
| Gray | Convert all colours into the Gray model (and then into the gray model). |

continued ...

| option | meaning |
|---|---|
| dvipsnames | Load the predefined DVIPS colours. |
| svgnames | Load the predefined SVG colours. |
| x11names | Load the predefined X11 colours. |
| prologue | Write the list of all colour names (dvipsnames) into the PostScript header; this is important when creating documents via DVIPS. |
| table | Load the colortbl package for coloured table rows. |
| hyperref | Support the hyperref package. |
| showerrors | (default) Output an error message on undefined colours. |
| hideerrors | Output an error message only if an undefined colour is used (and set it to black). |

Table 8.9: Supported colour models ($L, M, N$ are natural numbers).

| name | base colours | parameter range | Standard |
|---|---|---|---|
| rgb | red, green, blue | $[0, 1]$ | |
| cmy | cyan, magenta, yellow | $[0, 1]$ | |
| cmyk | cyan, magenta, yellow, black | $[0, 1]$ | |
| hsb | hue, saturation, brightness | $[0, 1]$ | |
| gray | gray | $[0, 1]$ | |
| RGB | Red, Green, Blue | $\{0, 1, \ldots, L\}$ | $L = 255$ |
| HTML | RRGGBB | $\{000000, \ldots, FFFFFF\}$ | |
| HSB | Hue, Saturation, Brightness | $\{0, 1, \ldots, M\}$ | $M = 240$ |
| Gray | Gray | $\{0, 1, \ldots, N\}$ | $N = 15$ |
| wave | lambda (nm - nanometre) | $[363, 814]$ | |

## 8.8.1 Definition of colours through numerical values

The colours black, **white**, red, green, blue, cyan, magenta and yellow should be defined by every driver and can be accessed directly through their names. xcolor also defines the additional base colours gray, lightgray, darkgray, brown, lime, olive, orange, pink, purple, violet and teal.

```
\color[model]{specification}
\textcolor[model]{specification}{text}
```

08-08-1

Now the text is green and now a bit magenta and now blue and now green again.

```
\usepackage{xcolor}

Now the text is \color[rgb]{0,1,0} green and
now \textcolor[cmyk]{0,1,0,0}{a bit magenta}
and {\color[rgb]{0,0,1}now blue} and now green again.
```

The \definecolor command is already defined by the color package, but is extended by xcolor. The following commands are available for further colour definitions:

```
\definecolor          \providecolor          \colorlet
\definecolorset       \providecolorset
\definecolorseries
```

Furthermore, xcolor defines the current colour (*current color* in PostScript) as the dot; it can be accessed like any other colour. In the following example, the current (dot) colour is changed several times to $80\%$ (\color{.!80}) of its current value, which tends gradually towards white. The following \colorbox on the other hand uses the complementary current colour (-.) for the background to make \iCol visible.

1 2 3 4 5 6 7 8 9 10 11

1 2 3 4 5 6 7 8 9 10 11

```
\usepackage{xcolor,multido}
\newcommand*\CBox[2][]{\color{.!80}\colorbox{.}{%
    \rule[-3ex]{0pt}{7ex}{\color{#1}\Large#2}}}

\color{red}\multido{\iC=1+1}{11}{\CBox[black]{\iC}}\\
\color{red}\multido{\iC=1+1}{11}{\CBox[-.]{\iC}}
```

08-08-2

Unlike command names, colour names may contain numbers; this is especially helpful for colours like *Grey40* to remind you how they were made. You can also specify these percentages when the colour is selected: \textcolor{black!40}{black40}→black40. xcolor allows additional characters as well, but these should be used with caution to retain compatibility with other packages and future versions.

```
\definecolor [type] {name}{model}{colour specification}
\providecolor [type] {name}{model}{colour specification}
\colorlet{name} [num model] {colour}
\definecolorset [type] {model}{prefix}{suffix}{set specification}
\providecolorset [type] {model}{prefix}{suffix}{set specification}
\definecolorseries{name}{base model}{method} [b model] {b specification}
                 [s model] {s specification}
\resetcolorseries [number] {name}
```

The \providecolor and \providecolorseries commands work in the same way as the LaTeX \providecommand command. If a colour or colour series of the same name exists already, it is not redefined to prevent overwriting.

```
\definecolor{MyOrange}{cmyk}{0,0.42,1,0}    \definecolor[named]{Blue}{rgb}{0,0,0.8}
\providecolor{MyGrey}{gray}{0.75}           \definecolor{MyBlack}{named}{Black}
\colorlet{MyRGBO}[rgb]{MyOrange}
```

> Remember: \definecolor always has local scope, but \definecolorseries applies globally!

The above definitions provide five new colours that can be used in addition to the predefined ones. This can be seen in the following example, which makes the additional colour names of the dvips program available through the dvipsnames and prologue package options. \colorlet uses the colour *MyOrange*, defined in the CMYK colour model, as basis. It is converted into the rgb model and then called *MyRGBO*.

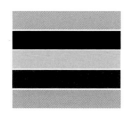

08-08-3

```
\usepackage[dvipsnames,prologue]{xcolor}
\definecolor{MyOrange}{cmyk}{0,0.42,1,0}
\definecolor[named]{Blue}{rgb}{0,0,0.8}
\definecolor{MyGrey}{gray}{0.75}
\definecolor{MyBlack}{named}{Black}
\colorlet{MyRGBO}[rgb]{MyOrange}
\newcommand*\col[1]{\color{#1}\rule{3cm}{5mm}}

{\col{MyOrange}}\\{\col{Blue}}\\
{\col{MyGrey}}\\{\col{MyBlack}}\\{\col{MyRGBO}}
```

The table option is only necessary when using coloured tables, for example in Table 8.8 on page 154 and 8.9 on page 155.

xcolor supports the definition of colour series through three commands. The first two are just extended versions of \definecolor:

```
\definecolorset{rgb}{}{}{red,1,0,0;green,0,1,0;blue,0,0,1}
\providecolorset{rgb}{}{H}{red,0.5,0,0;green,0,0.5,0;blue,0,0,0.5}
```

The first example defines the three RGB base colours and the second three new base colours with the suffix *H* – *redH*, *greenH* and *blueH*. \providecolorset could have been replaced by \definecolorset, as no corresponding colour names exist already. The reverse would not have been possible; the three RGB base colours red, green and blue are defined already by xcolor as well as PSTricks.

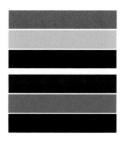

08-08-4

```
\usepackage{xcolor}
\definecolorset{rgb}{}{}{%
  red,1,0,0;green,0,1,0;blue,0,0,1}
\providecolorset{rgb}{}{H}{%
  red,0.5,0,0;green,0,0.5,0;blue,0,0,0.5}
\newcommand*\col[1]{\color{#1}\rule{3cm}{5mm}}

{\col{red}}\\{\col{green}}\\
{\col{blue}}\\[4pt]
{\col{redH}}\\{\col{greenH}}\\{\col{blueH}}
```

The third command, \definecolorseries, lets you specify an entire colour series by giving a start and end colour as well as the number of intermediate steps, for example a series from black to white in 200 steps.

```
\definecolorseries{testA}{rgb}{last}{black}{white}
\resetcolorseries[200]{testA}%  defines a series with 200 colours
```

The \definecolorseries command "logically" defines the series, while \resetcolorseries executes it "physically" by calculating the intermediate steps and defining all intermediate colours internally in a kind of field. Individual colours of the field can be accessed through their index – \testA!![*index*].

08-08-5

```
\usepackage{xcolor,multido}
\definecolorseries{testA}{rgb}{last}{blue}{white}
\resetcolorseries[200]{testA}% 200 colour steps
\definecolorseries{testB}{rgb}{step}[rgb]{%
    0.95,0.85,0.55}{0.17,0.47,0.37}
\resetcolorseries[200]{testB}
\linethickness{0.004\linewidth}

\multido{\nC=1+1}{200}{\hspace*{0.004\linewidth}%
    \color{testA!![\nC]}\line(0,1){40}}\\[5pt]
\multido{\nC=1+1}{200}{\hspace*{0.004\linewidth}%
    \color{testB!![\nC]}\line(0,1){40}}
```

The way the intermediate steps are calculated depends on the chosen method.
- {*b model*}{*b specification*} Specify the first colour.
- {*s model*}{*s specification*} Calculate the intermediate steps depending on method:
  - step, grad: The optional argument is meaningless and {*s specification*} is a vector whose dimension is determined by {*base model*}, e. g. [hsb]{0.1,-0.2,0.3}.
  - last: Specify the last colour, e. g. [rgb]{0.1,0.5,0.5}.

The documentation of xcolor has more details as to how the intermediate steps are calculated. [6] The easiest way of defining a colour series is through the last option, as shown in the following two examples. The first refers to the CMYK model and the second one to the HSB model.

```
\usepackage{xcolor,multido}
\definecolorseries{C}{cmyk}{last}{white}[cmyk]{1,0,0,0}\resetcolorseries[10]{C}
\definecolorseries{M}{cmyk}{last}{white}[cmyk]{0,1,0,0}\resetcolorseries[10]{M}
\definecolorseries{Y}{cmyk}{last}{white}[cmyk]{0,0,1,0}\resetcolorseries[10]{Y}
\definecolorseries{K}{cmyk}{last}{white}[cmyk]{0,0,0,1}\resetcolorseries[10]{K}
\makebox[30mm][l]{cyan (C):}%
\multido{\nColr=0+1}{10}{\colorbox{C!![\nColr]}{0.\nColr}}\\
\makebox[30mm][l]{magenta (M):}%
\multido{\nColr=0+1}{10}{\colorbox{M!![\nColr]}{0.\nColr}}\\
\makebox[30mm][l]{yellow (Y):}%
\multido{\nColr=0+1}{10}{\colorbox{Y!![\nColr]}{0.\nColr}}\\
\makebox[30mm][l]{black (K):}%
\multido{\nColr=0+1}{10}{\colorbox{K!![\nColr]}{0.\nColr}}
```

08-08-6

| | | | | | | | | | | |
|---|---|---|---|---|---|---|---|---|---|---|
| cyan (C): | 0.0 | 0.1 | 0.2 | 0.3 | 0.4 | 0.5 | 0.6 | 0.7 | 0.8 | 0.9 |
| magenta (M): | 0.0 | 0.1 | 0.2 | 0.3 | 0.4 | 0.5 | 0.6 | 0.7 | 0.8 | 0.9 |
| yellow (Y): | 0.0 | 0.1 | 0.2 | 0.3 | 0.4 | 0.5 | 0.6 | 0.7 | 0.8 | 0.9 |
| black (K): | 0.0 | 0.1 | 0.2 | 0.3 | 0.4 | 0.5 | 0.6 | 0.7 | 0.8 | |

```
\usepackage{xcolor,multido}
\definecolorseries{H}{hsb}{last}[hsb]{0,1,1}[hsb]{1,1,1}\resetcolorseries[10]{H}
\definecolorseries{S}{hsb}{last}[hsb]{.1,0,1}[hsb]{.1,1,1}\resetcolorseries[10]{S}
\definecolorseries{B}{hsb}{last}[hsb]{1,1,0}[hsb]{1,1,1}\resetcolorseries[10]{B}
```

```
\makebox[30mm][l]{Hue (H):}%
\multido{\nColr=0+1}{10}{\colorbox{H!![\nColr]}{0.\nColr}}\\
\makebox[30mm][l]{Saturation (S):}%
\multido{\nColr=0+1}{10}{\colorbox{S!![\nColr]}{0.\nColr}}\\
\makebox[30mm][l]{Brightness (B):}%
\multido{\nColr=0+1}{10}{\colorbox{B!![\nColr]}{\color{white}0.\nColr}}\\
```

08-08-7

| Hue (H): | 0.0 | 0.1 | 0.2 | 0.3 | 0.4 | 0.5 | 0.6 | 0.7 | 0.8 | 0.9 |
| --- | --- | --- | --- | --- | --- | --- | --- | --- | --- | --- |
| Saturation (S): | 0.0 | 0.1 | 0.2 | 0.3 | 0.4 | 0.5 | 0.6 | 0.7 | 0.8 | 0.9 |
| Brightness (B): | 0.0 | 0.1 | 0.2 | 0.3 | 0.4 | 0.5 | 0.6 | 0.7 | 0.8 | 0.9 |

## 8.8.2 Colour specifications

– Specification by name; the name of the current colour is dot (.).
– Specification by expression with syntax:

*prefixname*! *value1*! *name1*!... ! *valueN*! *nameNsuffix*

*prefix* If a minus sign (−) is given, the colour is converted to the complementary one.

*name* Model and colour parameters of *name* create the temporary colour \temp.

*value1!name1* The new colour consists of *value1*% of the colour *temp* and (100-*value1*)% of the colour *name1* and is saved as new temporary colour \temp. This step is repeated for all further *!value!name*. If a *suffix* is defined, the temporary colour corresponds to the colour series *name*.

*suffix* May take one of the values !!+, !!++, !!+++, etc. The number of plus signs (+) refers to the base colour series.

Table 8.10 shows some examples of colour expressions and the equivalent RGB code. The right half of the table shows the use of the complementary colours, which are added to those from the first half. Colour plus complementary colour results in white with RGB value 1 1 1.

**Table 8.10:** Colour expressions and the equivalent RGB triple.

| colour expression | RGB triple | | | colour expression | RGB triple | | |
| --- | --- | --- | --- | --- | --- | --- | --- |
| red | 1 | 0 | 0 | -red | 0 | 1 | 1 |
| red!75 | 1 | 0.25 | 0.25 | -red!75 | 0 | 0.75 | 0.75 |
| red!75!blue!100 | 0.75 | 0 | 0.25 | -red!75!blue!100 | 0.25 | 1 | 0.75 |
| red!75!blue!405 | 0.9 | 0.6 | 0.7 | -red!75!blue!40 | 0.1 | 0.4 | 0.3 |
| red!75!blue!40!cyan!50 | 0.95 | 0.8 | 0.55 | -red!75!blue!40!cyan!50 | 0.05 | 0.2 | 0.45 |

```
\usepackage{pstricks}

\psframebox[linecolor={red!70!green},
  fillcolor=yellow!90!cyan, fillstyle=solid,
  doubleline=true,doublesep=5pt,framesep=10pt,
  doublecolor=-yellow!90!cyan]{\Large RGB%
    \textcolor{red!72.75}{RGB}\color{-green}RGB}
```

In addition to the "normal" colour expressions, xcolor also supports "extended" colour expressions, which are expressed as a mixture of colours.

*core model,suml:expr1,fac1;expr2,fac2;...;exprN,facN*

Each colour in the expression is followed by an integer factor – the weight of the colour.

08-08-9

### 8.8.3 Use of predefined colours (named colours)

The *named colours* that are provided by the used driver, for example dvips, allow for easier definition of new colours – \color[*named*]{*SpringGreen*} chooses the predefined colour SpringGreen. Alternatively, you can define a new colour with the same properties. xcolor lets you use the predefined colours for all output drivers.

\definecolor{*MyGreen*}{*named*}{*SpringGreen*}

After this definition, the colour \color{*MyGreen*} is available. All named colours can be requested through the package option. A summary of the available colour names for the dvipsnames, svgnames and x11names colour models are shown in tables 8.11, 8.12 and 8.13.

**Table 8.11:** List of all available colour names for the dvipsnames model.

| Apricot | Aquamarine | Bittersweet | Black | Blue |
|---|---|---|---|---|
| BlueGreen | BlueViolet | BrickRed | Brown | BurntOrange |
| CadetBlue | CarnationPink | Cerulean | CornflowerBlue | Cyan |
| Dandelion | DarkOrchid | Emerald | ForestGreen | Fuchsia |
| Goldenrod | Gray | Green | GreenYellow | JungleGreen |
| Lavender | LimeGreen | Magenta | Mahogany | Maroon |
| Melon | MidnightBlue | Mulberry | NavyBlue | OliveGreen |
| Orange | OrangeRed | Orchid | Peach | Periwinkle |
| PineGreen | Plum | ProcessBlue | Purple | RawSienna |
| Red | RedOrange | RedViolet | Rhodamine | RoyalBlue |
| RoyalPurple | RubineRed | Salmon | SeaGreen | Sepia |
| SkyBlue | SpringGreen | Tan | TealBlue | Thistle |
| Turquoise | Violet | VioletRed | White | WildStrawberry |
| Yellow | YellowGreen | YellowOrange | | |

**Table 8.12:** List of all available colour names for the svgnames model.

| | | | |
|---|---|---|---|
| AliceBlue | AntiqueWhite | Aqua | Aquamarine |
| Azure | Beige | Bisque | Black |
| BlanchedAlmond | Blue | BlueViolet | Brown |
| BurlyWood | CadetBlue | Chartreuse | Chocolate |
| Coral | CornflowerBlue | Cornsilk | Crimson |
| Cyan | DarkBlue | DarkCyan | DarkGoldenrod |
| DarkGray | DarkGreen | DarkGrey | DarkKhaki |
| DarkMagenta | DarkOliveGreen | DarkOrange | DarkOrchid |
| DarkRed | DarkSalmon | DarkSeaGreen | DarkSlateBlue |
| DarkSlateGray | DarkSlateGrey | DarkTurquoise | DarkViolet |
| DeepPink | DeepSkyBlue | DimGray | DimGrey |
| DodgerBlue | FireBrick | FloralWhite | ForestGreen |
| Fuchsia | Gainsboro | GhostWhite | Gold |
| Goldenrod | Gray | Grey | Green |
| GreenYellow | Honeydew | HotPink | IndianRed |
| Indigo | Ivory | Khaki | Lavender |
| LavenderBlush | LawnGreen | LemonChiffon | LightBlue |
| LightCoral | LightCyan | LightGoldenrodYellow | LightGray |
| LightGreen | LightGrey | LightPink | LightSalmon |
| LightSeaGreen | LightSkyBlue | LightSlateGray | LightSteelBlue |
| LightYellow | Lime | LimeGreen | Linen |
| Magenta | Maroon | MediumAquamarine | MediumBlue |
| MediumOrchid | MediumPurple | MediumSeaGreen | MediumSlateBlue |
| MediumSpringGreen | MediumTurquoise | MediumVioletRed | MidnightBlue |
| MintCream | MistyRose | Moccasin | NavajoWhite |
| Navy | OldLace | Olive | OliveDrab |
| Orange | OrangeRed | Orchid | PaleGoldenrod |
| PaleGreen | PaleTurquoise | PaleVioletRed | PapayaWhip |
| PeachPuff | Peru | Pink | Plum |
| PowderBlue | Purple | Red | RosyBrown |
| RoyalBlue | SaddleBrown | Salmon | SandyBrown |
| SeaGreen | Seashell | Sienna | Silver |
| SkyBlue | SlateBlue | SlateGray | SlateGrey |
| Snow | SpringGreen | SteelBlue | Tan |
| Teal | Thistle | Tomato | Turquoise |
| Violet | Wheat | White | WhiteSmoke |
| Yellow | YellowGreen | | |

**Table 8.13:** List of all available colours for the x11names model.

| | | | |
|---|---|---|---|
| AntiqueWhite1 | AntiqueWhite2 | AntiqueWhite3 | AntiqueWhite4 |
| Aquamarine1 | Aquamarine2 | Aquamarine3 | Aquamarine4 |
| Azure1 | Azure2 | Azure3 | Azure4 |

continued . . .

... x11names model continued

| | | | |
|---|---|---|---|
| Bisque1 | Bisque2 | Bisque3 | Bisque4 |
| Blue1 | Blue2 | Blue3 | Blue4 |
| Brown1 | Brown2 | Brown3 | Brown4 |
| Burlywood1 | Burlywood2 | Burlywood3 | Burlywood4 |
| CadetBlue1 | CadetBlue2 | CadetBlue3 | CadetBlue4 |
| Chartreuse1 | Chartreuse2 | Chartreuse3 | Chartreuse4 |
| Chocolate1 | Chocolate2 | Chocolate3 | Chocolate4 |
| Coral1 | Coral2 | Coral3 | Coral4 |
| Cornsilk1 | Cornsilk2 | Cornsilk3 | Cornsilk4 |
| Cyan1 | Cyan2 | Cyan3 | Cyan4 |
| DarkGoldenrod1 | DarkGoldenrod2 | DarkGoldenrod3 | DarkGoldenrod4 |
| DarkOliveGreen1 | DarkOliveGreen2 | DarkOliveGreen3 | DarkOliveGreen4 |
| DarkOrange1 | DarkOrange2 | DarkOrange3 | DarkOrange4 |
| DarkOrchid1 | DarkOrchid2 | DarkOrchid3 | DarkOrchid4 |
| DarkSeaGreen1 | DarkSeaGreen2 | DarkSeaGreen3 | DarkSeaGreen4 |
| DarkSlateGray1 | DarkSlateGray2 | DarkSlateGray3 | DarkSlateGray4 |
| DeepPink1 | DeepPink2 | DeepPink3 | DeepPink4 |
| DeepSkyBlue1 | DeepSkyBlue2 | DeepSkyBlue3 | DeepSkyBlue4 |
| DodgerBlue1 | DodgerBlue2 | DodgerBlue3 | DodgerBlue4 |
| Firebrick1 | Firebrick2 | Firebrick3 | Firebrick4 |
| Gold1 | Gold2 | Gold3 | Gold4 |
| Goldenrod1 | Goldenrod2 | Goldenrod3 | Goldenrod4 |
| Green1 | Green2 | Green3 | Green4 |
| Honeydew1 | Honeydew2 | Honeydew3 | Honeydew4 |
| HotPink1 | HotPink2 | HotPink3 | HotPink4 |
| IndianRed1 | IndianRed2 | IndianRed3 | IndianRed4 |
| Ivory1 | Ivory2 | Ivory3 | Ivory4 |
| Khaki1 | Khaki2 | Khaki3 | Khaki4 |
| LavenderBlush1 | LavenderBlush2 | LavenderBlush3 | LavenderBlush4 |
| LemonChiffon1 | LemonChiffon2 | LemonChiffon3 | LemonChiffon4 |
| LightBlue1 | LightBlue2 | LightBlue3 | LightBlue4 |
| LightCyan1 | LightCyan2 | LightCyan3 | LightCyan4 |
| LightGoldenrod1 | LightGoldenrod2 | LightGoldenrod3 | LightGoldenrod4 |
| LightPink1 | LightPink2 | LightPink3 | LightPink4 |
| LightSalmon1 | LightSalmon2 | LightSalmon3 | LightSalmon4 |
| LightSkyBlue1 | LightSkyBlue2 | LightSkyBlue3 | LightSkyBlue4 |
| LightSteelBlue1 | LightSteelBlue2 | LightSteelBlue3 | LightSteelBlue4 |
| LightYellow1 | LightYellow2 | LightYellow3 | LightYellow4 |
| Magenta1 | Magenta2 | Magenta3 | Magenta4 |
| Maroon1 | Maroon2 | Maroon3 | Maroon4 |
| MediumOrchid1 | MediumOrchid2 | MediumOrchid3 | MediumOrchid4 |
| MediumPurple1 | MediumPurple2 | MediumPurple3 | MediumPurple4 |
| MistyRose1 | MistyRose2 | MistyRose3 | MistyRose4 |
| NavajoWhite1 | NavajoWhite2 | NavajoWhite3 | NavajoWhite4 |

continued ...

## ... x11names model continued

| | | | |
|---|---|---|---|
| OliveDrab1 | OliveDrab2 | OliveDrab3 | OliveDrab4 |
| Orange1 | Orange2 | Orange3 | Orange4 |
| OrangeRed1 | OrangeRed2 | OrangeRed3 | OrangeRed4 |
| Orchid1 | Orchid2 | Orchid3 | Orchid4 |
| PaleGreen1 | PaleGreen2 | PaleGreen3 | PaleGreen4 |
| PaleTurquoise1 | PaleTurquoise2 | PaleTurquoise3 | PaleTurquoise4 |
| PaleVioletRed1 | PaleVioletRed2 | PaleVioletRed3 | PaleVioletRed4 |
| PeachPuff1 | PeachPuff2 | PeachPuff3 | PeachPuff4 |
| Pink1 | Pink2 | Pink3 | Pink4 |
| Plum1 | Plum2 | Plum3 | Plum4 |
| Purple1 | Purple2 | Purple3 | Purple4 |
| Red1 | Red2 | Red3 | Red4 |
| RosyBrown1 | RosyBrown2 | RosyBrown3 | RosyBrown4 |
| RoyalBlue1 | RoyalBlue2 | RoyalBlue3 | RoyalBlue4 |
| Salmon1 | Salmon2 | Salmon3 | Salmon4 |
| SeaGreen1 | SeaGreen2 | SeaGreen3 | SeaGreen4 |
| Seashell1 | Seashell2 | Seashell3 | Seashell4 |
| Sienna1 | Sienna2 | Sienna3 | Sienna4 |
| SkyBlue1 | SkyBlue2 | SkyBlue3 | SkyBlue4 |
| SlateBlue1 | SlateBlue2 | SlateBlue3 | SlateBlue4 |
| SlateGray1 | SlateGray2 | SlateGray3 | SlateGray4 |
| Snow1 | Snow2 | Snow3 | Snow4 |
| SpringGreen1 | SpringGreen2 | SpringGreen3 | SpringGreen4 |
| SteelBlue1 | SteelBlue2 | SteelBlue3 | SteelBlue4 |
| Tan1 | Tan2 | Tan3 | Tan4 |
| Thistle1 | Thistle2 | Thistle3 | Thistle4 |
| Tomato1 | Tomato2 | Tomato3 | Tomato4 |
| Turquoise1 | Turquoise2 | Turquoise3 | Turquoise4 |
| VioletRed1 | VioletRed2 | VioletRed3 | VioletRed4 |
| Wheat1 | Wheat2 | Wheat3 | Wheat4 |
| Yellow1 | Yellow2 | Yellow3 | Yellow4 |
| Gray0 | Green0 | Grey0 | Maroon0 |
| Purple0 | | | |

### 8.8.4  Colours in boxes

Colour definitions within a \savebox are always saved with the box and are therefore local so can't be overwritten from the outside.

```
\usepackage{xcolor}
\newsavebox{\X}\sbox{\X}{[black] and \color[cmyk]{0,0.6,0.8,0}[orange]}
Start with \usebox{\X} and back to black.\\
\color{green}Start with green, see \usebox{\X} and green again.
```

Start with [black] and [orange] and back to black.
Start with green, see [black] and [orange] and green again.

## 8.8.5 Page and box background colour

```
\pagecolor{name}
```

You can change the background colour of the entire page through \pagecolor, which uses the same syntax as \color. This sets the current page as well as all subsequent pages to the specified background colour. This definition is always global and doesn't make sense within a minipage or group.

Similar to the \fbox command, there are two commands to set the background colour in boxes, where \fcolorbox also supports setting the frame colour.

```
\colorbox{background colour}{text}
\fcolorbox{frame colour}{background colour}{text}
```

```
\usepackage{xcolor}
\definecolor{Light}{gray}{.80}  \definecolor{Dark}{gray}{.20}
\colorbox{red!40}{black on 40\%~red}\hfill%
\fcolorbox{red}{cyan!40}{black -- text, cyan -- background, red -- frame}\\
\colorbox{Light}{\textcolor{Dark}{light background}}\hfill%
\fcolorbox{red}{cyan!60}{\color{white}white -- text, cyan -- background, red -- frame}
```

| black on 40% red | | black – text, cyan – background, red – frame | 08-08-11 |
| light background | | white – text, cyan – background, red – frame | |

The other examples show how to use the \fbox parameters \fboxrule and \fboxsep, which control the line thickness and the space between inner box text and frame.

```
\usepackage{xcolor}
\setlength\fboxsep{10pt}\setlength\fboxrule{6pt}
\colorbox{yellow!40}{\color{blue}fun with xcolor}
\fcolorbox{red!40}{yellow}{fun with xcolor}
\setlength\fboxrule{1pt}\colorbox{green!40}{fun with xcolor}
\fcolorbox{blue}{green!40}{\color{blue}fun with xcolor}
```

| fun with xcolor | fun with xcolor | fun with xcolor | fun with xcolor | 08-08-12 |

## 8.8.6 Determine colour values

You can easily determine colour values or colour series with the xcolor package (Section 8.8.1). If for example you want to define a colour identical to one on an HTML page, just use the model of the same name. You can also use \convertcolorspec to transform a colour from another model and output the corresponding values.

08-08-13

HTML colour FF2006
rgb  :1,0.12549,0.02353
cmyk:0,0.87451,0.97647,0
hsb  :0.0174,0.97647,1

```
\usepackage{xcolor}

\definecolor{HTMLcolour}{HTML}{FF2006}% #FF2006
HTML colour \ttfamily\textcolor{HTMLcolour}{FF2006}\\
rgb :\convertcolorspec{HTML}{FF2006}{rgb}\RGBcolour
\textcolor[rgb]{\RGBcolour}{\RGBcolour}\\
cmyk:\convertcolorspec{HTML}{FF2006}{cmyk}\CMYKcolour
\textcolor[cmyk]{\CMYKcolour}{\CMYKcolour}\\
hsb :\convertcolorspec{HTML}{FF2006}{hsb}\HSBcolour
\textcolor[hsb]{\HSBcolour}{\HSBcolour}
```

Chapter **9**

# Bibliographies

## 9.1 Structure

In principle, there are four different ways to create a bibliography:
- Completely free layout without using existing commands or environments.
- Using the thebibliography environment.
- Using a BibTeX-compatible database and the external bibtex program.
- Using a BibTeX-compatible database and the biblatex package.

It only makes sense to use the second method if you require a small number of references, while the third and fourth methods are suitable for anything from a small number to a *very* large number of references. It usually doesn't make sense to use a custom layout. Nowadays there are many programs for literature and reference management that are able to produce BibTeX-compatible output.

## 9.2 The BibTeX program

The way BibTeX works is shown in Figure 9.1 on the next page. The external bibtex program or bibtex8 (the 8 Bit version) must be run independently of a LaTeX run. Most TeX editors do this automatically in the background if you have activated the corresponding option. The possible options are listed in Table 9.1.

bibtex creates a .bbl file from the specifications in the .aux file, which is read during subsequent LaTeX runs and included accordingly. The log file with the extension .blg should be consulted if the output doesn't correspond to expectations. Note that LaTeX only outputs an error message if the syntax is wrong – inconsistent specifications in the .bbl file don't trigger error messages.

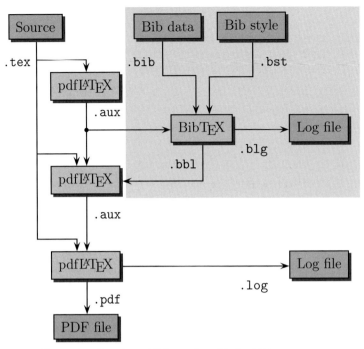

**Figure 9.1:** Creating a bibliography with the bibtex program.

**Table 9.1:** Summary of the possible options for the bibtex program.

| *name* | *description* |
| --- | --- |
| min-crossrefs | This parameter must be assigned a number, which is 2 by default. It determines the minimum number of references to non-cited literature necessary to insert it automatically into the bibliography even if no explicit reference exists. |
| terse | No output on stdout. |
| help | Output a short help. |
| version | Output the current version. |

> bibtex *options* ⟨*file*⟩ .aux
> bibtex8 *options* ⟨*file*⟩ .aux

*bibtex8* Because of the restriction to 7 Bit ASCII, the bibtex8 program was developed by Alejandro Aguilar Sierra and Neil Kempson. It sorts the authors correctly even if the names contain or start with non-ASCII characters. BibTEX8 has many more optional arguments, but the call is the same. A summary of the optional arguments is given in Table 9.2 on the facing page.

**Table 9.2:** Summary of the possible options for the bibtex8 program.

| short/long form | description |
|---|---|
| -? --help | Output help. |
| -7 --traditional | Original BibTeX mode. |
| -8 --8bit | Force 8-Bit mode without .csf (character set) file. |
| -c --csfile | Parameter is a .csf file (BibTeX character set file). |
| -d --debug | Type of debug information. Possible values are all, csf, io, mem, misc, search. |
| -s --statistics | Output internal statistics. |
| -t --trace | Output an execution trace. |
| -v --version | Output program version. |
| -B --big | Set large BibTeX capacity. |
| -H --huge | Set huge BibTeX capacity. |
| -W --wolfgang | Set really huge BibTeX capacity. |
| -M --min_crossrefs | Specification of the minimum number of required references for a bibliography entry to appear in the list automatically. |
| --mcites | Maximum number of \cites commands in the .aux file. |
| --mentints | Maximum number of integer entries in the .bib file. |
| --mentstrs | Maximum number of string entries in the .bib file. |
| --mfields | Maximum number of fields in the .bib file. |
| --mpool | Size of the string pool in bytes. |
| --mstrings | Maximum number of unique strings. |
| --mwizfuns | Maximum number of wizard functions. |

In order for 7 Bit BibTeX to sort the bibliography correctly, you should input non-ASCII characters in the TeX notation with additional braces.

```
author = "Jos{\'e} S{\'a}nchez"
author = "Ma{\ss}mann, R{\"u}diger"
author = {Fr{\c{c}}ois Ferdi{\'e}re}
title  = "{\OE}uvres compl{\'e}tes"
```

You can find appropriate character set files (.csf), required for a correct sorting with bibtex8, at $TEXMF/bibtex/csf. The following files are in the subdirectory /base:

```
88591lat.csf  % ISO 8859-1 (Unix/MS Windows), Latin countries
88591sca.csf  %                              Scandinavian countries
ascii.csf     % ASCII 0--127
cp437lat.csf  % IBM Code Page 437, Latin countries
cp850lat.csf  % IBM Code Page 850, Latin countries
cp850sca.csf  % IBM Code Page 850, Scandinavian countries
cp866rus.csf  % Code Page 866, Russian
```

The directory $TEXMF/doc/resources contains additional special versions for these files; by default the file 88591lat.csf is used.

```
voss@shania:~> bibtex8 test
The 8-bit codepage and sorting file: 88591lat.csf
The top-level auxiliary file: test.aux
The style file: plain.bst
Database file #1: test8.bib
```

When using bibtex8, you don't need to use the special encoding for accents and umlauts shown on the previous page. The following example would have a different order for the bibliography if you were using the bibtex program instead.

## References

[Ör07]  Hérbèrt Öre. Allgemeine und sprachenspezifische Probleme bei der Entwicklung eines Textsatzsystems am Beispiel von TeX. Vortrag im Institut für germanistische Sprachwissenschaft, Friedrich-Schiller-Universität Jena, 2007.

[Pat88]  Oren Patashnik. BibTeXing, February 1988. CTAN: //biblio/bibtex/contrib/doc/btxdoc.pdf.

```
\usepackage{url}
% bibtex8 <file>

foo\cite{btxdoc,hv2007}\clearpage
\bibliographystyle{alpha}
\bibliography{data/UTF8}
```

`09-02-1`

### 9.2.1 Workflow

After a first LaTeX run, the next step depends on which packages you are using. In the simplest case, bibtex or bibtex8 is run with the .aux file of the document as a parameter. After this, at least another LaTeX run is required, depending on the structure of the document.

### 9.2.2 Bibliography styles for BibTeX

The standard distributions of TeX, like TeXlive or MiKTeX, should have the following BibTeX styles (.bst files) available. Missing entries are marked with –. The list below is only current so long as the TeXlive distribution here is not changed. You can also create custom styles interactively with latex makebst.

| .bst name | description |
| --- | --- |
| aaai-named | American Association for Artificial Intelligence |
| aabbrv | – |
| aalpha | – |
| abbrv | standard style file |
| abbrvdin | according to DIN 1505 |
| abbrv-fr | French version of abbrv |
| abbrvhtml | extended with an html field |
| abbrvnat | same with natbib package |
| abbrvnat-fr | French version |
| abbrvurl | modification of abbrv for URL entries |
| abbrv-letters | – |
| abstract | modified standard style ('alpha') |
| achemso | style for American Chemical Society publications |
| achicago | inspired by the Chicago Manual of Style |
| acm | similar to abbrv, adapted for ACM Transactions |
| acm-fa | Farsi version |
| acmtrans | ACM Transactions style, based on the Chicago style |
| active2006 | numeric style for English texts for Active2006 (Sixth International Symposium on Active Noise and Vibration Control) |
| address-html | style by Christophe Geuzaine |
| address | ditto |

continued ...

| `.bst name` | *description* |
|---|---|
| `address-ldif` | – |
| `address-vcard` | – |
| `adrconv` | style for address databases |
| `adrfax` | ditto |
| `aer` | American Economic Review |
| `aertt` | modified style `alpha` |
| `agecon` | Agricultural Economics |
| `agsm` | from the Harvard series (Peter Williams) |
| `agu` | for journals of the AGU (American Geophysical Union) |
| `agufull` | same, without restriction of the number of authors |
| `aiaa` | AIAA (American Institute of Aeronautics and Astronautics) – technical conference papers |
| `aichej` | American Institute of Chemical Engineers |
| `aipauth4-1` | – |
| `aipauth4-1long` | – |
| `aipnum4-1` | – |
| `aipnum4-1long` | – |
| `ajae` | American Journal of Agricultural Economics |
| `alpha` | standard BⁱᵦTEX style file |
| `alpha-fr` | French version |
| `alphadin` | DIN 1505, part 2 from 1984 |
| `alphahtml` | exports HTML-compatible code |
| `alphahtmldate` | ditto |
| `alphahtmldater` | ditto |
| `alphaurl` | modification of the `abbrv` style, to be able to specify URL entries |
| `alpha-letters` | style derived from `alpha` (Thomas van Oudenhove) |
| `amsalpha` | alphabetical label bibliography for AMS (American Mathematical Society) publications |
| `ametsoc` | AMS journals |
| `amsplain` | same with numeric labels |
| `amsra` | based on `amsxport.dtx` (options are bst, sort, alpha) |
| `amsrn` | ditto (options are bst, sort, plain) |
| `amsrs` | ditto (options are bst, sort, short) |
| `amsru` | ditto (options are bst, plain) |
| `amsry` | ditto (options are bst, sort, alpha, y2k) |
| `angew` | Royal Society of Chemistry |
| `annotate` | style based on alpha |
| `annotation` | style based on plain |
| `anotit` | – |
| `apa` | adapted from `apalike` with features from `astron` (Sake J. Hogeveen) |
| `apacann` | APA annotated bibliography style |
| `apacannx` | same with author index |
| `apacite` | reference list similar to the APA manual |
| `apacitex` | same with short explanations |
| `apalike` | adapted from `alpha` style; requires the `apalike` package |
| `apalike-fr` | French version |
| `apalike2` | apalike style |
| `apalike-letters` | apalike style |
| `aplain` | apalike style |
| `apecon` | Applied Economics |

continued …

| `.bst` name | description |
|---|---|
| apsr | from the Harvard series (Peter Williams) |
| apsrev | revTEX-compatible style (Patrick W. Daly) |
| apsrev4-1 | ditto |
| apsrev4-1long | ditto |
| apsrevM | ditto |
| apsrmp4-1 | ditto |
| apsrmp4-1long | ditto |
| apsrmpM | ditto |
| apsrmp | ditto |
| asaetr | style for ASAE (American Society for Agricultural Engineers) |
| ascelike | style for ASCE (American Society of Civil Engineers) |
| astron | style for astronomy journals; requires astron package |
| aunsnot | – |
| aunsrt | – |
| authordate1 | for references in "author-date" style with the authordate1-4 package |
| authordate2 | ditto |
| authordate3 | ditto |
| authordate4 | ditto |
| bababbr3-fl | for babelbib – multilingual bibliographies (options are bst, bststd, bstshort, bstthree, namevara) |
| bababbr3-lf | ditto (options are bst, bststd, bstshort, bstthree, namevarb) |
| bababbr3 | ditto (options are bst, bststd, bstshort, bstthree) |
| bababbrv-fl | ditto (options are bst, bststd, bstshort, namevara) |
| bababbrv-lf | ditto (options are bst, bststd, bstshort, namevarb) |
| bababbrv | ditto (options are bst, bststd, bstshort) |
| babalpha-fl | ditto (options are bst, bststd, bstsorted, bstalpha, namevara) |
| babalpha-lf | ditto (options are bst, bststd, bstsorted, bstalpha, namevarb) |
| babalpha | ditto (options are bst, bststd, bstsorted, bstalpha) |
| babalpha2 | ditto |
| babamspl | ditto (options are bst, bstams) |
| babplai3-fl | ditto (options are bst, bststd, bstthree, namevara) |
| babplai3-lf | ditto (options are bst, bststd, bstthree, namevarb) |
| babplai3 | ditto (options are bst, bststd, bstthree) |
| babplain-fl | ditto (options are bst, bststd, namevara) |
| babplain-lf | ditto (options are bst, bststd, namevarb) |
| babplain | ditto (options are bst, bststd) |
| babplain-neu | ditto |
| babplain-orig | ditto |
| babplain-spielen | ditto |
| babunsrt-fl | ditto (options are bst, bststd, bstunsorted, namevara) |
| babunsrt-lf | ditto (options are bst, bststd, bstunsorted, namevarb) |
| babunsrt | ditto (options are bst, bststd, bstunsorted) |
| bbs | BBS (Behavioral and Brain Sciences), adapted from apalike with the features from astron by Sake J. Hogeveen |
| bibtoref | UNIX-compatible format, based on the style by Kannan Varadhan |
| biblatex | style for bibliography with biblatex |
| biochem | American Chemical Society |
| birthday | see adrconv |
| cbe | Council of Biology Editors, used by (among others) Evolution, American Naturalist, … |

continued …

| `.bst name` | description |
|---|---|
| cc | Computational Complexity |
| cc2 | same with `natbib` |
| cell | style for biological journals |
| ChemCommun | Chemistry Community |
| ChemEurJ | Chemistry – A European Journal |
| chicago | style inspired by the 13th edition of the Chicago Manual of Style |
| chicagoa | same with annotation support |
| chicago-annote | ditto |
| cje | Canadian Journal of Economics |
| classic | – |
| cont-ab | style for conTEXt |
| cont-au | ditto |
| cont-no | ditto |
| cont-ti | ditto |
| cv | Curriculum Vitae |
| databib | – |
| dcbib | – |
| dcu | member of the Harvard family |
| dinat | "author-year" style |
| disser | Russian bibliographies |
| disser-s | ditto |
| dk-abbrv | Danish version (Arne Jorgensen) |
| dk-alpha ditto | dk-apali ditto     dk-plain ditto     dk-unsrt ditto |
| dtk | style for the "TEXnische Komödie" of DANTE e. V. |
| ecca | Economica |
| econometrica | Econometrica style for the `harvard` package |
| econometrica-fr | French version |
| ecta | Econometrica |
| elsart-harv | Harvard-compatible style of Elsevier (Patrick W. Daly) |
| elsart-num | ditto |
| elsarticle-num-names | ditto |
| elsart-num-names | ditto |
| elsart-num-sort | ditto |
| email-html | style by Christophe Geuzaine |
| email | see `adrconv` |
| en-mtc | – |
| erae | European Review of Agricultural Economics |
| fbs | Frontiers in Bioscience |
| figbib | – |
| figbib1 | – |
| finplain | Finnish version (Antti-Juhani Kaijanaho) |
| fr-mtc | – |
| frplainnat-letters | special French version |
| gatech-thesis-losa | for a list of symbols or abbreviations of the `gatech-thesis` class (Jose Luis Diaz and Javier Bezos) |
| gatech-thesis | ditto |
| gerabbrv | special version for the `bibgerman` package |
| geralpha | ditto |
| gerapali | ditto |
| gerplain | ditto |

continued …

| .bst name | description |
|---|---|
| gerunsrt | ditto |
| glsplain | part of the gloss distribution (Jose Luis Diaz and Javier Bezos) |
| glsshort | ditto |
| gost71s | style for GOST 7.1-84 vd970321 (Maksym Polyakov) |
| gost71u | ditto |
| gost780s | ditto |
| gost780u | ditto |
| hc-de | special German style (Christian Siefkes) |
| hc-en | same for English |
| humanbio | inspired by the Human Biology journal |
| humannat | same for Human Nature and American Anthropologist |
| IEEEtran | style for IEEE (Institute of Electrical and Electronics Engineers) – unsorted |
| IEEEtranM | ditto |
| IEEEtranMN | ditto |
| IEEEtranN | ditto – unsorted natbib version |
| IEEEtranS | ditto – sorted |
| IEEEtranSA | ditto – alpha sorted |
| IEEEtranSN | ditto– sorted natbib version |
| ieeepes | style for articles of IEEE Instructions (Volker Kuhlmann) |
| ieeetr | IEEE (Institute of Electrical and Electronics Engineers), derived from the "plain" style |
| ieeetr-fa | ditto |
| ieeetr-fr | ditto |
| ier | International Economic Review |
| ijmart | Israel Journal of Mathematics |
| ijqc | International Journal of Quantum Chemistry |
| imac | IMAC (International Modal Analysis Conference) style (Joseph C. Slater) |
| inlinebib | style for footnote references (René Seindal) |
| InorgChem | Inorganic Chemistry |
| iopart-num | IOP (Institute of Physics) journal |
| is-abbrv | modification of the btxbst style with optional support for CODEN, ISBN, ISSN, LCCN and PRICE fields |
| is-alpha | same in "alpha" style |
| is-plain | same in "plain" style |
| is-unsrt | same in "unsorted" style |
| itaxpf | International Tax and Public Finance |
| JAmChemSoc | Journal of the American Chemical Society |
| JAmChemSoc_all | ditto |
| jas99 | style for Journal of Atmospheric Science and Journal of Applied Meteorology |
| jbact | ditto |
| jcc | style jcc2005 for Journal of Computational Chemistry |
| jmb | Journal of Molecular Biology and Journal of Theoretical Biology (Tom Schneider) |
| jmr | style by Peter Williams |
| jneurosci | Journal of Neuroscience |
| jox | style for the jurabib package |
| jpc | Journal for Physics and Chemistry |
| jpe | Journal of Political Economy |

continued . . .

| .bst name | description |
|---|---|
| jphysicsB | Harvard-compatible style (Peter Williams) |
| jtb | for bibliographies in the format of the Journal of Theoretical Biology |
| jthcarsu | for the Journal of Thoracic and Cardiovascular Surgery |
| jurabib | style for the jurabib package (Jens Berger) |
| jurarsp | for court decisions (Lucas Wartenburger) |
| jureco | part of the jurabib package |
| jurunsrt | ditto |
| klunamed | Kluver style (publishing house) |
| klunum | ditto |
| kluwer | ditto |
| letter | style by Christophe Geuzaine |
| ltugbib | for the harvardcite option of the ltug* LaTeX document class |
| mbplain | plainbst adapted for the multibib package (Thorsten Hansen) |
| mbunsrtdin | DIN 1505, part 2 from 1984 |
| mslapa | special style for the mslapa package (Michael Landy) |
| munich | – |
| named | support for short (year-only) citations |
| namunsrt | derived from unsrt |
| nar | Journal of Nucleic Acid Research, derived from unsrt |
| natdin | DIN 1505, parts 2 and 3 |
| naturemag | Nature Journal (Peter Czoschke) |
| nddiss2e | modified abbrvnat |
| nederlands | special Harvard style (Werenfried Spit) |
| newapa | special support for abbreviated author lists and year-only citations |
| newapave | ditto |
| oega | Austrian Society for Agricultural Economics |
| opcit | opcit project – references as footnote (Federico Garcia) |
| pccp | Physical Chemistry Chemical Physics |
| perception | Pion Journal Perception |
| phaip | style for several physics journals |

| phapalik ditto | phcpc ditto | phiaea ditto | phjcp ditto |
| phnf ditto | phnflet ditto | phone ditto | phpf ditto |
| phppcf ditto | phreport ditto | phrmp ditto | |

| .bst name | description |
|---|---|
| plabbrv | special Polish version (Boguslaw Lichonski) |
| plain | standard BibTeX style |
| plain-fa | Farsi version |
| plain-fr | French version |
| plaindin | DIN 1505, parts 2 and 3 |
| plainhtml | exports compatible HTML code |
| plainhtmldate | ditto |
| plainhtmldater | ditto |
| plainnat | plain for the natbib package (Patrick W. Daly) |
| plainnat-fr | same for French |
| plain-letters | modification of plain |
| plainnat-letters | same for natbib |
| plainurl | modification of abbrv with URL fields |
| plainyr | like "plain", but sorted by year, author, title |
| plalpha | Polish version of alpha |
| plplain | same for plain |
| plunsrt | same for unsrt |

continued …

| .bst name | description |
|---|---|
| psuthesis | Pennsylvania State University |
| refer | bibliography in "refer" format, based on style by Kannan Varadhan |
| regstud | Regional Studies |
| revcompchem | Reviews in Computational Chemistry |
| rsc | Royal Society of Chemistry |
| rusnat | — |
| sageep | Symposium on the Application of Geophysics to Environmental & Engineering (SAGEE) |
| savetrees | — |
| siam | SIAM (Society for Industrial and Applied Mathematics) style (Howard Trickey) |
| siam-letters | style adapted to siam (Thomas van Oudenhove) |
| siam-fr | like siam for French |
| spiebib | for SPIE (International Society of Optical Engineering) proceedings |
| sweabbrv | Swedish version of abbrv |
| sweplain | same for plain |
| sweplnat | same for plain with natbib package |
| sweunsrt | same for unsrt |
| tandfx | Taylor and Francis Reference Style |
| texsis | style by Bernd Dammann |
| thesnumb | — |
| thubib | — |
| unsrt | standard style |
| unsrt-fa | Farsi version |
| unsrt-fr | French version |
| unsrtdin | DIN 1505 |
| unsrthtml | with html field |
| unsrtnat | same for the natbib package |
| unsrtnat-fr | French version |
| unsrturl | modification of unsrt for URL entries |
| xagsm | Harvard-compatible style for AGSM (Australian Graduate School of Management, Peter Williams). |
| usmeg-a | style for the University of Stellenbosch |
| usmeg-n | ditto |
| ussagus | ditto |
| vancouver | for manuscripts of the Biomedical Journal |
| worlddev | World Development |
| xagsm | — |
| xplain | corresponds to the "plain" style |

## 9.3 The biblatex package

The biblatex package by Philipp Lehman tries to lift the restrictions of BibTeX with respect to style files. It moves the formatting of the references and the bibliography to TeX so that changes can be made in the document itself. BibTeX is only required to sort the entries of the bibliography (cf. figures 9.2 and 9.3 on the facing page). For full UTF8 support you need to install the Biber program, which is already part of the TeX Live and MikTeX distribution. Like natbib, biblatex supports the numeric references that are the default in LaTeX as well as

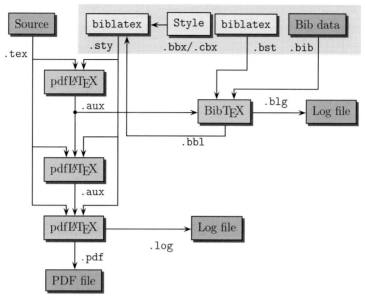

**Figure 9.2:** Bibliography creation with the biblatex package and the BⁱⁱⁱTₑX program.

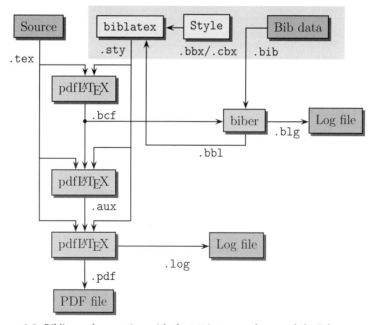

**Figure 9.3:** Bibliography creation with the biblatex package and the Biber program.

the author-year scheme. Furthermore, `biblatex` provides styles for author-title references like the `jurabib` package and alphanumeric references like the `alpha` style. The requested style is passed as a package option to `biblatex`, e. g. `style=authoryear`. You can also configure different citation styles for the references and the bibliography; this is done by using the `citestyle` and `bibstyle` options, instead of `style`. `biblatex` covers many of the citation styles that previously required separate packages. Some of the different styles and examples are listed in Table 9.4.

**Table 9.4:** Some citation styles of biblatex. *angenendt, companion, vazques-de-parga* and *springer* were all referenced; *geer* was also included through \nocite. For authoryear and authortitle, only *angenendt* was referenced.

| citation style | output |
|---|---|
| numeric | [1, 4, 3, 5] |
| numeric-comp | [1, 3–5] |
| numeric-verb | [1]; [4]; [3]; [5] |
| alphabetic | [Ang02; Spr50; GMS94; VLUR93] |
| alphabetic-verb | [Ang02]; [Spr50]; [GMS94]; [VLUR93] |
| authoryear | Angenendt 2002 |
| authortitle | Angenendt, "In Honore Salvatoris" |

```
\usepackage[style=alphabetic,backend=biber]{biblatex} \bibliography{examples}
Aristoteles.~\cite{aristotle:rhetoric,averroes/bland,aristotle:physics,aristotle:poetics}
\printbibliography
```

Aristoteles. [Ari77; Ave82; Ari29; Ari68]

09-03-1

## References

[Ari29]  Aristotle. *Physics.* Trans. by P. H. Wicksteed and F. M. Cornford. New York: G. P. Putnam, 1929.

[Ari68]  Aristotle. *Poetics.* Ed. by D. W. Lucas. Clarendon Aristotle. Oxford: Clarendon Press, 1968.

[Ari77]  Aristotle. *The Rhetoric of Aristotle with a commentary by the late Edward Meredith Cope.* Ed. and comm. by Edward Meredith Cope. 3 vols. Cambridge University Press, 1877.

[Ave82]  Averroes. *The Epistle on the Possibility of Conjunction with the Active Intellect by Ibn Rushd with the Commentary of Moses Narboni.* Ed. and trans. by Kalman P. Bland. Moreshet: Studies in Jewish History, Literature and Thought 7. New York: Jewish Theological Seminary of America, 1982.

### 9.3.1 Structure of the BibTeX file

The BibTeX database for `biblatex` is in principle similar to a normal BibTeX database. However, it introduces a number of new fields (e. g. `bookauthor`), which are either used by the adapted styles already or are available to be used in adapted styles. The fields range from `redactor` for the editor to `shorthand` for an abbreviation for the citation and to `subtitle` for subtitles.

We can't cover all the new fields here, but will focus on those that are of special interest to the arts. You can find additional information in the `biblatex` documentation. [15]

biblatex distinguishes between different kinds of fields:
- Text fields, like title, where the contents are output as they are.
- Range fields, like page or year, where a simple dash (-) is replaced by an en dash (LATEX input --, output –).
- Numeric fields, like edition or month, which are either output as a number or as a word.
- Date fields, like date or urldate for a last-visited date, which require the special input format YYYY-MM-DD, e. g. 2011-03-17 for 17th March 2011.
- Verbatim fields, like url or doi, whose content may contain certain special characters, e. g. underscores (_) or tildes (~).

Furthermore, there are key fields that may contain a special fixed value. An example of this is pagination, which may contain the values page, column, line, verse, paragraph or none. This field determines the type of pagination to be used when citing something. Usually, this is pages (page), but some encyclopaedias for example are counted by column (column). For poems, a verse could be referenced. In law publications, paragraphs can be referred to. If pagination is set accordingly, the language-dependent specification or its abbreviation in the optional argument of \cite selects the type. If none is selected, no pagination specification is output.

Apart from the fields mentioned above, there are also list fields that consist of several units separated by and. In traditional BIBTEX, this type of field is only available for author and editor; in biblatex this corresponds to the name lists, which can be split into four parts – first name, name prefix (e. g. "of"), last name and name suffix (e. g. "Senior"). There is also an additional type of list field in biblatex – literal lists. Fields of this type are a restricted version of the name lists that are only split on the "and". The fields publisher, institution (or school), organization and location (or address) are such literal lists. The location of a publication should therefore be given as follows.

```
location = {New York and Toronto and Berlin and Tokyo and Madrid},
```

The advantage is that the number of places (publishers, institutions etc.) to be output can be limited through the maxitems and minitems package options. The default values are 3 for maxitems and 1 for minitems. The example above would be output as "New York etc." with the default setting. biblatex also recognizes commas as separators, but the maxitems/minitems functionality is not available for it. For name lists (authors/publishers), the options are called maxnames and minnames. They can be defined globally (for all bibliographies in a document) as well as separately for each individual bibliography.

Apart from the new fields, there are also entry types that aren't available in standard BIBTEX. These are:
- @collection for books with self-contained entries that usually don't have an author, but one or more publishers, e. g. encyclopaedias or anthologies.
- @online for internet sources; the types @electronic and @www can be used synonymously. The url field is also available in other entry types – articles that are also published online should be added using @article whereas @online is meant for websites, blogs, etc.
- @patent for patents.
- @periodical for individual issues of journals (e. g. special issues). If they have a separate title, you can specify it in the issuetitle field. This type of entry is used in

a different way than in jurabib, where @periodical is meant for essays in journals that are cited by volume and not by year. In biblatex this is possible with @article entries.

biblatex defines a number of entry types that are not used in the standard styles. They are either ignored or refer to a different entry type. Examples are @reference and @inreference, which represent encyclopaedias and articles in encyclopaedias. The standard styles treat these types like @collection and @incollection. These entry types can be used and adapted in custom bibliography styles. You can find a complete list of these types in the biblatex documentation. [15]

**URLs and last-visited dates**

The increasing number of online sources usually implies specifying the last date when the source was checked. biblatex supports this through the field entry urldate, which expects a specification in journal notation: YYYY-MM-DD.

```
@Online{biblatex,
  sorttitle  = {biblatex package},
  author     = {Lehman, Philipp},
  title      = {\texttt{The biblatex package}},
  subtitle   = {{Programmable} bibliographies and citations},
  version    = {1.4c},
  date       = {2011-05-12},
  url        = {http://mirror.ctan.org/macros/latex/biblatex/doc/biblatex.pdf},
  urldate    = {2011-06-04},
  annotation = {The official \texttt{biblatex} documentation.}
}
```

09-03-2

... biblatex. [1]

# References

[1] Philipp Lehman. *The biblatex package. Program-mable bibliographies and citations.* Version 1.4c. 12th May 2011. URL: http://mirror.ctan.org/macros/latex/biblatex/doc/biblatex.pdf (visited on 04/06/2011).

```
\usepackage[backend=biber]{biblatex}
\bibliography{demo11}

\ldots\
\texttt{biblatex}.~\cite{biblatex}

\printbibliography
```

## 9.3.2  Customization

It is often necessary to customize the display in minor ways, but these customizations usually can't be done through package options. Instead, you have to redefine the commands in the preamble. These changes and the package options can also be put into the biblatex.cfg file; this applies them globally, so they don't have to be made in each document separately. All the definitions are in biblatex.def and the files with the extensions .bbx, .cbc and .lbx.

**Customize individual elements**

As an example, we want to stop titles of journal articles being enclosed in quotation marks. The titles in the references are formatted by the field format "citetitle", which is defined in

`.biblatex.def` as follows.

```
\DeclareFieldFormat{citetitle}{\mkbibemph{#1}}
\DeclareFieldFormat[article]{citetitle}{\mkbibquote{#1}}
```

Titles in references are typeset in italics and titles of literature of type `@article` are enclosed in quotation marks. The `\mkbibemph` command emphasizes the text like `\emph`; the `\mkbibquote` command from the `biblatex` package is based on `\enquote` from the `csquotes` package [14], *csquotes* which is strongly recommended if `biblatex` is used. These commands can be changed to omit the italics or the quotation marks.

```
\DeclareFieldFormat{citetitle}{#1\isdot}
\DeclareFieldFormat[article]{citetitle}{#1\isdot}
```

Similar to `@article`, you can change the "citetitle" of other types as well. The display in the bibliography, however, is controlled by other field formats, though these can also be changed.

```
\DeclareFieldFormat{title}{#1\isdot}
\DeclareFieldFormat[article]{title}{#1\isdot}
(*\ldots*)
```

You can change the appearance of all other fields in the same manner; however, it is worth noting that not all fields differentiate between reference and bibliography.

## Display and order of names

The formatting of names is not controlled through `\DeclareFieldFormat`, in contrast to the other fields of a BibTeX entry. This is mostly because of the complexity of displaying names, which can be split into four components, each of which have a separate command. Author names in small caps can be achieved through

```
\renewcommand*{\mkbibnamelast}[1]{\textsc{#1}}
```

You can customize first names (`\mkbibnamefirst`), name prefixes (`\mkbibnameprefix`) and name suffixes (`\mkbibnameaffix`) in a similar way to the last name (`\mkbibnamelast`).
To change the order of the names, e. g. "lastName, f." instead of "firstName lastName" in references, you must adapt the name formats. The name format "labelname" is responsible for references.

```
\DeclareNameFormat{labelname}{%
  \ifcase\value{uniquename}%
    \usebibmacro{name:last}{#1}{#3}{#5}{#7}%
  \or
    \ifuseprefix
      {\usebibmacro{name:first-last}{#1}{#4}{#5}{#8}}
      {\usebibmacro{name:first-last}{#1}{#4}{#6}{#8}}%
  \or
    \usebibmacro{name:first-last}{#1}{#3}{#5}{#7}%
  \fi
  \usebibmacro{name:andothers}}
```

Explaining all the details is beyond the scope of this book, but it is obvious that different commands are called. The names ("name:last", "name:first-last" and "name:last-first") already indicate that they are responsible for the order of the names. These commands take four arguments from the eight possible arguments below:

| #1 last name | #2 last name (initials) | #3 first name |
| #4 first name (initials) | #5 name prefix | #6 name prefix (initials) |
| #7 name suffix | #8 name suffix (initials) | |

To reverse the order in the literature references and abbreviate first names (i.e. "lastName, f."), you would use the following definition:

```
\DeclareNameFormat{labelname}{\ifuseprefix
    {\usebibmacro{name:last-first}{#1}{#4}{#5}{#8}}
    {\usebibmacro{name:last-first}{#1}{#4}{#6}{#8}}%
  \usebibmacro{name:andothers}}
```

The bibliography uses the "sortname" name format; in all other cases, the "default" name format is used. The name formats are, like the field formats, defined in the biblatex.def file.

## 9.3.3  biblatex – examples

The BibTeX program was used to sort the entries. The example file examples.bib, which is included with the biblatex package, was used as literature database. The first and the last references are the same so that the behaviour of the style files with multiple references can be seen. The current list of biblatex styles is given in Table 9.5. These styles usually have additional options to enable additional forms of output; corresponding descriptions can be found in the documentation. Note that if you use language-dependent fields, there may be problems if the language wasn't defined through the document class.

Table 9.5: Summary of packages that provide additional styles for biblatex.

| style | description | example |
| --- | --- | --- |
| apa | American Psychological Association | 09-03-3 |
| authoryear-icomp-tt | authoryear-comp and authoryear-ibid | 09-03-4 |
| chem-angew | Applied Chemistry journal | 09-03-5 |
| chem-biochem | Biochemistry journal | 09-03-6 |
| chicago | Chicago Manual of Style | 09-03-7 |
| footnote-dw | full citation as footnote | 09-03-8 |
| authoryear-dw | author-year style | 09-03-9 |
| historian | default | 09-03-10 |
| jura | law | 09-03-11 |
| mla | Modern Language Association | 09-03-12 |
| nature | Nature journal | 09-03-13 |
| science | Science journal | 09-03-14 |
| historische-zeitschrift | | 09-03-15 |

**American Psychological Association – `style=apa`**

A style by Philip Kime for publications in the APA style, which is in widespread use.

```
\usepackage[style=apa,backend=biber]{biblatex}
\DeclareLanguageMapping{american}{american-apa}
\bibliography{examples}
\ldots, die Verweise.~%
\cite{shore}; \cite{averroes/bland}; \cite{brandt}; \cite{ctan};
\cite{jaffe}; \cite{kant:kpv}; \cite{geer}; \cite{shore}
%@article: @book: @incollection: @online: @collection: @inbook: @thesis: @article:
\printbibliography
```

..., die Verweise. Shore, 1991; Averroes, 1982; Brandt and Hoffmann, 1987; "CTAN," 2006; Jaffé, 1885–1888; Kant, 1968; Geer, 1985; Shore, 1991

09-03-3

# References

Averroes. (1982). *The epistle on the possibility of conjunction with the active intellect by ibn rushd with the commentary of moses narboni* (K. P. Bland, Ed. & Trans.). Moreshet: Studies in Jewish History, Literature and Thought. New York: Jewish Theological Seminary of America.

Brandt, A. von, & Hoffmann, E. (1987). Die nordischen Länder von der Mitte des 11. Jahrhunderts bis 1448. In F. Seibt (Ed.), *Europa im Hoch- und Spätmittelalter* (2, pp. 884–917). Handbuch der europäischen Geschichte. Stuttgart: Klett-Cotta.

CTAN. (2006). Ctan: The comprehensive tex archive network. (2006). Retrieved 1 October 2009, from http://www.ctan.org

Geer, I. de. (1985). *Earl, saint, bishop, skald – and music: The orkney earldom of the twelfth century. a musicological study.* (Doctoral dissertation, Uppsala Universitet, Uppsala).

Jaffé, P. (Ed.). (1885–1888). *Regesta pontificum romanorum ab condita ecclesia ad annum post christum natum* MCXCVIII. Leipzig,

Kant, I. (1968). Kritik der praktischen Vernunft. In *Kants Werke. Akademie Textausgabe:Vol. 5. Kritik der praktischen Vernunft. Kritik der Urtheilskraft* (pp. 1–163). Berlin: Walter de Gruyter.

Shore, B. (1991, March). Twice-born, once conceived: Meaning construction and cultural cognition. *American Anthropologist.* New ser., *93*(1), 9–27.

`style=authoryear-icomp-tt`

An author-year style by Thomas Titz, with compact repeated citations and an ibidem algorithm.

```
\usepackage[style=authoryear-icomp-tt,backend=biber]{biblatex}  \bibliography{examples}
\ldots, the references.~%
\cite{shore}; \cite{averroes/bland}; \cite{brandt}; \cite{ctan};
\cite{jaffe}; \cite{kant:kpv}; \cite{geer}; \cite{shore}
%@article: @book: @incollection: @online: @collection: @inbook: @thesis: @article:
\printbibliography
```

09-03-4

..., the references. Shore 19911991; Averroes 19821982; Brandt and Hoffmann 19871987; CTAN 20062006; Jaffé 1885–18881885–1888; Kant 19681968; Geer 19851985; Shore 19911991

# References

Averroes (1982). *The Epistle on the Possibility of Conjunction with the Active Intellect by Ibn Rushd with the Commentary of Moses Narboni.* Ed. and trans. by Kalman P. Bland. Moreshet: Studies in Jewish History, Literature and Thought 7. New York: Jewish Theological Seminary of America.

Brandt, Ahasver von and Erich Hoffmann (1987). 'Die nordischen Länder von der Mitte des 11. Jahrhunderts bis 1448'. In: *Europa im Hoch- und Spätmittelalter.* Ed. by Ferdinand Seibt. Handbuch der europäischen Geschichte 2. Stuttgart: Klett-Cotta, pp. 884–917.

CTAN (2006). *CTAN. The Comprehensive TeX Archive Network.* URL: http://www.ctan.org (visited on 01/10/2009).

Geer, Ingrid de (1985). 'Earl, Saint, Bishop, Skald – and Music. The Orkney Earldom of the Twelfth Century. A Musicological Study'. PhD thesis. Uppsala: Uppsala Universitet.

Jaffé, Philipp, ed. (1885–1888). *Regesta Pontificum Romanorum ab condita ecclesia ad annum post Christum natum* MCXCVIII. 2nd ed. 2 vols. Leipzig.

Kant, Immanuel (1968). 'Kritik der praktischen Vernunft'. In: *Kants Werke. Akademie Textausgabe.* Vol. 5: *Kritik der praktischen Vernunft. Kritik der Urtheilskraft.* Berlin: Walter de Gruyter, pp. 1–163.

Shore, Bradd (Mar. 1991). 'Twice-Born, Once Conceived. Meaning Construction and Cultural Cognition'. In: *American Anthropologist.* New ser. 93.1, pp. 9–27.

**Applied Chemistry journal – `style=chem-angew`**

A style by Joseph Wright.

```
\usepackage[style=chem-angew,backend=biber]{biblatex} \bibliography{examples}
\ldots, the references.~%
\cite{shore}; \cite{averroes/bland}; \cite{brandt}; \cite{ctan};
\cite{jaffe}; \cite{kant:kpv}; \cite{geer}; \cite{shore}
%@article: @book: @incollection: @online: @collection: @inbook: @thesis: @article:
\printbibliography
```

..., the references. [1]; [2]; [3]; [4]; [5]; [6]; [7]; [1]

09-03-5

# References

[1]   B. Shore, *American Anthropologist* **1991**, *93*, 9–27.

[2]   Averroes, *The Epistle on the Possibility of Conjunction with the Active Intellect by Ibn Rushd with the Commentary of Moses Narboni* (Ed.: K. P. Bland), Jewish Theological Seminary of America, New York, **1982**.

[3]   A. von Brandt, E. Hoffmann in *Europa im Hoch- und Spätmittelalter* (Ed.: F. Seibt), Klett-Cotta, Stuttgart, **1987**, pp. 884–917.

[4]   CTAN, The Comprehensive TeX Archive Network, 2006, http://www.ctan.org (visited on 01/10/2009).

[5]   *Regesta Pontificum Romanorum ab condita ecclesia ad annum post Christum natum* MCX-CVIII (Ed.: P. Jaffé), Leipzig, 2nd ed., **1885–1888**.

[6]   I. Kant in, *Kants Werke. Akademie Textausgabe, Vol. 5*, Walter de Gruyter, Berlin, **1968**, pp. 1–163.

[7]   I. de Geer, PhD thesis, Uppsala Universitet, Uppsala, **1985**.

**Biochemistry journal – `style=chem-biochem`**

A style by Joseph Wright.

```
\usepackage[style=chem-biochem,backend=biber]{biblatex} \bibliography{examples}
\ldots, the references.~%
\cite{shore}; \cite{averroes/bland}; \cite{brandt}; \cite{ctan};
\cite{jaffe}; \cite{kant:kpv}; \cite{geer}; \cite{shore}
%@article: @book: @incollection: @online: @collection: @inbook: @thesis: @article:
\printbibliography
```

09-03-6

..., the references. (*1*); (*2*); (*3*); (*4*); (*5*); (*6*); (*7*); (*1*)

# References

(1)   Shore, B. (1991). Twice-Born, Once Conceived (Meaning Construction and Cultural Cognition). *American Anthropologist*, *93*, 9–27.

(2)   Averroes *The Epistle on the Possibility of Conjunction with the Active Intellect by Ibn Rushd with the Commentary of Moses Narboni*; Bland, K. P., Ed.; Moreshet: Studies in Jewish History, Literature and Thought 7; Jewish Theological Seminary of America: New York, 1982.

(3)   Brandt, A. von, Hoffmann, E. In *Europa im Hoch- und Spätmittelalter*; Seibt, F., Ed.; Handbuch der europäischen Geschichte 2; Klett-Cotta: Stuttgart, 1987, pp 884–917.

(4)   CTAN (The Comprehensive TeX Archive Network). http://www.ctan.org (accessed 1st Oct. 2009).

(5)   *Regesta Pontificum Romanorum ab condita ecclesia ad annum post Christum natum* MCX-CVIII, 2nd ed.; Jaffé, P., Ed.; Leipzig, 1885–1888.

(6)   Kant, I. In *Kants Werke. Akademie Textausgabe*; Walter de Gruyter: Berlin, 1968; Vol. 5, pp 1–163.

(7)   Geer, I. de Earl, Saint, Bishop, Skald – and Music. Ph.D. Thesis, Uppsala Universitet, Uppsala, 1985.

### Chicago Manual of Style – `style=biblatex-chicago`

A style by David Fussner, especially for the arts, which follows the 15th edition of the Chicago Manual of Style.

```
\usepackage[strict,babel=other,bibencoding=inputenc,backend=biber]{biblatex-chicago}
\bibliography{examplesA}
\ldots, the references.~\cite{shore}; \cite{averroes/bland}; \cite{brandt};
\cite{ctan}; \cite{jaffe}; \cite{kant:kpv}; \cite{geer}; \cite{shore}
%@article: @book: @incollection: @online: @collection: @inbook: @thesis: @article:
\printbibliography
```

..., the references. Bradd Shore, "Twice-Born, Once Conceived: Meaning Construction and Cultural Cognition," *American Anthropologist*, n.s., 93, no. 1 (March 1991): 9–27; Averroes, *The Epistle on the Possibility of Conjunction with the Active Intellect by Ibn Rushd with the Commentary of Moses Narboni*, ed. and trans. Kalman P. Bland, Moreshet: Studies in Jewish History, Literature and Thought 7 (New York: Jewish Theological Seminary of America, 1982); Ahasver von Brandt and Erich Hoffmann, "Die nordischen Länder von der Mitte des 11. Jahrhunderts bis 1448," in *Europa im Hoch- und Spätmittelalter*, ed. Ferdinand Seibt, Handbuch der europäischen Geschichte 2 (Stuttgart: Klett-Cotta, 1987), 884–917; "CTAN: The Comprehensive TeX Archive Network," 2006, `http://www.ctan.org` (accessed October 1, 2009); Philipp Jaffé, ed., *Regesta Pontificum Romanorum ab condita ecclesia ad annum post Christum natum* MCX-CVIII, 2nd ed., 2 vols. (Leipzig, 1885–1888); Immanuel Kant, "Kritik der praktischen Vernunft," in *Kritik der praktischen Vernunft. Kritik der Urtheilskraft*, vol. 5 of *Kants Werke. Akademie Textausgabe* (Berlin: Walter de Gruyter, 1968), 1–163; Ingrid de Geer, "Earl, Saint, Bishop, Skald – and Music: The Orkney Earldom of the Twelfth Century. A Musicological Study" (PhD diss., Uppsala Universitet, 1985); Shore, "Twice-Born, Once Conceived"

09-03-7

## References

Averroes. *The Epistle on the Possibility of Conjunction with the Active Intellect by Ibn Rushd with the Commentary of Moses Narboni*. Edited and translated by Kalman P. Bland. Moreshet: Studies in Jewish History, Literature and Thought 7. New York: Jewish Theological Seminary of America, 1982.

Brandt, Ahasver von, and Erich Hoffmann. "Die nordischen Länder von der Mitte des 11. Jahrhunderts bis 1448." In *Europa im Hoch- und Spätmittelalter*, edited by Ferdinand Seibt, 884–917. Handbuch der europäischen Geschichte 2. Stuttgart: Klett-Cotta, 1987.

"CTAN: The Comprehensive TeX Archive Network." 2006. `http://www.ctan.org` (accessed October 1, 2009).

Geer, Ingrid de. "Earl, Saint, Bishop, Skald – and Music: The Orkney Earldom of the Twelfth Century. A Musicological Study." PhD diss., Uppsala Universitet, 1985.

Jaffé, Philipp, ed. *Regesta Pontificum Romanorum ab condita ecclesia ad annum post Christum natum* MCX-CVIII. 2nd ed. 2 vols. Leipzig, 1885–1888.

Kant, Immanuel. "Kritik der praktischen Vernunft." In *Kritik der praktischen Vernunft. Kritik der Urtheilskraft*, vol. 5 of *Kants Werke. Akademie Textausgabe*, 1–163. Berlin: Walter de Gruyter, 1968.

Shore, Bradd. "Twice-Born, Once Conceived: Meaning Construction and Cultural Cognition." *American Anthropologist*, n.s., 93, no. 1 (March 1991): 9–27.

### Footnotes – `style=footnote-dw`

A style by Dominik Waßenhoven for literature references in footnotes. The style is similar to the `verbose-inote` style, which is part of `biblatex`. In repeated references it points to the number of the footnote of the first reference.

```
\usepackage[style=footnote-dw,backend=biber]{biblatex} \bibliography{examples}
\ldots, the references.~%
A\footcite{shore}; B\footcite{averroes/bland}; C\footcite{brandt}; D\footcite{ctan};
E\footcite{jaffe}; F\footcite{kant:kpv}; G\footcite{geer}; H\footcite{shore}
%@article: @book: @incollection: @online: @collection: @inbook: @thesis: @article:
\printbibliography
```

09-03-8

..., the references. A[1]; B[2]; C[3]; D[4]; E[5]; F[6]; G[7]; H[8]

## References

Averroes: The Epistle on the Possibility of Conjunction with the Active Intellect by Ibn Rushd with the Commentary of Moses Narboni, ed. and trans. by Kalman P. Bland (Moreshet: Studies in Jewish History, Literature and Thought 7), New York 1982.

Brandt, Ahasver von and Erich Hoffmann: Die nordischen Länder von der Mitte des 11. Jahrhunderts bis 1448, in: Ferdinand Seibt (ed.): Europa im Hoch- und Spätmittelalter (Handbuch der europäischen Geschichte 2), Stuttgart 1987, pp. 884–917.

CTAN. The Comprehensive TeX Archive Network, 2006, URL: http://www.ctan.org (visited on 01/10/2009).

Geer, Ingrid de: Earl, Saint, Bishop, Skald – and Music. The Orkney Earldom of the Twelfth Century. A Musicological Study, PhD thesis, Uppsala: Uppsala Universitet, 1985.

Jaffé, Philipp (ed.): Regesta Pontificum Romanorum ab condita ecclesia ad annum post Christum natum MCXCVIII, 2nd ed., 2 vols., Leipzig 1885–1888.

Kant, Immanuel: Kritik der praktischen Vernunft, in: idem: Kants Werke. Akademie Textausgabe, vol. 5: Kritik der praktischen Vernunft. Kritik der Urtheilskraft, Berlin 1968, pp. 1–163.

Shore, Bradd: Twice-Born, Once Conceived. Meaning Construction and Cultural Cognition, in: American Anthropologist, new ser. 93.1 (Mar. 1991), pp. 9–27.

---

[1] Bradd Shore: Twice-Born, Once Conceived. Meaning Construction and Cultural Cognition, in: American Anthropologist, new ser. 93.1 (Mar. 1991), pp. 9–27.

[2] Averroes: The Epistle on the Possibility of Conjunction with the Active Intellect by Ibn Rushd with the Commentary of Moses Narboni, ed. and trans. by Kalman P. Bland (Moreshet: Studies in Jewish History, Literature and Thought 7), New York 1982.

[3] Ahasver von Brandt/Erich Hoffmann: Die nordischen Länder von der Mitte des 11. Jahrhunderts bis 1448, in: Ferdinand Seibt (ed.): Europa im Hoch- und Spätmittelalter (Handbuch der europäischen Geschichte 2), Stuttgart 1987, pp. 884–917.

[4] CTAN. The Comprehensive TeX Archive Network, 2006, URL: http://www.ctan.org (visited on 01/10/2009).

[5] Philipp Jaffé (ed.): Regesta Pontificum Romanorum ab condita ecclesia ad annum post Christum natum MCXCVIII, 2nd ed., 2 vols., Leipzig 1885–1888.

[6] Immanuel Kant: Kritik der praktischen Vernunft, in: idem: Kants Werke. Akademie Textausgabe, vol. 5: Kritik der praktischen Vernunft. Kritik der Urtheilskraft, Berlin 1968, pp. 1–163.

[7] Ingrid de Geer: Earl, Saint, Bishop, Skald – and Music. The Orkney Earldom of the Twelfth Century. A Musicological Study, PhD thesis, Uppsala: Uppsala Universitet, 1985.

[8] Shore: Twice-Born, Once Conceived (see n. 1).

### Author-title – `style=authortitle-dw`

A style by Dominik Waßenhoven for the author-title citation style. It is an adaptation of the style of the same name in biblatex (`authortitle`). Additional options enable special handling of repeated citations and references with the same authors.

```
\usepackage[style=authortitle-dw,backend=biber]{biblatex} \bibliography{examples}
\ldots, the references.~%
\cite{shore}; \cite{averroes/bland}; \cite{brandt}; \cite{ctan};
\cite{jaffe}; \cite{kant:kpv}; \cite{geer}; \cite{shore}
%@article: @book: @incollection: @online: @collection: @inbook: @thesis: @article:
\printbibliography
```

..., the references. Shore: Twice-Born, Once Conceived; Averroes: Possibility of Conjunction; Brandt/Hoffmann: Die nordischen Länder; CTAN; Jaffé (ed.): Regesta Pontificum Romanorum; Kant: Kritik der praktischen Vernunft; Geer: Earl, Saint, Bishop, Skald – and Music; Shore: Twice-Born, Once Conceived

09-03-9

## References

Averroes: The Epistle on the Possibility of Conjunction with the Active Intellect by Ibn Rushd with the Commentary of Moses Narboni, ed. and trans. by Kalman P. Bland (Moreshet: Studies in Jewish History, Literature and Thought 7), New York 1982.

Brandt, Ahasver von and Erich Hoffmann: Die nordischen Länder von der Mitte des 11. Jahrhunderts bis 1448, in: Ferdinand Seibt (ed.): Europa im Hoch- und Spätmittelalter (Handbuch der europäischen Geschichte 2), Stuttgart 1987, pp. 884–917.

CTAN. The Comprehensive TeX Archive Network, 2006, URL: http://www.ctan.org (visited on 01/10/2009).

Geer, Ingrid de: Earl, Saint, Bishop, Skald – and Music. The Orkney Earldom of the Twelfth Century. A Musicological Study, PhD thesis, Uppsala: Uppsala Universitet, 1985.

Jaffé, Philipp (ed.): Regesta Pontificum Romanorum ab condita ecclesia ad annum post Christum natum MCXCVIII, 2nd ed., 2 vols., Leipzig 1885–1888.

Kant, Immanuel: Kritik der praktischen Vernunft, in: idem: Kants Werke. Akademie Textausgabe, vol. 5: Kritik der praktischen Vernunft. Kritik der Urtheilskraft, Berlin 1968, pp. 1–163.

Shore, Bradd: Twice-Born, Once Conceived. Meaning Construction and Cultural Cognition, in: American Anthropologist, new ser. 93.1 (Mar. 1991), pp. 9–27.

## History – style=historian

Sander Gliboff provides a style that is based on the Turabian Manual for Writers, a variant of the Chicago Manual of Style.

```
\usepackage[style=historian,backend=biber]{biblatex} \bibliography{examples}
\ldots, the references.~%
\cite{shore}; \cite{averroes/bland}; \cite{brandt}; \cite{ctan};
\cite{jaffe}; \cite{kant:kpv};        \cite{geer};    \cite{shore}
%@article: @book: @incollection: @online: @collection: @inbook: @thesis: @article:
\printbibliography
```

09-03-10

..., the references. Bradd Shore. "Twice-Born, Once Conceived: Meaning Construction and Cultural Cognition." *American Anthropologist,* new ser., 93, no. 1 (Mar. 1991): 9–27; Averroes. *The Epistle on the Possibility of Conjunction with the Active Intellect by Ibn Rushd with the Commentary of Moses Narboni.* Trans. and ed. Kalman P. Bland. New York: Jewish Theological Seminary of America, 1982; Ahasver von Brandt and Erich Hoffmann. "Die nordischen Länder von der Mitte des 11. Jahrhunderts bis 1448." In *Europa im Hoch- und Spätmittelalter,* ed. Ferdinand Seibt, 884–917. Stuttgart: Klett-Cotta, 1987; "CTAN: The Comprehensive TeX Archive Network." 2006. URL: http://www.ctan.org (accessed 10/01/2009); Philipp Jaffé, ed. *Regesta Pontificum Romanorum ab condita ecclesia ad annum post Christum natum* MCXCVIII. 2 vols. 2nd ed. Leipzig, 1885–1888; Immanuel Kant. "Kritik der praktischen Vernunft." In *Kritik der praktischen Vernunft. Kritik der Urtheilskraft.* Vol. 5 of *Kants Werke. Akademie Textausgabe,* 1–163. Berlin: Walter de Gruyter, 1968; Ingrid de Geer. "Earl, Saint, Bishop, Skald – and Music: The Orkney Earldom of the Twelfth Century. A Musicological Study." PhD diss., Uppsala Universitet, 1985; Shore, "Twice-Born, Once Conceived "

## References

Averroes. *The Epistle on the Possibility of Conjunction with the Active Intellect by Ibn Rushd with the Commentary of Moses Narboni.* Translated and edited by Kalman P. Bland. New York: Jewish Theological Seminary of America, 1982.

Brandt, Ahasver von and Erich Hoffmann. "Die nordischen Länder von der Mitte des 11. Jahrhunderts bis 1448." In *Europa im Hoch- und Spätmittelalter,* edited by Ferdinand Seibt, 884–917. Stuttgart: Klett-Cotta, 1987.

"CTAN: The Comprehensive TeX Archive Network." 2006. URL: http://www.ctan.org (accessed 10/01/2009).

Geer, Ingrid de. "Earl, Saint, Bishop, Skald – and Music: The Orkney Earldom of the Twelfth Century. A Musicological Study." PhD diss., Uppsala Universitet, 1985.

Jaffé, Philipp, editor. *Regesta Pontificum Romanorum ab condita ecclesia ad annum post Christum natum* MCXCVIII. 2 vols. 2nd ed. Leipzig, 1885–1888.

Kant, Immanuel. "Kritik der praktischen Vernunft." In *Kritik der praktischen Vernunft. Kritik der Urtheilskraft.* Vol. 5 of *Kants Werke. Akademie Textausgabe,* 1–163. Berlin: Walter de Gruyter, 1968.

Shore, Bradd. "Twice-Born, Once Conceived: Meaning Construction and Cultural Cognition." *American Anthropologist,* new series, 93, no. 1 (March 1991): 9–27.

### Law – `style=biblatex-jura`

Ben E. Hard provides a style for German law citations according to the specifications of the Nomos publisher.

```
\usepackage[style=biblatex-jura,backend=biber]{biblatex} \bibliography{examples}
\ldots, die Verweise.~%
A\footcite[1]{shore}; B\footcite[3]{averroes/bland}; C\footcite[5]{brandt};
E\footcite[77]{jaffe}; F\footcite[10]{kant:kpv};
G\footcite[9]{geer}; H\footcite[123][Abs.3 S.4]{shore}
\printbibliography
```

..., die Verweise. A[1]; B[2]; C[3]; E[4]; F[5]; G[6]; H[7]

09-03-11

## References

*Averroes*, The Epistle on the Possibility of Conjunction with the Active Intellect by Ibn Rushd with the Commentary of Moses Narboni, ed. and trans. by *Kalman P. Bland* (Moreshet: Studies in Jewish History, Literature and Thought 7), New York 1982.

*Ahasver von Brandt* and *Erich Hoffmann*, Die nordischen Länder von der Mitte des 11. Jahrhunderts bis 1448, in: *Ferdinand Seibt* (ed.), Europa im Hoch- und Spätmittelalter (Handbuch der europäischen Geschichte 2), Stuttgart 1987, pp. 884–917.

*Ingrid de Geer*, Earl, Saint, Bishop, Skald – and Music. The Orkney Earldom of the Twelfth Century. A Musicological Study, PhD thesis, Uppsala: Uppsala Universitet, 1985.

*Philipp Jaffé* (ed.), Regesta Pontificum Romanorum ab condita ecclesia ad annum post Christum natum MCXCVIII, 2nd ed.2 vols., Leipzig 1885–1888.

*Immanuel Kant*, Kritik der praktischen Vernunft, in: *idem*: Kants Werke. Akademie Textausgabe, vol. 5: Kritik der praktischen Vernunft. Kritik der Urtheilskraft, Berlin 1968, pp. 1–163.

*Bradd Shore*, Twice-Born, Once Conceived. Meaning Construction and Cultural Cognition, in: American Anthropologist, new ser. 93.1 Mar. 1991, pp. 9–27.

---

[1] *Shore*, Twice-Born, Once Conceived, American Anthropologist, 1991, (1).

[2] *Averroes*, Possibility of Conjunction, p. 3.

[3] *Brandt/Hoffmann*, Die nordischen Länder, in: *Seibt* (ed.), Europa im Hoch- und Spätmittelalter, (5).

[4] *Jaffé*, Regesta Pontificum Romanorum, p. 77.

[5] *Kant*, Kritik der praktischen Vernunft, in: *idem*: Kritik der praktischen Vernunft. Kritik der Urtheilskraft, vol. 5, p. 10.

[6] *Geer*, Earl, Saint, Bishop, Skald – and Music, p. 9.

[7] 123 *Shore*, Twice-Born, Once Conceived, American Anthropologist, 1991, (Abs.3 S.4).

**Modern Language Association – `style=mla`**

This style by James Clawson realizes the specifications of the MLA. This style is an author-page style – only author names and page numbers are used unless several works by the same author are cited, in which case the title of the cited work is added as well. The MLA style could therefore also be called an author-title style. Online sources can't be used with this.

```
\usepackage[style=mla,backend=biber]{biblatex}
\usepackage{hyperref}
 \bibliography{examples}
\ldots, the references.~%
A\autocite{shore}; B\autocite{averroes/bland}; C\autocite{brandt}; %D\autocite{ctan};
E\autocite{jaffe}; F\autocite{westfahl:frontier}; G\autocite{geer}; H\autocite{shore}
%@article: @book: @incollection: @online: @collection: @inbook: @thesis: @article:
\printbibliography
```

09-03-12

..., the references. A(Shore); B(Averroes); C(Brandt and Hoffmann); E(Jaffé); F(Westfahl); G(Geer); H(Shore)

# Works Cited

Averroes. *The Epistle on the Possibility of Conjunction with the Active Intellect by Ibn Rushd with the Commentary of Moses Narboni*. Ed. and trans. Kalman P. Bland. New York: Jewish Theological Seminary of America, 1982. Print. Moreshet: Studies in Jewish History, Literature and Thought 7.

Brandt, Ahasver von and Erich Hoffmann. "Die nordischen Länder von der Mitte des 11. Jahrhunderts bis 1448." *Europa im Hoch- und Spätmittelalter*. Ed. Ferdinand Seibt. Handbuch der europäischen Geschichte 2. Stuttgart: Klett-Cotta, 1987. 884–917. Print. Handbuch der europäischen Geschichte 2.

Geer, Ingrid de. "Earl, Saint, Bishop, Skald – and Music: The Orkney Earldom of the Twelfth Century. A Musicological Study." Diss. Uppsala Universitet, 1985. Print.

Jaffé, Philipp, ed. *Regesta Pontificum Romanorum ab condita ecclesia ad annum post Christum natum* MCXCVIII. 2nd ed. 2 vols. Leipzig, 1885–1888. Print.

Shore, Bradd. "Twice-Born, Once Conceived: Meaning Construction and Cultural Cognition." *American Anthropologist* ns 93.1 (Mar. 1991): 9–27. Print. Ns.

Westfahl, Gary, ed. *Space and Beyond: The Frontier Theme in Science Fiction*. Westport, Conn. and London: Greenwood, 2000. Print.

### Nature journal – `style=nature`

This style by Joseph Wright allows numeric references with a bibliography, according to the specifications of the Nature journal.

```
\usepackage[style=nature,backend=biber]{biblatex} \bibliography{examples}
\ldots, the references.~%
A\autocite{shore}; B\autocite{averroes/bland}; C\autocite{brandt}; D\autocite{ctan};
E\autocite{jaffe}; F\autocite{kant:kpv}; G\autocite{geer}; H\autocite{shore}
%@article: @book: @incollection: @online: @collection: @inbook: @thesis: %@article:
\printbibliography
```

..., the references. A[1]; B[2]; C[3]; D[4]; E[5]; F[6]; G[7]; H[1]

09-03-13

# References

1. Shore, B. Twice-Born, Once Conceived. Meaning Construction and Cultural Cognition. *American Anthropologist. newseries* **93**, 9–27 (Mar. 1991).

2. Averroes. *The Epistle on the Possibility of Conjunction with the Active Intellect by Ibn Rushd with the Commentary of Moses Narboni* (ed Bland, K. P.)trans. by Bland, K. P. *Moreshet: Studies in Jewish History, Literature and Thought* 7 (Jewish Theological Seminary of America, New York, 1982).

3. Brandt, A. von & Hoffmann, E. in *Europa im Hoch- und Spätmittelalter* (ed Seibt, F.) *Handbuch der europäischen Geschichte* 2, 884–917 (Klett-Cotta, Stuttgart, 1987).

4. *CTAN. The Comprehensive TeX Archive Network* <http://www.ctan.org> (2006).

5. *Regesta Pontificum Romanorum ab condita ecclesia ad annum post Christum natum* MCXCVIII (ed Jaffé, P.) 2nd ed. 2 vols. (Leipzig, 1885–1888).

6. Kant, I. in. *Kants Werke. Akademie Textausgabe.* **5**: *Kritik der praktischen Vernunft. Kritik der Urtheilskraft* 1–163 (Walter de Gruyter, Berlin, 1968).

7. Geer, I. de. *Earl, Saint, Bishop, Skald – and Music. The Orkney Earldom of the Twelfth Century. A Musicological Study* PhD thesis (Uppsala Universitet, Uppsala, 1985).

### Science journal – `style=science`

This style by Joseph Wright allows numeric references with a bibliography, according to the specifications of the Science journal.

```
\usepackage[style=science,backend=biber]{biblatex} \bibliography{examples}
\ldots, the references.~%
\autocite{shore}; \autocite{averroes/bland}; \autocite{brandt}; \autocite{ctan};
\autocite{jaffe}; \autocite{kant:kpv}; \autocite{geer}; \autocite{shore}
%@article: @book: @incollection: @online: @collection: @inbook: @thesis: @article:
\printbibliography
```

09-03-14   ..., the references. (*1*); (*2*); (*3*); (*4*); (*5*); (*6*); (*7*); (*1*)

# References

1.  B. Shore, *American Anthropologist*, new ser. **93**, 9–27 (Mar. 1991).

2.  Averroes, *The Epistle on the Possibility of Conjunction with the Active Intellect by Ibn Rushd with the Commentary of Moses Narboni*, ed. and trans. by K. P. Bland (Jewish Theological Seminary of America, New York, 1982).

3.  A. von Brandt, E. Hoffmann, in *Europa im Hoch- und Spätmittelalter*, ed. by F. Seibt (Klett-Cotta, Stuttgart, 1987), pp. 884–917.

4.  *CTAN, The Comprehensive TeX Archive Network* (2006; http://www.ctan.org).

5.  P. Jaffé, Ed., *Regesta Pontificum Romanorum ab condita ecclesia ad annum post Christum natum* MCXCVIII, 2 vols. (Leipzig, ed. 2, 1885–1888).

6.  I. Kant, in, *Kants Werke. Akademie Textausgabe*, vol. 5: *Kritik der praktischen Vernunft. Kritik der Urtheilskraft* (Walter de Gruyter, Berlin, 1968), vol. 5, pp. 1–163.

7.  I. de Geer, PhD thesis, Uppsala Universitet, 1985.

## Journal – `style=historische-zeitschrift`

This style by Dominik Waßenhoven is a citation style according to the guidelines of the *Historische Zeitschrift*. The scheme is a full citation for the first reference and "author, short title (like ref. N, p)" for all subsequent references, where p stands for page number.

```
\usepackage[style=historische-zeitschrift,backend=biber]{biblatex}
\bibliography{examples}
\ldots, die Verweise.~A\footcite{shore}; B\footcite{averroes/bland};
C\footcite{brandt}; D\footcite{ctan}; E\footcite{jaffe}; F\footcite{kant:kpv};
G\footcite{geer}; H\footcite{shore}
%@article: @book: @incollection: @online: @collection: @inbook: @thesis: @article:
\printbibliography
```

..., die Verweise. A[1]; B[2]; C[3]; D[4]; E[5]; F[6]; G[7]; H[8]

09-03-15

# References

*Averroes*, The Epistle on the Possibility of Conjunction with the Active Intellect by Ibn Rushd with the Commentary of Moses Narboni. Ed. and trans. by Kalman P. Bland. (Moreshet: Studies in Jewish History, Literature and Thought, vol. 7.) New York 1982.

*Ahasver von Brandt/Erich Hoffmann*, Die nordischen Länder von der Mitte des 11. Jahrhunderts bis 1448, in: Ferdinand Seibt (ed.), Europa im Hoch- und Spätmittelalter. (Handbuch der europäischen Geschichte, vol. 2.) Stuttgart 1987, 884–917.

CTAN. The Comprehensive TeX Archive Network. 2006. URL: http://www.ctan.org (visited on 10/01/2009).

*Ingrid de Geer*, Earl, Saint, Bishop, Skald – and Music. The Orkney Earldom of the Twelfth Century. A Musicological Study. PhD thesis. Uppsala: Uppsala Universitet 1985.

*Philipp Jaffé* (ed.), Regesta Pontificum Romanorum ab condita ecclesia ad annum post Christum natum MCXCVIII. 2 vols. 2nd ed. Leipzig 1885–1888.

*Immanuel Kant*, Kritik der praktischen Vernunft. In: Kants Werke. Akademie Textausgabe. Vol. 5: Kritik der praktischen Vernunft. Kritik der Urtheilskraft. Berlin 1968, 1–163.

*Bradd Shore*, Twice-Born, Once Conceived. Meaning Construction and Cultural Cognition, in: American Anthropologist. New ser. 93.1, Mar. 1991, 9–27.

---

[1] *Bradd Shore*, Twice-Born, Once Conceived. Meaning Construction and Cultural Cognition, in: American Anthropologist. New ser. 93.1, Mar. 1991, 9–27.

[2] *Averroes*, The Epistle on the Possibility of Conjunction with the Active Intellect by Ibn Rushd with the Commentary of Moses Narboni. Ed. and trans. by Kalman P. Bland. (Moreshet: Studies in Jewish History, Literature and Thought, vol. 7.) New York 1982.

[3] *Ahasver von Brandt/Erich Hoffmann*, Die nordischen Länder von der Mitte des 11. Jahrhunderts bis 1448, in: Ferdinand Seibt (ed.), Europa im Hoch- und Spätmittelalter. (Handbuch der europäischen Geschichte, vol. 2.) Stuttgart 1987, 884–917.

[4] CTAN. The Comprehensive TeX Archive Network. 2006. URL: http://www.ctan.org (visited on 10/01/2009).

[5] *Philipp Jaffé* (ed.), Regesta Pontificum Romanorum ab condita ecclesia ad annum post Christum natum MCXCVIII. 2 vols. 2nd ed. Leipzig 1885–1888.

[6] *Immanuel Kant*, Kritik der praktischen Vernunft. In: Kants Werke. Akademie Textausgabe. Vol. 5: Kritik der praktischen Vernunft. Kritik der Urtheilskraft. Berlin 1968, 1–163.

[7] *Ingrid de Geer*, Earl, Saint, Bishop, Skald – and Music. The Orkney Earldom of the Twelfth Century. A Musicological Study. PhD thesis. Uppsala: Uppsala Universitet 1985.

[8] *Shore*, Twice-Born, Once Conceived (see n. 1).

## Partial bibliographies

This example by Rolf Niepraschk shows some of the possibilities offered by biblatex.

```
\usepackage[style=authoryear,backref=false,hyperref=auto,
  abbreviate=true,sorting=nyt,bibencoding=inputenc,block=ragged,
  backend=biber]{biblatex}
\setlength\bibitemsep{0.5\baselineskip plus 0.3\baselineskip minus 0.1\baselineskip}
\renewcommand*{\bibsetup}{%
  \interlinepenalty=5000\relax \widowpenalty=10000\relax
  \clubpenalty=5000\relax % 10000
  \raggedbottom\frenchspacing\sloppy\emergencystretch=4em}
\makeatletter
\usepackage{marginnote}
\newcommand*\formatItemCnt[1]{}
\newcommand*\@formatItemCnt[1]{\edef\@tempa{\ifnum#1<100\relax 0\fi
  \ifnum#1<10\relax 0\fi#1}{\fboxsep=2pt\fbox{\footnotesize\sffamily\@tempa}}}
\newcommand*\enableBibItemCount{\let\formatItemCnt=\@formatItemCnt}
\AtEveryBibitem{\raggedright\ifx\formatItemCnt=\@formatItemCnt\@tempswatrue\fi
  \if@tempswa\marginnote[\formatItemCnt{\the\value{instcount}}]%
      {\formatItemCnt{\the\value{instcount}}}\fi}
\makeatother
\bibliography{klassiker}
\nocite{*}


\enableBibItemCount
\defbibheading{Goe}{\section*{Literature by Johann Wolfgang Goethe}}
\defbibheading{AGoe}{\section*{Literature on Johann Wolfgang Goethe}}
\defbibnote{AGoe}{This section only shows part of the literature on
                Johann Wolfgang Goethe.}
\defbibheading{Sch}{\section*{Literature by Friedrich Schiller}}
\defbibheading{ASch}{\section*{Literature on Friedrich Schiller}}
\defbibnote{ASch}{This section only shows part of the literature on
                Friedrich Schiller.}
\defbibfilter{Sch}{\keyword{Friedrich Schiller}}
\defbibfilter{ASch}{\keyword{About Friedrich Schiller}}
\defbibfilter{Goe}{\keyword{Johann Wolfgang Goethe}}
\defbibfilter{AGoe}{\keyword{About Johann Wolfgang Goethe}}
\printbibliography[heading=Goe,filter=Goe]
\printbibliography[heading=AGoe,prenote=AGoe,filter=AGoe]
\printbibliography[heading=Sch,filter=Sch]
\printbibliography[heading=ASch,prenote=ASch,filter=ASch]
```

09-03-16

## Literature by Johann Wolfgang Goethe

Goethe, Johann Wolfgang (1769). *Frühe Gedichte*. Verlag A. 62 pp.

— (1788). *Späte Gedichte*. Verlag B. 73 pp.

— (1847). *Aus dem Nachlaß*. Verlag C. 34 pp.

## Literature on Johann Wolfgang Goethe

This section only shows part of the literature on Johann Wolfgang Goethe.

Bogen, Ellen (1966). *Goethes Tod*. Verlag DDD. 205 pp.

Silie, Peter (1921). *Goethes Leben*. Verlag CCC. 387 pp.

## Literature by Friedrich Schiller

Schiller, Friedrich (1779). *Frühe Gedichte*. Verlag A. 62 pp.

— (1798). *Späte Gedichte*. Verlag B. 73 pp.

— (1820). *Aus dem Nachlaß*. Verlag C. 34 pp.

## Literature on Friedrich Schiller

This section only shows part of the literature on Friedrich Schiller.

Bogen, Ellen (1965). *Schillers Tod*. Verlag DDD. 175 pp.

Silie, Peter (1920). *Schillers Leben*. Verlag CCC. 320 pp.

# Appendix

## A.1  Installing packages

Packages that for legal or other reasons are not part of a distribution, must be installed manually by the user. The process differs depending on the distribution and operating system, but only in terms of the location of the installed package. During compilation, TEX looks for the files in the order *current directory* – $TEXMFHOME – $TEXMFLOCAL – $TEXMF. The environment variables represent a particular location, for example:

```
TEXMFHOME:   /home/voss/texmf
TEXMFLOCAL:  /usr/local/texlive/2010/../texmf-local
TEXMF:       /home/voss/.texlive2010/texmf-config,
             /home/voss/.texlive2010/texmf-var,
             /home/voss/texmf,
             !!/usr/local/texlive/2010/texmf-config,
             !!/usr/local/texlive/2010/texmf-var,
             !!/usr/local/texlive/2010/texmf,
             !!/usr/local/texlive/2010/../texmf-local,
             !!/usr/local/texlive/2010/texmf-dist}
```

For custom files, you should choose the $TEXMFHOME or $TEXMFLOCAL location so that the files aren't overwritten when the distribution is updated – it only uses $TEXMF. For MiKTEX, these directories are the root directories, which can be shown through the menu MiKTEX▷Settings▷Roots. You can also amend them there if no local directory is present.

If the package you want to install is already available locally, you just need to copy the files into a TDS-compatible directory tree below the root. An overview is given below:

**tex**  TEX files.

      **context**  ConTEXt files.

> ...
>
> **generic** Files that are needed by different formats, for example prologue files for PostScript.
>
> ...
>
> **lualatex** LuaL#TeX files.
> **luatex** LuaTeX files.
> **latex** LATeX files.
>
> ...
>
> **xelatex** X∃LATeX files.
> **xetex** X∃TeX files.
>
> **fonts** Font-specific files.
>
> > **afm** Adobe font metrics.
> >
> > ...
> >
> > **map** Font map files.
> >
> > ...
> >
> > **opentype** Open Type fonts.
> >
> > ...
> >
> > **tfm** TeX font metrics.
> > **type1** Type 1 fonts (PostScript).
>
> **metafont** METAFONT files (no fonts).
> **metapost** METAPOST files.
> **bibtex** BɪʙTeX files.
>
> > **bib** Bibliography files.
> > **bat** BɪʙTeX style files.
> > **csf** Character set files for BɪʙTeX8.
>
> **scripts** Platform-independent executable files.
> **doc** Documentation.
> **source** Source files.

Adhering to this structure is crucial in order for TeX to find the files; recursive search only takes place in the current directory and $TEXMFHOME. For other directories, the structure outlined above is expected.

You should therefore put a new package for LATeX into a directory /tex/latex/MyDirectory, where MyDirectory can be an arbitrary name. After putting the new package into the directory, the package database of TeX needs to be updated. In TeX Live, this happens through the texhash or mktexlsr command.

```
voss@shania:~> texhash
texhash: Updating /usr/local/texlive/2010/texmf/ls-R...
texhash: Updating /usr/local/texlive/2010/texmf-config/ls-R...
texhash: Updating /usr/local/texlive/2010/texmf-dist/ls-R...
texhash: Updating /usr/local/texlive/2010/../texmf-local/ls-R...
texhash: Updating /usr/local/texlive/2010/texmf-var/ls-R...
texhash: Done.
```

In MiKTeX, the database is updated through MiKTeX▷Settings▷Refresh FNDB, where FNBD stands for *File Name Data Base* (cf. Figure A.1 on the next page). You can use the kpsewhich program to check whether the new package has been installed correctly – if the installation was successful, the current location of the file is given.

```
voss@shania:~> kpsewhich myTitlePage.sty
/usr/local/texlive/2010/../texmf-local/tex/latex/ZEDAT/myTitlePage.sty
```

In Windows, this can be done through a command line window:

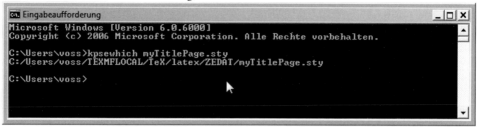

**Figure A.1:** Window to set parameters for MiKTEX.

If the to-be-installed package is available in the LaTeX format .dtx, you must first of all extract its contents; the format contains the package as well as the documentation. This applies primarily to packages available on CTAN (http://mirror.ctan.org). Usually a file with the same name and the extension .ins can be found there as well, which should be saved together with the .dtx file to a temporary directory. The .ins file is run through LaTeX or TeX, which extracts the various parts from the actual documentation file. In some cases, this file is missing and the normal .dtx file is run through LaTeX. As an alternative to using the .dtx file, you may be able to download a .zip file of the package from CTAN and unpack it to a temporary directory. Either way, you can now move the files from the temporary directory into the appropriate place within the TDS structure of the local TeX root directory outlined above, and update the database. The documentation can be compiled by treating the .dtx file like a normal LaTeX file.

## A.2 Outdated packages

On CTAN, outdated packages are moved into the *obsolete branch*, if a package author informs the CTAN maintainers about this fact. However, outdated packages are still needed in the TEX distributions in order to translate old documents error-free as before. On the web, you will find a lot of LaTeX templates that use obsolete packages. To keep track of what is outdated and replaced by newer packages Table A.1 lists the most important packages that were frequently used in the past but nowadays are outdated or replaced by newer packages.

**Table A.1:** List of outdated document classes and packages and the alternatives for LaTeX.

| outdated | alternative | outdated | alternative |
|---|---|---|---|
| a4 | geometry or typearea | a4wide | geometry or typearea |
| ae | lmodern | amsltx11 | amsmath |
| anysize | geometry or typearea | backrefx | backref |
| bitfield | bytefield | caption2 | caption |
| csvtool | datatool | doublespace | setspace |
| epsf | graphicx | epsfig | graphicx |
| euler | eulervm | eurotex | inputenc |
| dinat | natdin | dinbrief | scrlttr2 |
| fancyheadings | fancyhdr | floatfig | floatflt |
| glossary | glosseries | HA-Prosper | powerdot |
| here | float | isolatin | inputenc |
| isolatin1 | inputenc | mathpple | mathpazo |
| mathptm | mathptmx | nthm | ntheorem |
| palatino | mathpazo | prosper | powerdot |
| ps4pdf | pst-pdf | psfig | graphicx |
| pslatex | mathptmx, helvet, beramono | pst-char | pst-text |
| pst-vue3d | pst-solides3d | pstcol | pstricks |
| raggedr | ragged2e | subfigure | floatrow |
| scrlettr | scrlttr2 | scrpage | scrpage2 |
| seminar | powerdot | t1enc | fontenc |
| times | mathptmx | umlaut | fontenc |
| umlaute | fontenc | utopia | fourier |
| vmargin | geometry or typearea | zefonts | lmodern |

## A.3 File extensions

`.aux`    auxiliary file for LaTeX which can collect commands for an intermediate state between two or more LaTeX runs

`.bbl`    bibliography output file, created by BibTeX or biber

`.bib`    bibliograpy database

`.blg`    bibliography log file, created by BibTeX or biber

`.cfg`    config file

`.clo`    document class option file

`.cls`    document class file

`.cnf`    TeX config file `texmf.cnf`, also defines the search paths

`.dvi`    device independent file, one of the possible output formats of a LaTeX run

`.def`    definition file for class files and packages

`.enc`    font encoding file

`.eps`    encapsulated PostScript file

`.fd`    font definition file (encoding and family)

`.fmt`    format file (binary format)

`.glo`    glossary log file, created by makeindex with a glossary style file

`.idx`    index auxiliary file, which collects all index entries from the source document

`.ilg`    index log file, created by makeindex

`.ind`    index file, created after running makeindex

`.jpg`    joint photographic experts group

`.ldf`    language definition file

`.loa`    list of algorithms

`.lof`    list of figures

`.log`    log file of a LaTeX run

`.lot`    list of tables

`.ltx`    (latex) source file, alternative extension to `.tex` (also used for LaTeX kernel files)

| | | | |
|---|---|---|---|
| `.map` | font mapfile | `.mf` | MetaFont file |
| `.mp` | MetaPost file | `.pdf` | portable document format |
| `.pfa` | PostScript font (ASCII) | `.pfb` | PostScript font (binary) |
| `.png` | portable network graphics | `.pool` | `pdftex.pool` internal used strings |
| `.pro` | PostScript prologue file | `.sty` | package style file |
| `.tex` | LaTeX source file | `.tfm` | tex font metrics file |
| `.toc` | table of contents | `.vf` | virtual font definition |

# Bibliography

[1] Paul W. Abrahams, Karl Berry and Kathryn Hargreaves. TeX for the Impatient, 2003.      CTAN: /info/impatient/book.pdf

[2] Claudio Beccari. "Typesetting mathematics for science and technology according to ISO 31/XI". *TUGboat Journal*, 18(1):39–47, 1997.      http://www.tug.org/TUGboat/Articles/tb18-1/tb54becc.pdf

[3] Michael Downes. Short Math Guide for LaTeX. American Mathematical Society, 2002.      http://www.ams.org/tex/short-math-guide.html

[4] Victor Eijkhout. TeX by Topic, 1992.      http://www.eijkhout.net/tbt/

[5] Stephen G. Hartke. "A survey of Free Math Fonts for TeX and LaTeX". *The PracTeX Journal*, 01, 2006.      http://tug.org/pracjourn/2006-1/hartke/hartke.pdf

[6] Uwe Kern. Color extensions with the xcolor package, 2007. Version 2.11.      CTAN: /macros/latex/contrib/xcolor/

[7] Donald E. Knuth. "The TeXbook". Addison Wesley Professional, 21st edition, 1986.

[8] Markus Kohm. "Satzspiegelkonstruktionen im Vergleich". *Die TeXnische Komödie*, 14(4):28–48, 2002.      http://www.dante.de/dante/DTK/PDF/komoedie_2002_4.pdf

[9] Markus Kohm and Jens-Uwe Morawski. "KOMA-Script – Eine Sammlung von Klassen und Paketen füer LaTeX 2ε". DANTE/LOB-media.de, Heidelberg/Berlin, 3rd edition, 2008.

[10] Helmut Kopka and Patrick W. Daly. "Guide to LaTeX". Addison-Wesley, Reading, MA, 4th edition, 2004.

[11] Leslie Lamport. "Das LaTeX Handbuch". Addison-Wesley, Bonn, Germany, 1995. ISBN 0-201-15790-X.

[12] Richard Lawrence. "Math=Typography?" *TUGboat Journal*, 24(2):165–168, 2003.      http://www.tug.org/TUGboat/Articles/tb24-2/tb77lawrence.pdf

[13] Philipp Lehman. The Font Installation Guide, 2004.
CTAN: /info/Type1fonts/fontinstallationguide/fontinstallationguide.pdf

[14] Philipp Lehman. "The csquotes package. Context sensitive quotation facilities", 2008.
CTAN: macros/latex/contrib/csquotes

[15] Philipp Lehman. "The biblatex package. Programmable bibliographies and citations", 2009.
CTAN: macros/latex/contrib/biblatex

[16] Frank Mittelbach and Michel Goossens. "The LaTeX Companion". Addison-Wesley, Reading, MA, 2nd edition, 2006.

[17] Scott Pakin. The Comprehensive LaTeX Symbol List. CTAN, 2009.
CTAN: /info/symbols/comprehensive/symbol-a4.pdf

[18] Sebastian Rahtz and Heiko Oberdiek. Hypertext marks in LaTeX: a manual for hyperref, 2009.
http://www.tug.org/applications/hyperref/ftp/doc/manual.pdf

[19] Keith Reckdahl. Using Imported Graphics in LaTeX and pdfLaTeX, 2006.
CTAN: /info/epslatex/english/epslatex.pdf

[20] B. N. Taylor. Guide for the Use of the International System of Units (SI) – 10.5.4 Multiplying numbers. National Institute of Standard and Technology, 2008.
http://physics.nist.gov/Pubs/SP811/sec10.html

[21] LaTeX3 Project Team. LaTeX $2_\varepsilon$ fontselection, 2000.
http://www.latex-project.org/guides/fntguide.pdf

[22] Mark Trettin. l2tabu – Das LaTeX $2_\varepsilon$-Sündenregister oder Veraltete Befehle, Pakete und andere Fehler, 2007.
CTAN: /info/l2tabu/german/l2tabu.pdf

[23] Georg Verweyen. "Silbentrennung & Co.", 2007.
http://homepage.ruhr-uni-bochum.de/Georg.Verweyen/silbentrennung.html

[24] Herbert Voß. "Typesetting mathematics with LaTeX". UIT, Cambridge, UK, 2010.

[25] Herbert Voß. "PSTricks – Graphics for TeX and LaTeX". UIT, Cambridge, 1st edition, 2011.

[26] Herbert Voß. "Typesetting tables with LaTeX". UIT, Cambridge, UK, 2011.

[27] Dominik Waßenhoven. "Bibliographien erstellen mit biblatex (Part 2)". *Die TeXnische Komödie*, 4/08:31–61, 2008.
http://biblatex.dominik-wassenhoven.de

# Index of commands and concepts

To make it easier to use a command or concept, the entries are distinguished by their "type" and this is often indicated by one of the following "type words" at the beginning of an entry:

> boolean, counter, document class, env., file, file extension, font, font encoding, key value, keyword, length, option, package, program, rigid length, or syntax.

The absence of an explicit "type word" means that the "type" is either a TeX or LaTeX "command" or simply a "concept".

Use by, or in connection with, a particular package is indicated by adding the package name (in parentheses) to an entry.

An italic page number indicates that the command is demonstrated in a source code snippet or in an example on that page.

When there are several page numbers listed, **bold** face indicates a page containing important information about an entry.

# H

\H, 54
 h notation, 42
 h value, 38
 HA-Prosper package, 202
 half value, 22, 26
 half* value, 26
 half+ value, 25, 26
 half- value, 26
 hang value (caption), 133, 134, 137, 138
\hangindent rigid length, 74
 hangindent Option (caption), 135–137
 hanginside value (floatrow), 143
 hangleft value (floatrow), 143
 hangoutside value (floatrow), 143
 hangright value (floatrow), 143
 Harvard, 171–173, 176
 harvard package, 173
\hbadness TeX counter, 78
\hbox, 59, 78
\hdotsfor (amsmath), 90
 header, 26, 57
 header line, 26
\headheight rigid length, 74
 headings value, 26, 60
\headsep rigid length, 74
\height rigid length, 74
 height Option (graphicx), *131*
 heightadjust Option (floatrow), 139, 141
 Helvetica, 108
 here package, 202
 hexadecimal number, 69
\hexnumber@, 69
 hfil value (floatrow), 142
\hfill, **54**, 72, 73
 hfill value (floatrow), 142
 hhline package, 49
 High Energy Physics, 19
 historian value (biblatex), 183
 historische-zeitschrift value (biblatex), 183, *196*
\hline, **54**, 73
\hoffset rigid length, 74
\hphantom, 54
\href (hyperref), 149
\hrulefill, 54
\hspace, **54**, 65, 73
\hspace*, 54
 ht notation, 42
 htm value (hyperref), 147
 HTML, 171
 html value (hyperref), 147
 HTML code, 175
\Huge, **54**, 94, 96
\huge, **54**, 94
 Human Biology, 174
 Human Nature and American Anthropologist, 174
 hypcap Option (caption), 137

 hypcapspace Option (caption), 137
 hyperfigures Option (hyperref), 147
 hyperfootnotes Option (hyperref), 147
 hyperindex Option (hyperref), 147
 hyperref Option (hyperref), 144
 hyperref package, 143–145, 149, 155
\hypersetup (hyperref), 145, 146, **149**
 hypertex Option (hyperref), 147
 hypertexnames Option (hyperref), 147
 hyphen, 33
 hyphenation, 34
\hyphenation, 32, **54**, 54
 hyphenation algorithm, 33
 hyphenation point, 64

# I

\i, 54
 identifier, 133
.idx file extension, 57, 203
 IEEE, 174
 IEEE conference paper, 19
 IEEE Instructions, 174
 IEEE transactions, 19
\IfFileExists, 54
.ilg file extension, 203
 IMAC, 174
 implicit Option (hyperref), 147
 in, 71
\include, **54**, 55
\includegraphics (graphicx), **55**, **130**, 130, *131*
\includegraphics* (graphicx), **55**, **130**, 130
\includeonly, 16, **54**, 54
.ind file extension, 46, 203
\indent, 55
 indentation, 28
 indention Option (caption), 133, 136, 137
 index, 46
\index, 57
 index package, 145
 index file, 57
 Information Mapping, 20
\infty, *72*
 Inorganic Chemistry, 174
\input, 6, 54, **55**, 55
 input character, 5
 input encoding, 129, 130
 inputenc package, 7, 130
\inputencoding (inputenc), 130
\InputIfFileExists, 55
.ins file extension, 201
 Institute of Electrical and Electronics Engineers, 174
 Institute of Physics, 174
 International Association of Geodesy, 19
 International Congress on Sound and Vibration, 19
 International Economic Review, 174
 International Journal of Quantum Chemistry, 174
 International Modal Analysis Conference, 174

# U

# People

# Typesetting tables with LaTeX

## Herbert Voss

This is the first-ever book dedicated to typesetting tables in LaTeX. With LaTeX you can create just about any kind of table, from simple to extremely complex. But while the table capabilities in LaTeX are powerful, they can be daunting at first sight or when you require a sophisticated layout. This book describes the additional LaTeX packages that are available to simplify your task, and gives ready-to-run examples of each, to get you working as quickly as possible, and present your data in the most effective way.

With this book you will learn:

– How to typeset tables, from basic to advanced.
– How to use advanced features, such as color and multi-page tables.
– How add-on LaTeX tables packages can simplify or enhance your work.

### Contents

1. Introduction to LaTeX's table-handling
2. LaTeX packages for tables
3. Using color in tables
4. Multi-page tables
5. Tips and tricks
6. Examples

### Praise for the German Edition

*"A concise reference book for those who may already have used LaTeX but aren't aware of the powerful capabilities provided by LaTeX's extra tables packages."*

**ISBN: 9781906860257**
**240 pages**

ALSO PUBLISHED BY UIT

# Typesetting mathematics with LaTeX

## Herbert Voss

From a simple equation to a mathematical treatise, this practical guide offers an in-depth review of the mathematics typesetting aspects of the industry-leading typesetting software, LaTeX. Among the topics discussed in this manual are the software's special mathematics mode, how to embed mathematics in line with normal text, color in math expressions, and fonts and math.

Handy features include a list of mathematical symbols for quick-reference, a survey of a wide range of additional mathematics packages – with a particular emphasis on the American Mathematical Society packages – and ready-to-run examples to enable you to get going quickly.

This book will:

– Save you time by quickly giving you the detailed command syntax you require.
– Improve your mathematical typesetting by providing a reference to all the available commands.
– Show the advantages of the packages from the American Mathematical Society.
– Show you how to choose suitable math fonts, illustrated with convenient samples of font output.

### Contents

**ISBN: 9781906860172**
**304 pages**

ALSO PUBLISHED BY UIT

# Practical TCP/IP

## Designing, using, and troubleshooting
## TCP/IP networks on Linux and Windows

### Niall Mansfield

*Reprinted first edition*

## Key benefits

1. Explore, hands-on, how your network really works. Build small test networks in a few minutes, so you can try anything out without affecting your live network and servers.

2. Learn how to troubleshoot network problems, and how to use free packet sniffers to see what's happening.

3. Understand how the TCP/IP protocols map onto your day-to-day network operation – learn both theory and practice.

## What readers have said about this book

*"Before this book was released I was eagerly searching for a book that could be used for my Linux-based LAN-course. After the release of this book I stopped my searching immediately"* **Torben Gregersen, Engineering College of Aarhus**.

*"Accuracy is superb – written by someone obviously knowledgable in the subject, and able to communicate this knowledge extremely effectively."*

*"You won't find a better TCP/IP book!"*

*"An excellent book for taking your computer networking career from mediocre to top notch."*

*"Covers TCP/IP, and networking in general, tremendously."*

*"This book has been touted as the 21st-century upgrade to the classic TCP/IP Illustrated (by Richard W. Stevens). These are big boots to fill, but Practical TCP/IP does an impressive job. In over 800 pages of well-organized and well-illustrated text, there is no fat, but rather a lean and – yes – practical treatment of every major TCP/IP networking concept."*

*"It's an ideal book for beginners, probably the only one needed for the first and second semesters of a university networking course. ... (But it is not a book just for beginners. ...)"*

**ISBN: 9781906860363**
**880 pages**

# PSTricks

## Graphics and PostScript for LaTeX

## Herbert Voss

A comprehensive guide to creating and including graphics in TeX and LaTeX documents. It is both a reference work and a tutorial guide.

PSTricks lets you produce very high-quality PostScript graphics, by programming rather than interactive drawing. For designers, data publishers, scientists and engineers, generating graphics from data or formulas instead of having to draw manually allows large data collections or complex graphics to be created consistently and reliably with the minimum of effort.

There are many special-purpose extensions, for visualizing data, and for drawing circuit diagrams, barcodes, graphs, trees, chemistry diagrams, etc.

Numerous examples with source code (freely downloadable) make it easy to create your own images and get you up to speed quickly.

## Contents

**1.** Introduction  **2.** Getting Started  **3.** The Coordinate System  **4.** Lines and Polygons  **5.** Circles, Ellipses and Curves  **6.** Points  **7.** Filling  **8.** Arrows  **9.** Labels  **10.** Boxes  **11.** Custom styles and objects  **12.** Coordinates  **13.** Overlays  **14.** Basics  **15.** Plotting of Functions and Data  **16.** Nodes and Connections  **17.** Trees  **18.** Manipulating Text and Characters  **19.** Filling and Tiling  **20.** Coils, Springs and Zigzag Lines  **21.** Exporting PSTricks Environments  **22.** Color Gradients and Shadows  **23.** Three-Dimensional Figures  **24.** Creating Circuit Diagrams  **25.** Geographic Projections  **26.** Barcodes  **27.** Bar Charts  **28.** Gantt Charts  **29.** Mathematical Functions  **30.** Euclidean Geometry  **31.** Additional Features  **32.** Chemistry Diagrams  **33.** UML Diagrams  **34.** Additional PSTricks Packages  **35.** Specials  **36.** PSTricks in Presentations  **37.** Examples

## Praise for the German Edition

*"A nice Christmas present – for me!"*

*"A detailed current description of PSTricks and the huge variety of PSTricks packages that are available, and written by an experienced LaTeX package developer."*

*"Searching through loads of different pieces of documentation is a thing of the past. This single compendium is a quick reference to everything I need."*

**ISBN: 9781906860134**
**900 pages**

# More about this book

**Register your book:** receive updates, notifications about author appearances, and announcements about new editions. *www.uit.co.uk/register*

**News:** forthcoming titles, events, reviews, interviews, podcasts, etc. *www.uit.co.uk/news*

**Join our mailing lists:** get email newsletters on topics of interest. *www.uit.co.uk/subscribe*

**How to order:** get details of stockists and online bookstores. If you are a bookstore, find out about our distributors or contact us to discuss your particular requirements. *www.uit.co.uk/order*

**Send us a book proposal:** if you want to write – even if you have just the kernel of an idea at present – we'd love to hear from you. We pride ourselves on supporting our authors and making the process of book-writing as satisfying and as easy as possible. *www.uit.co.uk/for-authors*

UIT Cambridge Ltd.
PO Box 145
Cambridge
CB4 1GQ
England

Email: *inquiries@uit.co.uk*
Phone: **+44 1223 302 041**